Swoon

Manchester University Press

Swoon

A poetics of passing out

Naomi Booth

MANCHESTER UNIVERSITY PRESS

Copyright © Naomi Booth 2021

The right of Naomi Booth to be identified as the author of this work has been asserted by them in accordance with the Copyright, Designs and Patents Act 1988.

Published by Manchester University Press
Oxford Road, Manchester M13 9PL

www.manchesteruniversitypress.co.uk

British Library Cataloguing-in-Publication Data
A catalogue record for this book is available from the British Library

ISBN   978 1 5261 0118 1   hardback
ISBN   978 1 5261 7160 3   paperback

First published 2021
Paperback published 2022

The publisher has no responsibility for the persistence or accuracy of URLs for any external or third-party internet websites referred to in this book, and does not guarantee that any content on such websites is, or will remain, accurate or appropriate.

Typeset
by New Best-set Typesetters Ltd

For Mr Firth, Miss Briscoe and Joe Peters, with gratitude

Contents

List of illustrations	*page* viii
Acknowledgements	ix
Introduction: A poetics of passing out	1
1 Heart-stopped transformations: Swooning in late medieval literature	27
2 'Fall'n into a pit of ink': Shakespearean swoons and unreadable body-texts	59
3 Feeling too much: The swoon and the (in)sensible woman	93
4 'Dead born': Shadow resurrections and artistic transformations	123
5 Vampiric swoons and other dark ecologies	157
6 Lovesick, lesbian swoons and the romantic art of sinking	190
Passing out: Contemporary catatonia	218
Select bibliography	222
Index	229

Illustrations

1 Rogier van der Weyden, *The Descent from the Cross*, c.1435, Museo del Prado — page 27
2 Giotto di Bondone, *Crucifixion*, c.1310, Lower Church, Basilica of San Francesco d'Assisi, Assisi — 33
3 Alfred Elmore, Depiction of the church scene in *Much Ado about Nothing*, 1846 — 61
4 Pierre André Brouillet, A Clinical Lesson at the Salpêtrière (*Une leçon clinique à la Salpêtrière*), 1887 — 171

Acknowledgements

My greatest thanks go to Nicholas Royle for his generous support of this project in its early stages. Sara Crangle and Laura Marcus also provided invaluable feedback. My thanks too to the AHRC, who funded the initial research for this project. *Swoon* began life as a creative and critical hybrid, and I am indebted to Tom Chivers at Penned in the Margins who published the resulting work of fiction as *The Lost Art of Sinking* (2015). Parts of the chapters that follow were initially published in the following: the work on sensibility and swooning in Chapter 3 began life as 'Feeling too much: The swoon and the (in)sensible woman', in *Women's Writing* 21(4) (2014); the ideas on dark ecology and vampire narratives in Chapter 5 began as 'Dark ecology and queer amphibious vampires', in *Undercurrents: Journal of Critical Environmental Studies* 19 (2105); ideas about romance swooning in Chapter 6 were first developed in: 'The felicity of falling: Fifty Shades of Grey and the feminine art of sinking', in *Women: A Cultural Review* 26 (1–2) (2015) and 'Bathetic masochism and the shrinking woman', in *New Formations* 83 (2014). My thanks to the editors and publishers for permission to reprint, as well as for valuable reviews of this work.

I am extremely grateful to friends who've read this work along the way and/or provided much-needed support, including Camilla Bostock, Sabhbh Curran, Kieran Devaney, Michael Fake, Dulcie Few, Tom Houlton, Laura Joyce, Helen Jukes, Oliver Morgan, Sophie Nicholls and Alison Peirse. I've benefited tremendously from the intellectual generosity and advice of colleagues at three different universities (University of Sussex, York St John University and Durham University) while writing this book – especially from Janine Bradbury, Kim Campanello, Abi Curtis, Anne-Marie Evans,

Caleb Klaces, Catherine Packham, Barry Sheils and Katie Walter. Many thanks also to those who invited me to present this work in different forms and gave valuable feedback, including Alexander Beaumont, Beth Cortese, Steve Ely, Sarah Falcus, Nasser Hussain, Sarah Jackson, Sarah Lawson Welsh, and Helen Pleasance.

My thanks to all at Manchester University Press for their support for this book, to the anonymous peer reviewers who helped to shape it, and especially to Matthew Frost for his unfailing patience. Thank you also to the Faculty of Arts and Humanities at Durham University for a grant for the index and the beautiful illustrations we've been able to include.

I am grateful to my family for helping me not to despair of ever completing this book: Michael, Betty and Ruby-Rose, who helped and/or bore with me at crucial moments – I love you. Final thanks go to my parents, Jane and Ian, for supporting me in myriad ways.

Introduction:
A poetics of passing out

> In Bernini's statue *The Ecstasy of Saint Teresa*, she is lying back in a swoon with her mouth wide open. An angel stands over her. In one hand he holds an arrow, directed at her heart; the other teases the hem of her robe. Beams of light erupt from the sky. You can tell she is in both kinds of ecstasy.
>
> When I look at that sculpture, the folds of her marble dress, I can feel her lightness. Breathing life into stone. This is what it means to float.
>
> Abi Palmer, Sanatorium (2020)

As a teenager, it was a great disappointment to me that I had never swooned. There had been ample opportunities: we organised games in the school toilets that involved rounds of hyperventilation; we starved ourselves before important events; we told each other terrifying stories late at night, hoping to drive each other hysterical and faint with fear. At a religious festival, I linked hands with other girls and swayed, hoping to be slain in the spirit. The desire to swoon was partly borne, I think, from a desire to change the genre of my adolescence; from the hope that what was playing out as (sometimes gritty, mostly dull) kitchen-sink realism might become more heightened, more erotic, more mystical – rapturous even.

In my adolescent mind, the swoon was a means of transportation and transformation, which would function as it does in many works of literature, film and art: as a rapturous climax of the most intense forms of experience. The swoon promises the ecstasy – spiritual, aesthetic and erotic – that the writer Abi Palmer reads in Bernini's statue of the swooning Saint Teresa. Palmer's recent experimental text, *Sanatorium* (2020), provides an account of the writer's treatment for chronic illness, charting her journey to a thermal rehabilitation facility. Palmer's descriptions of the sanatorium she visits are interspersed with flashes of memory, which reveal the development of her medical conditions and of her prayer-like/heretical correspondence with Saint Teresa: 'Oh Teresa Sánchez de Cepeda y Ahumada, drown me with your thick and sacred thighs.'[1] Saint Teresa, or Teresa of Ávila, was a sixteenth-century Spanish mystic, known for her mortifications of the body, for long periods of incapacitation as well as her experiences of ecstasy, and for her 'embarrassment of raptures', which reportedly included levitation. After she had swooned, Teresa would begin to move upwards, instructing her sisters to hold her down, which Palmer describes as follows: 'Let us raise a glass now to Saint Teresa of Ávila, a mystic so pure that she kept floating off to heaven. Nuns had to sit on her stomach to stop her from levitating clean off into the sky.'[2] Descriptions of Teresa's swoons have led to recent speculation that she may have suffered from temporal lobe epilepsy.[3] Palmer positions Teresa as a subversive object of desire and a touchstone for her own potentially semi-mystical, erotic and often satirical depictions of falling, floating and illness. The opening line of Palmer's *Sanatorium*, 'Have you ever noticed that when we're near water I want to fuck?',[4] establishes a strong current of associations: sex, water, recuperation, illness, swooning ecstasy and subversion all converge in Palmer's supplication to Teresa to 'drown me with your thick and sacred thighs'.

Palmer's *Sanatorium* holds up the image of Saint Teresa to both erotically revere and critique the idealisation of female swooning in 'high art' and religious iconography. The contrast between the idealised image of Teresa's debilitating ecstasy, and the descriptions of Palmer sometimes struggling to walk, trying to float in a mouldy inflatable bathtub, left without adequate support to dress and clean herself ('I find myself wet and dizzy ... flopped on the bed in a damp towel, waiting for someone to get me dressed'),[5] is acute. Against Palmer's dizzyingly difficult experience of illness contrasts with the beauty of Bernini's sculpture. Palmer's response to the depiction of St Teresa highlights many of the features of swooning that are of interest to me in this poetics of passing out: she foregrounds the erotic appeal of certain kinds of female debility, an appeal that can seem both subversive and troubling; the rich confusion between states of ecstasy and agony; the speechless way in which the female body is made to signify in particular artistic traditions and medical discourses. She also shows us how important the swoon is in the history of artistic representation: Bernini's sculpture of *The Ecstasy of Saint Teresa* (1647–1652) is a celebrated masterpiece of High Roman Baroque. It is the triumph and high point of a certain kind of art. Palmer describes the effect of this depiction of swooning as one of uncanny artistic embodiment: 'When I look at that sculpture, the folds of her marble dress, I can feel her lightness. Breathing life into stone. That is exactly what it means to float.'[6] This iconisation of the female body overwhelmed and about to lift off is also a moment in which art 'takes off': in which stone seems to breathe and come to life. And as Palmer is looking at St Teresa, she is also *feeling her lightness*, becoming light-headed, becoming prone to a falling and floating herself. The swoon is the test of art's potential effectiveness and affectiveness: the most powerful depiction of swooning is one that makes the statue seem to breathe and that makes the viewer also feel faint. The artwork moves towards life and vitality; the viewer moves closer to unconsciousness. This is the poetics of passing out.

Fainting and falling aesthetes

A particularly showy example of passing-out as superlative aesthetic response is narrated by writer Chuck Palahniuk when he describes his audience fainting as he reads his now infamous story 'Guts':

> at a lunchtime reading, two ... men fainted. At the same moment in the story, both of them fell so hard that their chrome chairs flipped and clattered loud on the polished hardwood floor of the auditorium. The event broke down for a few moments while the fainters were coaxed back to life. By now, we had a pattern. [...]
>
> So far, 67 people have fainted while I've read Guts. For a nine-page story, some nights it takes 30 minutes to read. In the first half, you're pausing for so much laughter from your audience. In the second half, you're pausing as your audience is revived.
>
> My goal was to write a new form of horror story, something based on the ordinary world, without supernatural monsters or magic. Guts, and the book that contained it, would be a trapdoor down into some place dark. A place only you could go, alone. Only books have that power.[7]

Palahniuk's description of his readers swooning is a powerful piece of self-mythologising. Palahniuk describes people at his readings palling, screaming, crying, calling for ambulances, and frequently passing out – sixty-seven times, according to the headline of the article I quote from here. He narrates these faints with great care, detailing the exact moments of supposedly synchronised falls and the precise ways in which bodies slacken and sag and fall. His descriptions of bodies falling together are often uncanny; he wants the reader to feel unsettled by these accounts of an audience being exorbitantly unsettled. The faints are described as indexical: they attest to the effectiveness and affectiveness of Palahniuk's literary work, of his 'new form of horror'. And the singular power of 'books', in Palahniuk's account of them, is as a gateway to unconsciousness; 'a trapdoor down into some place dark'.

Palahniuk's account of a swooning reader-response is a kind of viral marketing: he sensationalises these faints in order to generate interest in his books; he offers passing out as a kind of incitement and possible dark reward of reading his work (read it if you dare). But Palahniuk's depiction of passing out in response to a work of art also taps into historical traditions (including Bernini's sculpture of St Teresa) that celebrate swooning as a mode of high mystical and/or aesthetic response.

An exploration of the long association between swooning and experiences of art and literature is at the heart of this book. This exploration will necessarily draw different discourses into close proximity: aesthetic theory, literature and narratives of the body (religious, medical, cultural and political) are all bound together in the depictions of swooning discussed here. This is not accidental disciplinary slippage on my part: it is deliberate promiscuity, because a swoon always invites us to look at things in different ways simultaneously: is this ecstasy or agony? Is this escape or surrender? Is this eroticism or subjection? Is this a matter of the body or the mind? Swooning, I argue, is ambivalent and polyvalent. We might see this more clearly if we examine the contentious attempt to create the psychiatric diagnosis of 'Stendhal Syndrome'. In 1989, the *New York Times*[8] reported on the work of Dr Graziella Magherini, who researched the phenomenon of tourists swooning in front of great works of art. Based in the Santa Maria Nuova Hospital in Florence, Magherini collected and published cases of people overwhelmed by their aesthetic experiences in the city. The following is an excerpt from her case notes:

> You could call it anguish by art. Some Faint, Some Soar [sic] Suddenly, in the presence of provocative paintings, sculptures or architecture, certain people fall apart. Some start to perspire heavily. Others experience rapid heart beat [sic] and stomach pains. A few even faint.[9]

The *New York Times* describes the collected cases of 'Stendhal Syndrome' as a catalogue of 'unnerved' and 'disorientated art-lovers': it is the 'emotional texture of the artwork that usually sets off reactions' in 'particularly sensitive subjects', Magherini claims. Another psychiatrist, Dr Reed Moskowitz of the New York University Medical Center, describes these overwhelmed subjects as extreme aesthetes, likening their experiences to religious rapture: 'These are people who have a great appreciation of beauty, and you're putting them in the Mecca of art.' The overlap between overwhelming artistic and religious experience is emphasised in Magherini's description of other cases of 'Stendhal Syndrome' at important tourist sites: 'She has heard of a similar phenomenon occurring in Jerusalem, a city of obviously immense religious significance, and in Ravenna, an artistically rich Italian city on the Adriatic Sea.' Magherini's diagnosis describes a psychosomatic response to art: sufferers are profoundly moved, sometimes literally knocked off their feet, by an aesthetic experience that has religious force and velocity.

Swooning in this medical account of it is a crucible of aesthetic and religious experience, of corporeality and psychiatric receptivity. Some of the medics interviewed for the *New York Times* piece are sceptical about the aesthetic turn involved in the diagnosis of 'Stendhal Syndrome': Dr Elliot Wineburg, a specialist in stress-related disorders, argues for instance that the symptoms described by Magherini could 'occur not just with sensitive people, but sick people'.[10] These sensitive aesthetes could in fact be tourists who are just tired and hungry, are otherwise ill, or who might be suffering with other psychiatric illnesses that 'would have come out sooner or later'. Scientists have recently returned to these cases and a study in 2014 attempted to use neuroscientific methods to map brain activity in subjects viewing works of art in Florence. The study suggests a continuing ambiguity around extreme physical reactions to works of art, concluding that: 'There is no scientific evidence to define the Stendhal Syndrome as a specific psychiatric disorder; on the other hand there is evidence that the same cerebral areas involved in emotional reactions are activated during the exposure to artworks.'[11]

It will come as no surprise to anyone interested in aesthetics that viewing art affects the viewer emotionally, and in ways that we can now begin to trace within the brain and the body. But the medical debate over 'Stendhal Syndrome' shows how passing out in relation to art causes problems for the integrity of 'disciplines' of study: it brings aesthetics and psychiatry and neuroscience into indeterminate and disorienting contact. The psychiatric terminology at issue here betrays the close proximity of the medical and the literary: 'Stendhal Syndrome' is derived from the pen name of French writer Henri Beyle – 'M. de Stendhal, Officer de Cavalrie' – as it appeared on the cover of his travelogue, *Rome, Naples et Florence*, when it published in an early version in 1817. Stendhal's highly stylised travel writing is affecting contemporary psychiatry and his literary rendering of the swoon is paradigmatic of the long tradition that prizes passing out as an exemplary aesthetic response. Permit me a digression into his work here to takes us further into the physiological-psychological-religious-aesthetic experience of the swoon.

In an expanded version of *Rome, Naples et Florence* published in 1826, Beyle provides an ecstatic account of his travels around Italy after the end of the Napoleonic wars. Stendhal, Beyle's narrator, doesn't, as the translator Richard N. Coe puts it, 'offer a factual guide to Italy'; rather he creates an 'idealised vision of Italy', even a 'theory of Italy – a theory which is complex, involving love and art no less than history and politics, and which, in point of fact, is nothing less substantial than a far-reaching exploration of *la casse au bonheur*'.[12] Stendhal's writing doesn't merely describe a place, then: it produces Italy as a utopian site through an imaginative rendering of geography, culture, politics, history and art; his version of Italy animates the liberal political and aesthetic sensibilities that Stendhal valued (and that he believed were under threat from illiberal regimes). And descriptions of experiences of being overwhelmed are crucial to Stendhal's performative theory of Italy and to his aspirational version of an aesthetically and politically responsive subject. Stendhal's most dramatic descriptions in this regard are situated in Florence. His travelogue tells us that he arrived in the city on January

22, 1817 in a state of excitement. When he caught a glimpse of the city his 'heart was beating wildly within [him]' and he was moved to rhapsody: '"Behold the home of Michelangelo, of Leonardo de Vinci," I mused within my heart. "Behold this noble city, the Queen of mediaeval Europe." Here, within these walls, the civilisation of mankind was born anew' (300).

For Stendhal, the city is immediately associated with the renewal of mankind and with all that has been admirable in recent cultural history. Stendhal quickly progresses to the Santa Croce and the tomb of Michelangelo, where, he tells us, the 'tide of emotion which overwhelmed me flowed so deep that it scarce was to be distinguished from religious awe. The mystic dimness which filled the church ... spoke volumes to my soul' (301). Stendhal meets a friar, whom he persuades to allow him into the north-east corner of the church, where Volterrano's frescoes are preserved. It is here, gazing at the artworks on the ceiling, that Stendhal achieves the most profound 'experience of ecstasy that, as far as I am aware, I have ever encountered through the painter's art':

> My soul, affected by the very notion of being in Florence, and by the proximity of those great men whose tombs I had just beheld, was already in a state of trance. Absorbed in the contemplation of sublime beauty, I could perceive its very essence close at hand; I could, as it were, feel the stuff of it beneath my fingertips. I had attained to that supreme degree of sensibility where the divine intimations of art merge with the impassioned sensuality of emotion. As I emerged from the porch of Santa Croce, I was seized with a fierce palpitation of the heart (that same symptom which, in Berlin, is referred to as an attack of nerves); the well-spring of life was dried up within me, and I walked with a constant fear of falling to the ground. (302)

Stendhal's sensibility, his ability to perceive and be affected by art, is described here as so acute that the 'intimations' of art, its insubstantial and abstract qualities, are experienced as physical and proximate: the 'stuff of it' might be felt by his fingertips. And this very physical experience of art dramatically affects his body: Stendhal's heart palpitates and he teeters at the edge of swooning. Stendhal is describing a sort of incarnation of aesthetic experience: the ineffable or divine elements of art have become as real as physical 'stuff'; the picture is (re)made in his flesh. We might think of this as a literalised version of what has more recently been theorised as affect, whereby the picture descends from the ceiling to knock the viewer off his feet. Either way, the body is profoundly affected and destabilised by art. The metaphysical becomes deeply physical here, a turn that has already been suggested in Stendhal's characterisation of the activities of different parts of his body: his heart 'muses', his soul is in a 'trance', the animate and inanimate, the conscious and the inert, the abstract and the physical, encroach upon one another in Stendhal's account of himself as aesthete.

Giulio J. Pertile's recent study of Renaissance fainting, *Feeling Faint*,[13] is a useful reminder that the idea of what it means to have a 'consciousness' is determined by time, place and philosophical tradition: early modern Europeans, for example, 'lacked a concept of consciousness' as we might now understand it.[14] Pertile uses moments of unconsciousness to trace developments in experiences and theories of 'consciousness'; he analyses literary depictions of swoons and faints to create a kind of shadow philosophy of what is lost or suspended in these moments: 'the transition from consciousness to its absence enforces close scrutiny of what, exactly, is lost'.[15] And he reminds us that, while different in some important respects, the notion of the 'soul', as an organ of perception, is historically closest to what we might now conceptualise as 'consciousness'. Stendhal (and much later, Joyce too – see Chapter 4), gestures backwards in this respect, in describing a soul that swoons; but he also creates a complicated sense-perception-matrix that is curiously contemporary, at least in terms of circumnavigating mind–body dualism.

In the aftermath of his 'fear of falling', Stendhal walks around Florence in an altered state of consciousness. One notable feature of his precarious perambulations is his sense of the past now being as physically immediate as the present. Stendhal thinks of the great medieval Florentines, of 'Castruccio Castracani, Uguccione della Faggiola, etc., as though I might come upon them face to face at the corner of each street' (305). He describes the architecture of the city impressing itself upon him so forcefully as to disturb his sense of temporal location: 'The power of this mediaeval architecture; I could believe that Dante was the companion of my steps … the traveller may well believe himself to be living in the year 1500' (305). Stendhal has been knocked off his feet, but he's also been knocked backwards: his newly disturbed experience of the physical and the aesthetic alters his experience of time, so much so that he feels he is watching the past play out in front of him in the city: 'I was, so to speak, a spectator who gazed upon the very tragedy of history' (308). The ghosts of the city have become more real to him than the 'insignificant creatures who throng the streets today' (305).

In Stendhal's account, then, the ultimate aesthete is physically affected by the work of art, is made faint by it, and is drawn into contact with the dead. In an attempt to create the diagnosis, 'Stendhal Syndrome', literature and psychiatry collapse into one another in trying to account for swooning. In Palahniuk's rendering of mass faints, the swoon literalises the effectiveness of literature as a 'trapdoor down into some place dark'. In each of these descriptions the swoon is prized, valued as a sign of high sensitivity – but it also ruptures disciplinary integrity: the medical, the literary, the religious and the hyperbolic coincide in the swoon. And what, then, if the ultimate experience of art and literature is a profound, morbid disturbance of consciousness and of discourse? If the 'greatest' works of art seem 'alive' but draw the viewer into faintness and into close proximity with death, then art and literature, begin to seem constitutively dizzying.

Swooning and the feint of a faint

For millennia, for perhaps as long as written traditions have existed, swoons have occupied a crucial place in narrative art. Swoons occur at moments of high emotional intensity: they often dramatise ecstasy and grief. Swooning can indicate a profound disturbance of the human body's balance, in literal fashion. Swooning can also denote a dangerous receptivity to passion, empathy and contagion. In the work that follows, I seek to show that swoons are presented in literature to be read and interpreted; and that they are often used by writers to explore bodily experiences that disturb or challenge dominant narratives of health. Swoons are intimately connected to explorations of sickness and of dying; they cluster in narratives that are preoccupied with femininity and queer sexuality; and they can be unsettling indicators of political instability (the swooning body as metonym of the body politic in disarray).

This book considers texts from a range of different historical periods; while there might be frustrations with this approach (for both the reader and the writer), I hope that it serves to demonstrate the valence of literary swoons across centuries and through different millennia. I am interested in the similarities we can trace across time, and in the ways that the swoons of early mystics might be dimly shadowed in the faints of, for instance, contemporary romance and erotic fiction. The swoon has a long and rich history of animating intense affective states and of depicting these states as powerfully destabilising: the long range of this study will, I hope, help us to understand this, and to see contemporary swoons as palimpsests of previous passings-out. I am also keenly interested in the differences that we can observe when we look at the long history of swooning: in particular, the ways that the swoon is inflected and re-inflected as ideas of the body, gender, race, sexuality and sickness shift through time. A literary history of swooning is also a history of crux points for how we have imagined the body.

Swooning, then, is a crucial part of how literary texts present and interrogate the human body; but its strange status is also fundamental, I will argue, to how we understand literary language. Some definitions of swooning describe it as a constitutively 'literary' phenomenon. One dictionary, for example, designates the verb form as 'a literary word for faint'.[16] Whatever it might mean for a word to be 'literary', whatever special, abyssal quality 'literary' language might have, swooning is closely associated with it. In Shakespeare's *Much Ado About Nothing* (1598), Hero swoons dramatically when she is wrongly accused of unfaithfulness, and her father describes her as fallen, 'Into a pit of ink, that the wide sea / Hath drops too few to wash her clean again'.[17] Hero's body is presented as overwhelmed by ink – by the means of writing; she is floundering in expressive excess which ironically prevents her expression, rendering her mute and unconscious (Hero's swoon is the starting point for my exploration of the readable body-text in Shakespeare's work in Chapter 2). I seek, through proposing a poetics of passing out, to show that the language of swooning is never straightforwardly descriptive: writing about swoons invokes a kind of swoon within and of language. When a swoon is depicted, the rectitude of language is cast into abeyance. Swooning is frequently used in texts to depict the most powerful affective experiences – experiences that are excessive, that are presented as *beyond the measure of language*. Swooning texts mime the failure of language to be adequate to emotional and physical extremes, falling back on the symbolic power of soma to speak when words fail. The literary swoon therefore dramatises a complex crisis of language: in crucial moments, the text defers to the body to speak to the reader but must render a fiction of the mutely speaking body through words. Swoon-texts fall back on the idea of the body as the ultimate mode of expression yet must construct that body through language. The literary swoon produces a phantom of physical experience through words and indicative silences.

The word 'swoon' predates the 'faint'[18] in the English language, and I seek to demonstrate in this book that swooning has a long history that exceeds the faint in terms of its complex suggestiveness and its aesthetic qualities. The literary swoon is performative: it is a creative practice that is never entirely reliable. For instance, the swoon at surface level might be taken as a mark of authenticity of feeling in a text, but it is simultaneously shadowed by showiness, exaggeration, dissimulation and cliché; it is always convulsed by the possibility of contrived performance. A brief example from the work of Dickens shows this in amusing fashion. In *Martin Chuzzlewit* (1842–44) many characters 'sink', often under the weight of their grief. But Sarah Gamp, a self-serving, opportunistic character who ostensibly nurses sick folk while helping herself to alcohol on their premises, shows that such swooning can be a contrivance: 'Mrs Gamp had tottered out first, for the better display of her feelings, in a kind of walking swoon; for Mrs Gamp performed swoons of different sorts, upon a moderate notice, as Mr Mould did Funerals.'[19] Dickens employs the swoon here as a satire of social performances of feeling. Mrs Gamp swoons on demand as part of a cynical, mannered performance that is designed to benefit her in any given situation. Mrs Gamp emphatically does *not* suffer a fainting fit; she is deliberately and repeatedly involved in the construction of a swooning performance 'for the better display' of her supposedly fine feelings. Mrs Gamp, then, does not swoon in any primarily physiological sense of the word. Her swoon is the feint of a faint.

A note on terminology will take us further here: the swoon is of course in close correspondence with the faint. You may have found that your first thought, on reading the word 'swoon', was to think of an involuntary, primarily bodily reaction, synonymous with fainting: the *OED* gives the first definition of the verb to swoon as 'falling into a fainting-fit; to faint'. But literary depictions of swooning destabilise the notion of a straightforwardly physiological destabilisation. A central premise of this book is that the swoon draws its audience into a relation with constructions of affect and aesthetics, with displays of feeling that are performative. I do, however, explore different forms of literary passing out – faints, falls, fits, seizures, sinkings – when they are coterminous with or seem to share the complex performative poetics that I attribute to the swoon.

The literary swoon, then, sinks between involuntary reaction and studied rhetorical flourish; between medical phenomenon and fiction; between bodily action and literary stylisation; between physiology and physiognomy; between private response and public legibility; between feeling and performance; between corporeality and textuality. In this study, the swoon is explored as an event of the body that always also calls for the practice of hermeneutics: it is a 'somatic testimony', in the sense that Mary Ann O'Farrell suggests of literary blushing,[20] which invites us to construct and deconstruct narratives of the body.

Literary-theoretical swoons: A whistle-stop tour

This poetics of passing out will draw on theories of literature and art that help us to understand depictions of a certain kind of falling. But thinking about swooning has also helped me to appreciate the prevalence of falling to much contemporary literary theory. Perhaps I am at risk of being dazzled by my own interests here, but I've come to believe that many of the most influential literary thinkers of the twentieth and twenty-first centuries are interested in the experience of being dizzied, and in producing dizzying effects, as fundamental features of literary encounter. Forgive me for the whistle-stop tour, as I attempt to demonstrate how widespread this interest in falling and faintness might be: Georges Bataille (1897–1962) and Maurice Blanchot (1907–2003), two prominent twentieth-century critics whose work has had a significant influence on the literary-critical landscape, might serve as brief initial examples. In Bataille's extended essay on *Eroticism* (1957), 'the longed-for swoon [*la défaillance*] [...] the desire to fall, to fail, to faint and to squander all one's reserves until there is no firm ground beneath one's feet [...] a moment of disequilibrium',[21] is presented as the ultimate vertiginous prize of physical eroticism as well as of mystical and aesthetic experience. In Bataille's thinking, the ultimate aim of aesthetics is a kind of loss or sacrifice of the self, dramatically enacted in the swoon (see Chapter 4 for a discussion of this in relation to Joyce's work).

Blanchot, a close contemporary of Bataille, similarly privileges experiences of the negative, of 'worklessness' or *désoeuvrement*, of moments of death in life, that can be found in works of literature, and responses to his work bear witness to its profoundly destabilising effects. Ullrich Haase and William Large describe Blanchot as a precursor of post-structuralism in presenting literary experience as a kind of vertiginous disequilibrium: 'the firmness of the ground beneath our feet is seemingly replaced by the infinite connections between words, where one word refers to another word and so on, and where they could not constitute a totality or complex of concepts that would designate a discernible reality'.[22] Blanchot's work encourages us to see literature as words that call truth into question, *including* literature's own truth: the ground beneath our feet and the words on the page become equally unstable and '[l]anguage then becomes the experience of the loss of mastery of the self'.[23]

Much twenty-first century work that has followed on from Blanchot and Bataille continues to describe reading, writing and criticism as processes of destabilisation. In *Insister of Jacques Derrida* (2007), Hélène Cixous describes Derrida's work as akin to childhood games that attempt to induce dizziness. And her writing about this process produces a vertiginous, veering effect through its shifting scope, tumbling temporalities and fluid narrative locations:

> – You remember when we used to spin like tops?
> I am sitting next to my brother, there is no time.
>
> – We tried to make ourselves dizzy, to catch vertigo, says my brother. As if one could catch what one runs after, like Jacques Derrida running after language that ran after him while trying to circumvent it.
>
> – We spun around on ourselves until we got dizzy.[24]

Derrida's approach to language, and language's returning chase, are animated with the dizzying, circular energy of impossible childhood play by Cixous; and her writing enacts literary response as an energetic whirl, charged with the possibility of failing and falling.

The possibility of falling is also crucial to Nicholas Royle's figurations of writing and thinking, which are in close correspondence with Derrida and Cixous. Royle's influential work on the uncanny describes, in its closing chapter, an autobiographical experience of a fall-faint-fit: 'I feel as if I'm falling, I'm experiencing some kind of seizure, an episode, an attack, a fit.'[25] Royle's fall is narrated in fits and starts alongside a discussion of the 'fall' as a fundamental to Freud's discussion of the uncanny:

> Freud's remarks on epileptic and similar fits in 'The Uncanny' are only reiterating what Jentsch had already seen and said [...]: such cases (and everything has to do with the 'case' as the 'fall') can produce the dawning of a 'dark knowledge' that unsettles any sense of the 'human psyche' as 'unified'.[26]

Royle reminds us of Freud's own 'dead faints' – witnessed by Jung and subject to spiralling self-analysis in Freud's personal correspondence – and of Derrida's postcards on falling. Royle's writing falls into a first-person experience through which the very idea of a singular, unified 'first-person' falls away: literary transference, deferred effects, ghostly and virtual archives, déjà vu – all of these complicating, doubling effects are bound up with writing and with falling in Royle's account of them.

Thinking about swooning must also draw on, and into focus, the recent 'affective turn' in literary and cultural criticism, and the work of contemporary critics who (re)examine relationships between bodies and texts. 'Affect theory', as described by Patricia T. Clough, extends the discussion of 'culture, subjectivity, identity, and bodies begun ... under the influence of poststructuralism and deconstruction' and has 'returned critical theory and cultural criticism to bodily matter'.[27] Clough cites critics such as Gilles Deleuze and Felix Guattari, Baruch Spinoza and Henri Bergson, as examples of thinkers who conceptualise 'affect as pre-individual bodily forces augmenting or diminishing a body's capacity to act'.[28] Affect theory, then, focuses our attention on physical capacities, investigating the potentiality of bodies to be affected by – among other things – art, and to affect the world in turn; it describes theoretical work that highlights the importance of bodily matter and physical dynamism to the aesthetic encounter, and focuses on experiences that are not confined to the usual boundaries of a singular subject/subjectivity.

Giulio J. Pertile suggests that affect theory invites us to rethink selfhood as 'a decentred assemblage of impersonal intensities' and he focuses on fainting as 'a paradigmatic example of affect's power to disrupt and overturn ordinary first-person cognition'.[29] He extends these ideas in fascinating ways to give a fuller account than is possible here of consciousness as the capacity to 'self-sense': consciousness as a form, itself, of affect. This poetics of passing out also suggests the 'paradigmatic' quality of the swoon, and seeks to show how the swoon might function in literary texts to register (impersonal) possibilities for change – as well as highlighting the ways that bodies are constricted, rendering the possibility for change dubious or unlikely. If the swoon temporarily suspends the self, or the self's sensing of itself, then regaining consciousness might highlight the brutal inescapability of certain constructions of personhood.

I want to spend some time looking at a particular swoon in Charles Johnson's story 'Exchange Value' (1981),[30] and the reading that Lauren Berlant gives of it in *Cruel Optimism* (2011),[31] to further explore the swoon's importance in relation to affect theory, disrupted selfhood and scenes of potential change. 'Exchange Value' tells the story of two young African American brothers who find a hoard of valuable objects when they break into the apartment of a seemingly impoverished neighbour, Miss Bailey – 'a hincty, halfbald West Indian woman with a craglike face who kept her doors barricaded' whom Cooter, our narrator, recalls having a 'queer, crab-like walk' (398–401). The discovery of a prodigious stash in Miss Bailey's place, a stash which includes dollars, stocks, purses, coins, 'unopened cases of Jack Daniel's, three safes cemented to the floor, hundreds of matchbooks, unworn clothes, a fuel-burning stove, dozens of wedding rings [...] two pianos, glass jars full of pennies, a set of bagpipes, an almost complete Model A Ford dappled with rust, and, I swear, three sections of a dead tree' (400), is a crucial turning-point in the story; it is a moment where everything could change for the two main characters. It is fast followed by the discovery of Miss Bailey's gruesome corpse, and the sight of her bloated, fly-blown body makes Cooter swoon: 'My eyes snapped shut. My knees failed; then I did a Hollywood faint' (401).

In her work on *Cruel Optimism*, Berlant focuses on the imaginative and cultural forces that infringe upon people's physical, emotional and political capacities to affect change – particularly in terms of what she calls 'life-building' and 'life-expending' activities within current conditions of capital. In the early stages of this work, she explores her concept of cruel optimism in part through a reading of Johnson's 'Exchange Value'. Berlant reads Cooter's stagey fall to tell us that these characters' bodies 'become suspended': 'the scene of potential change is somatic. Change is an impact lived in the body before anything understood, and it is simultaneously meaningful and ineloquent' (39). Berlant hints at the contradiction endemic to the depiction of 'speaking', swooning bodies in fiction here: the falling body signifies an important shift that is pre-conscious, a potential power that has not yet been understood. The body registers this impact ahead of language and consciousness. But it is important to add that Cooter's body can only speak to the reader of this possibility of change through words (Cooter's own description of his faint, ventriloquised on the page by Johnson).

Cooter's swoon is read by Berlant as a moment of 'self-abeyance'. Berlant moves from the faint to examine other ways that the narrative explores the energies and lives of the brothers in the context of racist structures of capitalism. I want to look at Cooter's faint in more detail here – in part because I think we could see it as a synecdochal figure for the much of Berlant's work on affect, literature and political change. Berlant describes her work on political depression as tracking 'practices of self-interruption, self-suspension, and self-abeyance that indicate people's struggle to change ... the terms of value in which their life-making activity has been cast' (27). She describes her writing as cataloguing moments of impasse, the suspension of habituated life, and exuberance in that impasse – descriptions that could also function as plausible definitions of swooning. She describes *Cruel Optimism* as 'a kind of proprioceptive history, a way of thinking about the represented norms of bodily adjustment as key to grasping the circulation of the present' (20). Berlant's brief examination of Cooter's swoon hints at the potential importance of the swoon for her proprioceptive work and for affect theory in general: the swoon is a hyperbolic moment of physical destabilisation, through which the body might dramatically register the pre-conscious conditions for change, however (im)possible that change may turn out to be.

Some further thoughts in this respect, building on Berlant's: when Cooter comes round from his faint, he briefly feels what we might describe, after Berlant, as an 'exuberance in the impasse'; that is the possibility of the alleviation of fear:

> I suddenly flashed on this feeling, once we left her flat, that all the fears Loftis and me had about the future be gone, 'cause Miss Bailey's property was the past – the power of that fellah Henry Conners trapped like a bottle spirit – which we could live off, so it was the future, too, pure potential: can *do*. [...] Be like Miss Bailey's stuff is raw energy, and Loftis and me, like wizards, could transform her stuff into anything else at will. All we had to do, it seemed to me, was decide exactly what to exchange it for. (402)

Johnson's story is haunted by the ambivalence of this potential change. Loftis soon makes his brother, Cooter, inventory and move every object from Miss Bailey's flat to their own. Cooter tries to start spending some of the money, but Loftis has begun his own process of metamorphosis: he becomes 'vaguer, *crabby*, like something out of the Book of Revelations' (402, my italics). Loftis becomes more and more like the reclusive spendthrift Miss Bailey. He boobytraps his flat, he refuses to spend any of the stash, he has begun to assume Miss Bailey's crustacean demeanour. When Cooter buys himself a jacket, Loftis lambasts him: 'As soon as you buy something you lose the power to buy something' (402). A few days later, Miss Bailey's body is discovered by the landlord, and Cooter watches as it is stretchered out of the building:

> [T]his dizzy old lady [...] I seen something in her face, like maybe she'd been poor as Job's turkey for thirty years, suffering that special Negro fear of using up what little we get in this life – Loftis, he call that entropy – believing in her belly, and for all her faith, jim, that there just ain't no more coming tomorrow from grace, or the Lord, or from her own labor [...] so when Connors will her his wealth, it put her through *changes*, she be spellbound, possessed by the promise of life, panicky about depletion, and locked now in the past 'cause *every* purchase, you know, has to be a poor buy: a loss of life. (403–4, my italics)

Cooter's reflections here relate to the provenance of the stash: Miss Bailey's former employer, a rich, white industrialist, left his entire fortune to his employee for her twenty years of service. But this windfall hasn't brought 'dizzy' Miss Bailey an escape from poverty.

Just before her death, Miss Bailey was begging for change and living on food handouts from the local Creole restaurant; when they break into her flat, Cooter and Loftis find a broken toilet surrounded by 'five Maxwell House coffee cans full of shit' (398); her corpse is haloed by squashed cockroaches and is infested by a fist-sized rat. The 'changes' that money has produced for Miss Bailey are not positive: she has become a morbid hoarder, living on handouts because of her fear of 'depletion'.

Loftis also refuses to realise the hoard's exchange value: he too becomes afraid of its depletion, or 'entropy', which is the effect, in Cooter's view, of the particular precarity of African American lives: that 'special Negro fear of using up what little we get'. Berlant describes this fear as the effect of a system of racist impoverishment that is so endemic that no individual's windfall and/or concomitant 'sensorial break' is enough to produce a change that can be fully realised.

At the close of the story, Cooter waits for his brother to return home. Loftis seems to have been out scavenging for coins and now falls into a deep sleep that is eerily corpse-like. Cooter is left hoping that things can be different; that the change-potential and *can do* of the hoard might be realised differently for them: 'Me, I wanted to tell Loftis how Miss Bailey looked four days ago, that maybe it didn't have to be like that for us – did it? – because we could change. Couldn't we?' (405). Cooter's earlier swoon may have registered the potential for change, but the anxious and ambivalent ending of this story is a powerful reminder that not all swooning bodies are equal, nor do they have equal access to realise the somatic potential for change.

Cooter's 'Hollywood faint' connects him ironically with a long line of fainting white women on screen. But his own swoon doesn't see him revive into Hollywood luxury: instead, he is cooped up in a flat with a broken bathroom, scrounging food, and waiting for his brother to return. He is haunted by the possibility that there will be no change: that in fact the morbid degradation of Miss Bailey, and the killing poverty of his own parents, will be repeated, will dog the brothers to death. Cooter's faint is powerfully poignant: it shows a moment of potential change blocked by forms of oppression that might repeat themselves, uncannily. If literary swoons are points of possible transformation, they can also, tragically, fail to produce the larger systemic breaks that are necessary for real change. Fainting bodies might then be so much collateral damage, the change-potential of the swoon commuted by systems of inequality into repetition and a prolepsis of death.

Swoon: An overview

It's my contention that reading swoons attentively can help to deepen our understanding of the complex relation between words, affective states, bodies and the work of fiction. Literary swoons often simultaneously inscribe and destabilise narratives of health. Swooning shows us that effective, affective writing compromises the body – that literary experience might darkly undermine our sense of physical integrity, of what constitutes a consciousness, of distinctions of time and space, of the living and the dead. It might even move our body towards strange and morbid states: horripilation, laughter, weeping, dizziness, swoon. This book poses the swoon as a dramatisation of destabilised states, and as an unsettling snagging-point for approaches to art and literature that proceed as though criticism and literary/artistic response is disinterested and/or disembodied. Kate Zambreno registers something similar when she interrogates modes of literary criticism that attempt to eradicate the (female) self: 'Taking the self out feels like obeying a gag order – pretending an objectivity where there is nothing objective about the experience of confronting and engaging with and swooning over literature.'[32] Literary swoons show us that to read literature and to experience art is to be powerfully and physically affected, that art and literature cannot be isolated from the body, nor from the ways in which cultures have narrated bodies at different times according to constructions of gender, sexuality, race and health. This is a poetics of passing out:

Chapter 1 Heart-stopped transformations: Swooning in late medieval literature

To the heart of things. In some of the earliest surviving works of literature, the swoon's symbolic power is bound up with the potential it allows for dramatic alteration: for conversion, for renewal, for sudden change, for spiritual revival into life from death. In the 'Life of Mary Magdalen' (*c*.1290), preserved in the Middle English compilation of saints' lives known as the *South English Legendary*, the swoon is bound up with religious renewal and transformation, and with the new life in 'Crist' that might come from a symbolic death. This early example also binds suffering in childbirth to swooning: the tale of Saint Marie anticipates the (apocryphal) artistic tradition of the Swoon of the Virgin during the Passion, bringing birth pangs and swooning together in an overwhelming agony that produces new life.

In this chapter I also examine the relationship between passivity and passing out in terms of the construction of gender in the most famous swoony text of medieval literature, Chaucer's *Troilus and Criseyde* (*c*.1380). Troilus, a 'weldy' knight, swoons spectacularly in this text and Chaucer provides us with a strikingly physiological account of the swoon: Troilus' heart, and the way it is violently overwhelmed, shows the potential dangerousness of swooning in the medieval medical and literary imagination. Criseyde also swoons at an important point in the text, and these paired but asymmetrical passings-out reveal much about mutuality and difference in the lovers' relationship. The radical claims made by contemporary theorist Leo Bersani in respect of masochism are considered here alongside the erotics of suffering rendered through the medieval literary swoon. I argue that attentively reading the swoons in Chaucer's poem helps us to understand its larger patterns of transformation and the way in which the text pivots between different generic possibilities.

Chapter 2 'Fall'n into a pit of ink': Shakespearean swoons and unreadable body-texts

The swooning Shakespearean body is mired in expressive crisis. The Shakespearean swoons that I focus on in this chapter are abyssal: they stage a fall into the dark depths of a body that is inaccessible to the modes of 'reading' attempted by other characters in the plays. I read swoons in *Much Ado About Nothing* (1598), *Julius Caesar* (*c*.1599) and *Othello* (1604), because these are plays in which bodies are explicitly presented as texts to be read and deciphered – and swooning reveals such processes of reading to be complex, fraught, and/or tragically flawed. Each swoon I draw into focus here occurs when the body cannot be parsed through the signifying systems available within the world of the play: when the systems by which bodies *mean* something – according to humoral theories of the body and/as character, or to emerging medical discourses, or via narratives of differentiation according to sex, race and religion, for example – break down under pressure.

Chapter 3 Feeling too much: The swoon and the (in)sensible woman

A plethora of passing out coincides with historic moments during which emotional demonstrativeness is highly valued and there is a flourish of swooning in eighteenth-century novels under the rubric of sensibility. In this chapter I argue that the literary swoon has a crucial status in the discourse of sensibility: the swoon is the most dramatic in a long list of textual somatic signs of sensitivity – sighs, blushes, tremblings, flinchings, agitations, palpitations, tears, fevers. But, paradoxically, the swoon pushes high sensibility over into insensibility. I read the swoon in sentimental literature as a test of the aspirations to produce a communicable, socially useful version of interior feeling through a new rhetoric of the body. The swoon is also an important component of evolving performances of gender: sentimental scenes of feminine swooning in the popular novels of this time fall back on the pleasures of regarding the inert female form, and there is complex scenography created around 'fallen women' (which might also pertain to other sentimental depictions of suffering, for instance of the conditions of slavery). Focusing on the differences in the depictions of feminine swooning in two novels set apart by forty years – Henry Mackenzie's *The Man of Feeling* (1771) and Jane Austen's *Sense and Sensibility* (1811) – I see their treatment of the swoon as symptomatic of differing attitudes towards the female body in relation to sensibility. As anxieties about sensibility and its representation in 'feminine' novels deepened towards the end of the eighteenth century, a morbid excessiveness of feminine feeling was linked to different types of falling: to the disastrous tumble of the 'fallen woman', to 'falling ill', and to 'falling into hysterics'.

Chapter 4 'Dead-born': Shadow resurrections and artistic transformations

Here I propose a series of connections between ways of imagining the task of writing and ways of imagining the swoon, whereby the swoon is offered as a model of artistic transformation. The swoon in the work of writers considered here is a shadow of dominant narratives of resurrection and rebirth: it is used to describe dark and 'death-born' processes of revivification, and we find it frequently in the work of nineteenth and early twentieth-century writers who seek to channel feminine morbidity in order to challenge masculinist discourses of health and power. If the swoon had become tarnished by associations with feminine incapacity by the end of the eighteenth century, the writers discussed here play on that association in order to devise new forms of writing and of politics. Recent work in disability studies, particularly from scholars formulating 'disability aesthetics', has demonstrated how the formal dimensions of artistic work are shaped in relation to ideas and lived experiences of the body: disability aesthetics rejects notions of the 'healthy body' as the crucible for the production of art. I (re)present the work of John Keats, Edgar Allan Poe and James Joyce to show that they revere a morbid process of swooning as the initiator of art, and in so doing they reject received narratives of health, virility and vitality. James Joyce's descriptions of souls that swoon is given special consideration here as part of his complex reconfiguration of the mind and the body in relation to the aesthetic.

Chapter 5 Vampiric swoons and other dark ecologies

The frequent swoons of vampire victims are blurred, altered states that are darkly and sensuously ecological: in vampire narratives, victims swoon into networks of predation, contagion, telepathy and environmental degradation. I see vampiric swoons as highly erotic and anxious imaginings of interconnection and interference. The swoon iconises a pleasurable *softening into receptivity* that allows incursions of one body into another; and of different minds into one another. In this chapter, I re-present some classic vampire texts – *The Vampyre* (1819), *Carmilla* (1872), *Interview with a Vampire* (1976) – focusing on the swoon as an initiation into a polymeric re-imagining of mind and body. The vampiric swoon produces a mesmerised, ecological continuity between victim and vampire which is, at its most extreme, telepathic. The most famous vampire text, *Dracula* (1897), coincides with the early development of psychoanalysis and the swoon-states of the novel express deep anxieties about interference and thought transference, anxieties that were also important to the early development of psychoanalysis and to Freud's treatment of swooning hysterics. I propose a set of correspondences between the vampiric swoon-states of *Dracula*, the early hypnotic treatment of hysteria, and psychoanalysis's anxious relation to telepathy and occult modes of thinking. Finally, I read mass-unconsciousness-events in the context of mass-extinction-events and zoonotic pandemics to think about violent, deadly, morbidly beautiful forms of interrelation.

Chapter 6 Lovesick, lesbian swoons and the romantic art of sinking

In an afterword to her novel *Carol* (1952), Patricia Highsmith describes her experience of a near-faint as the precursor to the composition of this novel. I suggest that Highsmith deploys fainting in a way that anticipates the work of 'crip theory' in challenging norms of sexuality and the healthy body concurrently: she valorises elements of sickness in order to challenge 'health' as construed by a heteronormative, homophobic culture. In doing so, she has produced a groundbreaking queer romance text, as well as a stimulating version of writing being produced from overwhelmed states and ill-health.

Feminine swooning has been made to function in different ways in relation to romance in works by female writers in the twentieth and early twenty-first centuries: we might see Highsmith's swoons as part of a strategy of innovation and transformation, but feminine romance swooning also risks repetition, bathos and cliché. In contrast to Highsmith's work, I read E. L. James's depictions of feminine sinking in the *Fifty Shades of Grey* (2012) novels alongside Alexander Pope's *Peri Bathous, or the Art of Sinking in Poetry* (1728) to argue that the sinking James depicts might be understood as a form of bathos, or disappointed hope: a falling into cliché ideas of gender submission. James's work sets itself up in relation to a number of historical works of literature, including Thomas Hardy's *Tess of the*

D'Urbervilles (1891), but travesties its literary precedents into bathos. Nostalgia – the desire for temporal sinking back – is embedded in these novels as the eroticisation of past female powerlessness, largely produced through (mis)readings of iconic literary moments, including swoons. This studied anachronism produces a romanticised re-imagining of past female abjection that denies a material history of suffering. As a final contrast to James's bathetic approach to the past (literary and otherwise), I veer at the last moment to the work of Angela Carter and to a very different re-imagining of gender relations, which hinges on a depiction of female faintness.

Passing out: Contemporary catatonia

To pass out of this book, I briefly consider two contrasting instances of contemporary swooning: Marianna Simnett's *Faint with Light* (2016), a light and sound installation which records Simnett repeatedly passing out; and the ubiquitous use of *swoon* as an online 'action'. I consider the latter in relation to the endemic irony David Foster Wallace referred to as 'sardonic exhaustion', and question what role swooning might have now in questions of the virtual, affect and embodiment.

*

I have tried in this study to cover a long sweep of literary history, in order to highlight modulations in literary depictions of swooning over time. I have tended to focus on well-known texts – texts that were popular and/or widely circulated, and/or texts that have been important to literary studies in (re)constructing particular literary periods. My hope is that by reading swoons in these particular texts carefully, an emerging poetics of passing out might help us to appreciate the fictional processes by which bodies have been produced in specific times and places – processes through which certain bodies are spectacularised, venerated, objectified, compromised, traduced, made pitiable; and by which some bodies are partially erased. This approach might fail in a number of ways, and thinking about the narrative quality of swooning has brought me into close contact with different kinds of failure – contending with narratives of revival and transformation that are also always shadowed by recidivism and death. I hope that others will extend this work and take it further where I have failed to do so. This is the incitement: that a poetics of passing out might complicate thinking, consciousness and language through its paradoxical privileging of representations of unconsciousness. That swooning is a work of creative undoing: literary language, subjectivity, the body, politics, life – all fall together.

Notes

1. Abi Palmer, *Sanatorium* (London: Penned in the Margins, 2020), p. 11.
2. *Ibid.*, p. 31.
3. Marcella Biro Barton, 'Saint Teresa of Avila: Did She have Epilepsy?' *The Catholic Historical Review* LXVIII(4) (1982).
4. Palmer, *Sanatorium*, p. 7.
5. *Ibid.*, p. 70.
6. *Ibid.*, p. 71.
7. Chuck Palahniuk, '67 people fainted as I read my horror story', *Telegraph* (June 7, 2005).
8. Clyde Haberman, 'Florence's Art Makes Some People go to Pieces', *New York Times* (May 15, 1981).
9. Dr Graziella Magherini, case notes quoted by Haberman, 'Florence's Art Makes Some People go to Pieces'.
10. Quoted by Haberman, 'Florence's Art Makes Some People go to Pieces'.
11. C. Innocenti, G. Fioravanti, R. Spiti, and C. Faravelli, 'The Stendhal Syndrome Between Psychoanalysis and Neuroscience', *Rivista di Psichiatria* 49(2) (2014 Mar.–Apr.), 61–6.
12. Richard N. Coe, 'Translator's Foreword' to Stendhal, *Rome, Naples and Florence*, trans. Richard N. Coe (London: John Calder, 1959), p. xviii. All further references to Stendhal's work are to this edition.
13. Giulio J. Pertile, *Feeling Faint: Affect and Consciousness in the Renaissance* (Evanston, IL: Northwestern University Press, 2019).
14. *Ibid.*, p. 3.
15. *Ibid.*, p. 6.
16. *The Free Dictionary (by Farlax)*, at www.thefreedictionary.com/swoon: '1. (Medicine / Pathology) a literary word for faint'.
17. William Shakespeare, *Much Ado About Nothing* (1598), 4.1.139–140, in *The Riverside Shakespeare*, 2nd edn (Houghton Mifflin Co., 1997); 'Through Line Numbers' as established by Charles Hinman in *The Norton Facsimile: The First Folio of Shakespeare* (1968).

18 The *Oxford English Dictionary* (*OED*; www.oed.com/), for instance, gives early uses of the verb 'to swoon' in *c.*1290 and 'to faint' in 1375.
19 Charles Dickens, *Martin Chuzzlewit* (Oxford: Oxford University Press, 1982 [1842–1844]), p. 787.
20 I draw here on some of the analyses made in respect of blushing, a 'somatic testimony' given considerably more attention in recent criticism than swooning. See, for example, Mary Ann O'Farrell's *Telling Complexions: The Nineteenth-Century Novel and the Blush* (Durham, NC and London: Duke University Press, 1997), where she describes the blush as 'an event of the body [...] And as an act of interpretation' (p. 4).
21 Georges Bataille, *Eroticism*, trans. Mary Dalwood (London: Penguin Books, 2001 [1957]), p. 240.
22 Ullrich Haase and William Large, *Maurice Blanchot* (London and New York: Routledge, 2001), p. 32.
23 *Ibid.*, p. 3.
24 Hélène Cixous, *Insister of Jacques Derrida*, trans. Peggy Kamuf (Edinburgh: Edinburgh University Press, 2007).
25 Nicholas Royle, *The Uncanny* (Manchester: Manchester University Press, 2003), p. 307.
26 *Ibid.*
27 Patricia T. Clough, 'The Affective Turn: Political Economy, Biomedia, and Bodies', in Melissa Gregg and Gregory J. Seigworth (eds), *The Affect Theory Reader* (Durham, NC and London: Duke University Press, 2010), pp. 206–225, at p. 206.
28 *Ibid.*, p. 207.
29 Pertile, *Feeling Faint*, pp. 15–16.
30 Charles Johnson, 'Exchange Value' (1981) in Joyce Carol Oates (ed.), *American Gothic Tales* (Penguin, 1996), pp. 398–405, at p. 401. All future references will be to this version of the text.
31 Lauren Berlant, *Cruel Optimism* (Durham, NC and London: Duke University Press, 2011). All future references will be to this version of the text.
32 Kate Zambreno, *Heroines* (California: Semiotext(e), 2012), p. 281.

1

Heart-stopped transformations: Swooning in late medieval literature

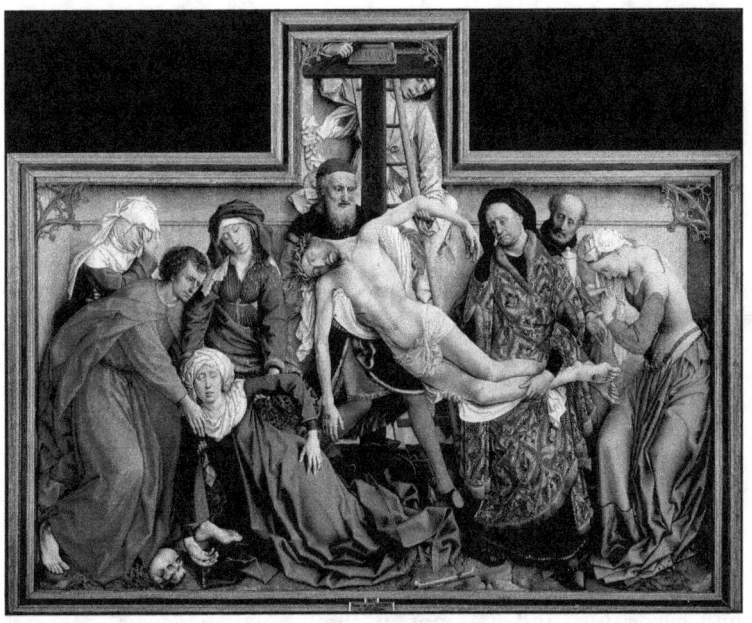

1 Rogier van der Weyden, *The Descent from the Cross*, c.1435, Museo del Prado

> To be true is to be vulnerable to death.
> Stephen A. Barney, 'Troilus Bound' (1972)[1]

In some of the earliest surviving literary examples of swooning, its symbolic power is bound up with the potential it allows for dramatic alteration: for conversion, for renewal, for sudden changes in direction, for revival into life from symbolic death. Saints and romance lovers alike are laid low by a swooning that is the low point of a parabola of possible transformation.[2] In this chapter I focus on instances of the swoon in late medieval literature where it allows for the possibility of dramatic change at the very edge of life; swooning in the literature of this period is often a phenomenon at the extreme of existence, connoting a dangerous vulnerability to death. There is a rich vocabulary for swooning at this time, and many of its forms are intimately connected to mortality. The verb form 'swelten', for instance, initially meant, '[t]o die, perish' (*c*.888),[3] but comes by *c*.1330 also to mean to swoon.[4] Another common form, 'swouen' (*c*.1250), is derived from the Old English *geswogan* (meaning insensible, or in a swoon), a past participle of *swogan*, which could mean to suffocate.[5] Coming round from a swoon is coming back to life from death.

The first swoons that I examine in this chapter are found in the 'Life of Mary Magdalen' (*c*.1290); in this text, the suggestiveness of swooning as a feint of death and resurrection in Christ, and as an expression of maternal suffering, is richly demonstrated. I then focus in detail on the most famous swoony text in medieval literature: Chaucer's *Troilus and Criseyde* (*c*.1380). Troilus' swoon has been the focus of a much recent criticism, some of it reflecting a post-medieval correspondence between swooning and femininity, whereby the swoon is seen to affect the representation of Troilus' masculinity.[6] I reconsider the relationship between passivity and passing out in terms of the construction of the gender of the swoon in these early appearances. As we shall see, in medieval literature swooning is common to both male and female characters in a way that contemporary readers might find surprising, and it is not in conflict with medieval concepts of masculine love. I am indebted in this discussion to Gretchen Mieszkowski, who, reading *Troilus and Crisyede* with and through Judith Butler's work, has shown that the anachronism of some modern responses to the text is a result of the spectacular way in which the swoon has been co-opted into the production of gender over the past six centuries, such that it can be said that the swoon 'acquires gender' through its literary performances in the eighteenth century and therefore appears to modern readers as a 'feminine' act.[7]

Chaucer provides us with a strikingly physiological account of swooning: Troilus' heart, and the way it is described as being violently overwhelmed, reflects the potential dangerousness of swooning in medieval medical and literary discourses. The swoon is one of the tortuous delights of courtly love; an exquisite formulation of physical suffering. It is a bedfellow of other figurations of a lover's disequilibrium and physical danger: it is contiguous with *falling* in love, lovesickness and heartbreak, for example. But the risk of death, I will argue, is key to the swoon's thrill. To claim that there is a connection between physical risk and eroticism in the literature of this period is not, of course, new. Slavoj Žižek has posited a relationship between courtly romance and personal jeopardy in deliberately anachronistic terms when he tells us that 'it is only with the emergence of masochism, of the masochistic couple, towards the end of [the nineteenth century] that we can now grasp the libidinal economy of courtly love'.[8] I hope to add something new to this account by thinking about the dangerousness of swooning in the context of theorisations of masochism that position it as a potential transformation in, and of, subjectivity.

Leo Bersani is perhaps the critic best-known for making this kind of radical claim about masochism as a 'self-shattering' of the subject, and I will read his work in order to help us think about the erotics of suffering rendered through literary swooning. I will re-present Troilus' swoon as a vulnerability he *shares* with Criseyde under the erotic charge of physical risk, and I will focus on Criseyde's own (often overlooked) swoon and its asymmetrical but paired relationship to Troilus', to think about the different kind of physical risk that it represents. In so doing, I want to suggest that attentively reading the swoons in the poem helps us to understand its larger patterns of possible transformation and of eventual failure – which is finally formalised as tragedy.

Saintly swooning in the 'Life of Mary Magdalen'

The 'Life of Mary Magdalen' (*sic*) is a saintly biography collected in the *Early South English Legendary* of approximately 1290,[9] and it contains some of the earliest surviving Middle English examples of swooning. There are numerous examples of earlier French depictions of swooning, many of which are detailed by Judith Weiss in her extensive work on medieval swooning.[10] Barry Windeatt suggests that swooning reaches a peak in the medieval period, in excess of anything that may have preceded it: 'It is not hard to find cases where instances of swooning were added to medieval versions of stories from earlier times and different cultures, and these cases might be presented as evidence that demonstrative sensibility is more pleasing to medieval taste than to taste before or since.'[11]

Swoons are crucial to the narrative in the hagiography of Mary Magdalene – and this particular legend may be from an earlier source than most of the rest of the *Legendary*.[12] In the 1290 version of Mary's life, saint 'Marie' is described as a beautiful woman, 'fair' beyond compare (63). But she is also 'sunful and forlein [unchaste]' (6); Marie is full of pride, and when she inherits a third of her parents' estate she wishes to adorn herself yet more exquisitely. The more beautiful she becomes, the narrator tells us, the more sinful and unwise (65). She pursues the desires of her flesh ('hire flechses wille' (51)) and lies with rich men for great reward ('gret mede' (54)): she becomes known to all as 'Sunfole wumman'. The decisive change from sinner to saint occurs after Marie's first encounter with 'Jhesu'. Marie approaches Jesus unbidden, kisses his feet, bathes them in her tears and dries them with her hair. She is absolved of her sins and becomes a bold and devoted evangelist of Christ.

After the Passion, the *Legendary* tells us, Christians were forced to flee from persecution. Marie boards a ship, which is blown to Marseilles. Here Marie sets about evangelising and petitioning for support, as the Christian group are destitute and close to starving. She encounters a rich 'Sarazen' prince and princess, who have travelled to Marseilles with their retinue. The prince listens to her preach because of her great beauty, but gives the Christians nothing. Marie presses her case with the princess, and the prince then asks for a proof of Marie's teachings. That night the princess conceives a long-hoped-for son, and the prince and princess immediately convert to Christianity. They set out on a pilgrimage across the Mediterranean, but are beset by storms: 'The se bigan to flowen [surge], and the wawes for to arise / Some bigonne to swounen, and heore heortene sore agrise [their hearts were afraid]' (351–352). The verb form 'swounen' is used here to describe falling into unconsciousness in the midst of the surging sea. The imagery of the waves rising and threatening to overwhelm the boat links the consequent swoon to an apprehension of being imminently overwhelmed. This swooning is also proximate with a figuration of the heart ('heortene') as the receptacle of strong, potentially overwhelming, feeling – in this case fear. As the sea rises, and the wind blows yet more strongly, the princess is forced to her bed, taken there by fierce contractions. Once there, she swoons often, we are told, and suffers keenly: 'Heo swounede ful ilomeliche and harde pinede tharefore' (355). Swooning is linked to the inundation of birth pangs, to the 'ful strongue throwes' of birth (354). The word 'throwes', used here to describe violent and uncontrollable contractions, likens the swooning experience of giving birth to the agony of death – the contraction as the chiasma of the 'death-throe'.[13]

The princess must swoon, the narrator tells us, '[s]o forto that hire youngue sone were of hure ibore' (365). But at the moment the child is born, 'the moder bigan to deye' (366). The infant is born into lamentation, bereft of his mother and of any other provider of milk. The ship's men request that the dead princess be thrown into the sea, believing that keeping her cadaver aboard might prolong the storm. But the prince pleads for a stay, for the sake of his son: 'Spariez for mi luytel sone, so that he mouwe habbe is lyf. / For yif is moder mouwe yuyt of hire suoweningue awake, / Thanne may mi luytel sone to hire tete take' (374–376). The prince's hope, then, is that this apparent death is, rather, the princess's continued 'suoweningue', and here we get the swoon in noun form. This form may, in fact, be the oldest: the *OED* tells us that 'to swounen' could be a back-formation, a shortened verb-form derived from the noun. This early form of swooning, then, connects the experience of being overwhelmed to the concomitant possibility of death – and to the hope of revival. 'To swounen' in the face of the potentially overwhelming waves is something from which the men recover. The princess's 'suoweningue' while giving birth, the prince hopes, might similarly be recoverable. We might see some correspondence between this and the swoons that feature in the contemporary French *chansons de geste*. In these heroic tales, Judith Weiss tells us: 'Swooning is never a symptom of weakness or effeminacy: rather, where it is not a sign of religious ecstasy it is a recognised response to overwhelming grief or physical pain, sympathetically received; it is closely associated with death, which on occasion is mistaken for it' (123). The prince hopes that just such a mistake is being made. But eventually he is persuaded to be parted from the princess's body. He spies a hill from the ship, upon which he lays her and the infant he is unable to feed, entrusting them to 'Jhesu Crist'.

The prince makes his pilgrimage to Rome and is baptised. On his passage back to Marseilles he passes the point where he has left his wife and child for dead. The ship comes in to land, and he climbs the hill to see their bodies, finding them in repose. He prays to 'swete Marie Maudeleine' that he might see his wife's body quicken, that she might stir again. And at his words:

> his wif bigan to wake,
>
> Of a swume heo schok and braid, and sone bigan awake,
>
> And seide, 'The hende Marie Maudeleyne, heo hath igive me space,
>
> Fram dethe to live heo havez me ibrought thoru hire Loverdes grace.'
> (486–489)

The princess shakes and starts out of her 'swume'. This variant form is used to figure the swoon as an interim 'space', an abeyance through which Marie has miraculously brought the princess from death to life. The swoon is bound up with religious renewal and transformation, with the new life in 'Crist' that might come from a symbolic death.

It is fitting that this early instance of swooning binds together childbirth, apparent death and spiritual rebirth because the most familiar exemplar of swooning for medieval audiences would come to be, by the fourteenth century, the Virgin Mary swooning during the Passion.[14] Weiss posits the flourishing of the swoon during and after the twelfth century as the result of a rise in 'approved emotional behaviour in both secular and religious contexts' (123), memorably described by Linda Georgianna as the 'cult of tears'.[15] This emotional valency is exhibited in popular artistic depictions of Mary's *compassio*, her strenuous weeping and fainting at the foot of the cross.

Mary's sympathetic swoon was likely to be seen, Amy Neff argues, as 'a sign of strength: the Virgin, by fainting ... shares Christ's suffering and death: it is like a labour which gives birth to the eternal Church'.[16] The belief in Mary's swoon persisted in the absence of any biblical authority, and Barry Windeatt suggests that 'the reference in Revelation 12.1–2 to 'a woman clothed with the sun' who 'being with child cried, travailing in birth, and pained to be delivered' might be adduced in support of the tradition that those

Swooning in late medieval literature

2 Giotto di Bondone, *Crucifixion*, c.1310, Lower Church, Basilica of San Francesco d'Assisi, Assisi

labour pangs that Mary was spared at the miraculous birth of Christ were experienced instead in labour-like agonies of empathetic *compassio* for her son's Passion, which came to include swooning' (213). The apocryphal *Gospel of Nicodemus* (*circa* fourth century) includes some interesting elaborations on the Passion in this respect, describing the Virgin's agony and faint in considerable detail:

> When, therefore, they came to the multitude of the crowd, the mother of God says to John: Where is my son? John says: Seest thou Him bearing the crown of thorns, and having His hands bound? And the mother of God, hearing this, and seeing Him, fainted, and fell backwards to the ground, and lay a considerable time. And the women, as many as followed her, stood round her, and wept. And as soon as she revived and rose up, she cried out with a loud voice: My Lord, my son, where has the beauty of thy form sunk? how shall I endure to see thee suffering such things?[17]

The contemporary poet Steve Ely's recent sequence of poems, *I Beheld Satan as Lightning Fall From Heauen* (2019),[18] responds to this tradition in presenting intense maternal (and paternal) suffering as different versions of falling. His poem 'Melencolia, I' intersperses the Nicodemus account of the Virgin's swoon with unsettling descriptions of different kinds of abjection – of a mother '[b]ug-eyed with the strain of eighteen labours / that sucked her out like cancer'. Ely describes the rendering of the swoon in Nicodemus as 'tendentious, voyeuristic, manipulative, melodramatic, pornographic – and intensely moving'.[19] His own work uses some of the same effects to produce a highly intimate and affecting account of parental loss, violence and guilt – showing the power that Mary's maternal swoon might still exert on our imaginings of childbirth.

The tale of Saint Marie anticipates these different traditions, bringing birth pangs and swooning together in an overwhelming agony that produces new physical and spiritual life.[20] It equates the intense experiences of birth and mothering with the most powerful forms of spiritual suffering. The princess's revival reveals the rich suggestiveness of swooning to imply both the possibility of death[21] (the ultimate risk in childbirth and of being overwhelmed) and the opportunity for revival and transformation. And it is this suggestiveness that later medieval allegories deploy when they continue to imagine great moments of spiritual ecstasy, vision and transition through the swoon.[22]

The swoon and 'self-shattering' suffering in Chaucer's *Troilus and Criseyde*

'While many different strong emotions incite faints in … medieval literature', Gretchen Mieszkowski writes, 'the most usual precipitator is love. Secular love allegories combine wounds with swoons to express at once falling in love and visionary insight into the heart of things.'[23] The combination of wounding and swooning can be felt in the later homonym 'swound' (which the *OED* dates to *c.*1440); and there's an echo of this in 'dswounds', 'zounds' and other variant oaths derived from 'God's wounds' in the early modern period. It is in the context of wounding that I now turn to the richness of the swoon as a figuration of danger and transformation in medieval romance.[24]

The most-remarked-upon swoon in medieval literature is performed by the sort of character we moderns might least expect to feel faint: the celebrated warrior of the Trojan war, Troilus of Chaucer's *Troilus and Criseyde* (c.1380).[25] And this apparent incongruity might go some way to account for the amount of modern critical attention this swoon has attracted. Jill Mann's article on 'Troilus' Swoon'[26] cautions us that Troilus swoons only once in Chaucer's poem: 'It is important to be reminded of this fact', she writes, 'because this isolated instance is sometimes casually multiplied and generalised, as if it were a frequent testimony to the emotional intensity of Troilus' love ... it is also largely responsible for the popular impression of Troilus as a passive and ineffectual lover' (319). Mann's article seeks to singularise this 'multiplied' swoon, and to downplay its status. She sees Troilus' swoon as just one part of what she describes as Chaucer's 'proces' of love, an idealised account of the 'miraculous fusion of the two wills into one, so that it is no longer possible to say whose will is dominant and whose is subjected' (324). In my reading of *Troilus*, I want to challenge the idea of 'proces' as a clean version of parity (in which no character dominates the other), instead proposing that eroticism in the poem is charged by the characters' respective exposures to risk. The swoon will be seen as the most emphatic dramatisation of Troilus' propensity to love sickness, to physical disintegration and to ecstatic self-shattering; and, I argue, this propensity is met by Criseyde's different and specific vulnerabilities, which are iconised in her own swoon. Criseyde's swoon[27] and its concomitant danger of death is overlooked by much criticism that takes the line that Criseyde is a pragmatist, bent on steely self-preservation. Paying attention to Criseyde's swoon, alongside the text's descriptions of her vulnerabilities, I suggest a new reading of erotic love in *Troilus and Criseyde* as a rendering of mutual but differentiated vulnerability: the asymmetries in the text's swoons show us how the two lovers, briefly paired, will finally be set on different courses.

Troilus' swoon is placed at the heart of the structure of Chaucer's poem. The importance of this position becomes clear if we consider how Chaucer rearranged his source materials when composing his work: in Windeatt's introduction to his translation of the text, he tell us that the Trojan war was a favourite subject matter for medieval writers, and of the many versions Chaucer had available to him, the overriding influence is Boccaccio's narrative poem *Il Filostrato*.[28] One of the ways Boccaccio distinguishes his work from earlier accounts is by making the story of Troilus and Criseyde its main subject, and the title of Boccaccio's work can be translated literally as, *Laid Prostrate by Love* or *The One Overwhelmed by Love*.[29] The idea of Troilus being laid out by love, of him being inundated and overwhelmed, is therefore crucial to Chaucer's main source. Boccaccio's account describes Troilus swooning at a moment of high drama: the point at which he hears that Criseyde is to be exchanged for a Trojan prisoner, Antenor, and is therefore about to be removed from Troy. Chaucer's poem, however, moves the swoon to an entirely different point in the narrative: in *Troilus and Criseyde* it occurs immediately before the point of consummation (the mid-point of the total number of lines of the poem); the swoon and sexual consummation become the centre of the text, around which the rest of the narrative rises and falls.[30] Chaucer's decision to move the swoon to this position makes Troilus' swoon crucial for how we understand the consummation between the two lovers, and to how we understand Chaucer's poetic vision as distinct from Boccaccio's.

Chaucer introduces a Troilus who is hubristically certain of himself and his imperviousness to love: he is a 'worthy kynges son' (I.226) who dismisses lovers as foolish and blind; he believes himself to be self-possessed; he knows of nothing with the power to move his heart against his will (I.227–228). And yet, with one look at Criseyde, the 'God of Love' afflicts his heart (I.224): Troilus is in a moment's glance knocked down from his elevated position, and he is now depicted as the prostrate humble servant, the subject, the enthralled: he is 'sodeynly moost subgit unto love' (I.231); the freedom his heart is now 'to hym [Love] thralle' (I.235). The reversal is further symbolised in the *Canticus Troili* in which Troilus metaphorically resigns his royal position and privilege to Criseyde: 'For myn estat roial I here resigne / Into hire hond, and with ful humble chere / Bicome hir man, as to my lady dere' (I.422–434). This is the basis for Mann's argument that there is a transformation of the relative power positions of Troilus and Criseyde as part of Chaucer's 'proces' of love (324). While the dynamics of power and agency are clearly of interest here, Mann describes a utopic equalising of social power between man and woman, between privileged and dispossessed. But Troilus never gives up his royal or social advantage over Criseyde, or his position as dominant character in the poem. The crucial reversal is in the dominance of Troilus' own will as opposed to the will of the 'God of Love'. Troilus submits to Love, rather than to Criseyde – who, after all, gains no material benefit from his submission.

One striking aspect of Troilus' first sight of Criseyde is the sense of physical danger that is described as concomitant with it – a danger that is inherent in the medieval concept of love, but is especially pronounced in this text. When Criseyde looks at Troilus, we are told, 'sodeynly hym thoughte he felte dyen, / Right with hire look, the spirit in his herte' (I.306–307). This image of damage to his heart is the start of a remarkable depiction in the poem of Troilus' love as a matter of life and death. The death of the 'spirit in his herte' can be understood in the context of the Galenic physiology that was prevalent in the Middle Ages. Galen, a Greek physiologist (c.AD 200) who influenced the study of anatomy for nearly 1,400 years, often invoked the theory of *complexio*, or temperament; that is, the balance of the elementary qualities of hot, wet, cold and dry in the body.[31] Each organ of the body was thought to have its own complexional quality: the ideal complexion was temperate, and imbalance was thought to cause sickness. Alongside the complexions, the body was imagined to be composed of other 'things natural' which included 'humors, members, virtues, operations and *spiritus*'.[32] *Spiritus* was imagined as a substance manufactured in the heart and transmitted through the body via the arteries, closely resembling the Greek concept of *pneuma* – a breath-like vital force.[33] So when we are told that Troilus feels as though his heart is on fire, affected by extraneous heat, and that he thinks the spirit of his heart is dying with Criseyde's look, we are being told that he perceives himself to be in a highly dangerous physiological state of disequilibrium.

These sorts of descriptions have led some critics to re-read courtly romance tropes of suffering in the context of contemporary theorisations of masochistic desire. Holly Crocker and Tison Pugh,[34] in their work on masculinity, masochism and pleasure, reflect on the presentation of Troilus in light of the work of contemporary critic

Leo Bersani, for instance. They describe Troilus' experience of love as a potentially 'ecstatic "shattering"', sharing some similarities with Bersani's formulation of masochism. In *The Freudian Body*,[35] Bersani re-reads Freud's *Three Essays on the Theory of Sexuality*[36] to argue that masochism is constitutionally essential to the development of childhood sexuality. This sexuality, Bersani argues, is the by-product of experiences when they reach a certain level of *intensity*. Intensity, Bersani tells us, is experienced as a shattering for the infant, and any intensity will be experienced as a sexual pleasure when it is strong enough to shatter a certain stability or equilibrium of the self. Bersani draws here on Jean Laplanche's theory of sexual excitement as an effect of *ébranlement*, of perturbation or shattering. The gap between the 'period of shattering stimuli and the development of resistant or defensive ego structures'[37] is psychically bridged by a strategic masochism, the development of a sexuality that finds pleasure in being shattered. It is in this sense that 'sexuality – at least in the mode in which it is constituted – could be thought of as a tautology for masochism'.[38] If sexuality is 'constituted as a kind of psychic shattering, as a threat to the stability and integrity of the self'[39] then Bersani can extrapolate that: 'sexuality would be that which is intolerable to the structured self'.[40] We are '"shattered" into an ego-shattering sexuality'[41] that is a kind of disintegration of the self rather than its triumph.[42]

We might see this idea of sexuality as a shattering, overwhelming experience being dramatised in the heightened sense of physical danger that accompanies the experience of desire for Troilus. It can seem extraordinary to the modern reader the extent to which Troilus conceives of and petitions for love in terms of the precariousness of his health, or 'hele'. In the early stages of the poem, before proclaiming his love, Troilus wishes for Criseyde's pity, 'er that I deyde!' and 'hele ... And lif is lost' (I.459–462). His love is described as manifesting like a sickness: he is sleep deprived, food becomes his enemy, and he looks decidedly peaky: 'He seyde he hadde a fevere and ferde amys [felt unwell]' (I.491). When Pandarus petitions Criseyde on Troilus' behalf, the matter is presented to her as the possibility for her to prevent the death of a virtuous man. The threat then escalates to become the possible deaths of both Troilus *and Pandarus* if she refuses Troilus' ardour: 'But if ye late hym deyen, I wol sterve [die] ... What mende ye, though we booth appaire [should perish]?'

(II.323, 329). Criseyde is repeatedly figured as the 'cure' for Troilus' affliction, the cure, even, for death: 'Lo, here his life, and from the deth his cure!' (I.319–329). And when she is finally persuaded to visit Troilus in his chamber at night it is because Pandarus exhorts her, twice, not to be so foolish as to put Troilus' life in jeopardy by letting him endure a night of jealousy.[43] Pandarus' cynical histrionics effectively manipulate Criseyde.

Windeatt writes of the tradition of love as a sickness which allows Chaucer to play with the ironies of illnesses feigned and real; but, Windeatt reminds us, this is 'always veined with seriousness, since some medieval medical writings did indeed recognise the lover's malady as a form of illness ... the intensity of the most important emotional transitions and experiences is throughout associated with the extremity of death'.[44] Pandarus might be working cynically, but Troilus is presented as believing in his own jeopardy. Marcia Smith Marzec reiterates this point, suggesting that the love malady, which is sometimes merely a literary convention, is here posited as a 'literal fact';[45] the 'symptoms of courtly love in Troilus correspond to medieval understanding of the incapacitation caused by the disease *amor heros*'.[46] We might even see later definitions of 'lovesickness' as evolutions of Chaucer's description of love here (and its resulting swoon): the OED, for instance, gives an early example from *Partonope of Blois* (1450) of 'lovesick' being '*Overwhelmed* by (esp. unrequited or unfulfilled) love' and surrounded by suffering: 'Lovesyke She was ... Grete greef She felt all a-boute.'[47]

The various prostrate states in which Troilus is presented in the early stages of the narrative prepare him (and the reader) for the physical crisis of his swoon – when Pandarus encourages Troilus to take him into his confidence about his love of Criseyde, for instance, Troilus initially says not a word: 'But longe he ley as stylle as he ded were' (I.722). His eyes are cast up in his head, so that Pandarus fears he will 'in frensie [...] falle, or elles soone dye' (I.727–728). Troilus seems close here to some kind of fatal fit. Pandarus tries to rouse him: 'What! Slombrestow as in a litergie?' (I.730). Litergie connotes a more serious state than we might now associate with the term lethargy: the *Middle English Dictionary* describes 'litergie' as 'a disease characterized by prolonged unconsciousness or coma'. Pandarus is a pragmatist in the game of love, one who threatens his own death with a sort of playful cynicism, and similarly threatens to swoon as part of his love parley with Criseyde (he cannot repeat all of Troilus' sorrowful words to Criseyde, else 'ye wol se me swowne' (II.574)). But for Troilus, the threat of death functions as more than an elaborate play to win his lady's affection. His tendency to prostrate states is emblematic of the physical jeopardy love has placed him in. The coincidence of love and disease; a profound, erotic disturbance of body and mind; desire that risks fatality: these are the dangerous states that will culminate in Troilus' swoon.

To the central swoon in question, then: Pandarus has finally manoeuvred Criseyde into Troilus' chamber, through the fabrication of a story about Troilus' jealousy. This story has been concocted without Troilus' knowledge or consent, and when he realises how upset his imputed jealousy has made Criseyde, he fears that all is lost. With each tear that Criseyde sheds, 'wel he felte aboute his herte crepe, [...] The crampe of deth to streyne hym by the herte' (III.1063–1065). The importance of the heart is emphasised in the repetition here. The beginning of the swoon is the creeping cramp of death, which clutches Troilus' heart. He feels he is as good as dead ('He felte he nas but deed' (III.1081)). He protests he is not to blame for the situation and then his heart begins to effect the swoon proper:

> Therwith the sorwe so his herte shette
>
> That from his eyen fil there nought a tere,
>
> And every spirit his vigour in knette,
>
> So they astoned or oppressed were.
>
> The felyng of his sorwe, or of his fere,
>
> Or of aught elles, fled was out of towne;
>
> And down he fel al sodeynly a-swowne. (III.1086–1092)

The swoon's physiological onset is described as a totalising contraction beginning in the heart. The heart shuts tightly; Troilus' tears are stopped up inside him; the vital spirits, essential for the function of the organs and the humours, are contracted in their force, as though stunned or overcome; all feeling flees. Then Troilus swoons. Windeatt tells us that even given the ubiquity of the swoon in medieval literature, Chaucer here gives us an 'unusually scientifically aware' depiction of the onset of a swoon.[48]

Troilus is immediately thrown onto the bed by Pandarus and finally awakens from his 'swough' after Criseyde's fervent whisperings of forgiveness and plentiful kisses. Both Pandarus and Criseyde chastise him for being unmanly: 'O thef, is this a mannes herte?' (III.1098); 'Is this a mannes game?' (III.1126). There has been a slew of criticism focusing on Troilus' passivity in relation to masculinity, largely prompted by this swoon: David Aers, for example, has described Troilus suffering from male-identity performance anxiety;[49] Windeatt describes the swoon as a deflation of male stereotypes;[50] Edward Condren likens Troilus to a Victorian maiden suffering under vapour attack and suggests the swoon is symbolic of the experience of premature ejaculation;[51] elsewhere the swoon is viewed as a response to the possibility of impotence.[52] These positions are summarised by Gretchen Mieszkowski, in her excellent work 'Revisiting Troilus's Faint', and she goes on describe the anachronistic assumptions that underlie them: commentators since the 1990s have, she argues, described Troilus as effeminate, emasculated, and even impotent, basing their analysis on his 'feminine' passivity as demonstrated in his swoon. Twenty-first-century critics and readers, she suggests, see Troilus as 'unmanly' because they think of '[f]ainting as a behaviour peculiar to women'.[53] However, these same readers:

> will be surprised to learn that there is no basis in medieval literature for reading Troilus's passivity or his faint as evidence of effeminacy. Neither passive loving nor fainting was identified with women more than with men in the literature of Chaucer's period. [...] Both men and women faint in medieval literature, heroes in particular faint, and there is nothing unmanly about the act of fainting. 'Traunce,' 'swelte,' and most often 'swouen' in various forms precede 'faint' as words for losing consciousness in Middle English, and even a cursory reading of the pronouns in the Middle English Dictionary's citations for them shows how much more often the swooners are male than female. Some faint because they are wounded in battle, but others faint for strong feelings of all sort: joy, misery, humiliation, remorse, and particularly love.[54]

Mieszkowski goes on to describe the ways in which Troilus' swoon might be seen as an extreme version courtly behaviour in the context of medieval romance: 'Being capable of extraordinarily intense, idealising love is an attribute of greatness in these romances, and fainting is a sign of that capacity. By romance convention it is the greatest warriors and the greatest lovers who faint.'[55] And if a medieval audience were likely to consider swooning a sign of 'effeminacy', she argues, Chaucer's Arcite, Aurelius and Mars, the romances' Lancelot, Florimont, Partonopeu, Generydes, Claris, and 'other battle-hardened, tournament-winning, giant- and dragon-slaying heroes would not have been depicted fainting'.[56]

We might see the recent critical response to the swoon, then, and its critique of Troilus' masculinity, as an anachronistic reading that reveals the remarkable transformation of the swoon over time in terms of what Mieszkowski calls its *gender acquisition*. Over the course of six centuries, Mieszkowski suggests, 'passive loving became gendered so exclusively female that its earlier stature as a powerful and appropriate form of male loving in romance sank out of sight. Male fainting follows a similar but more extravagant trajectory'.[57] The 'extravagant trajectory' of the swoon in terms of its gendered associations will be revisited in Chapter 3, where I consider the discourse of sensibility and the 'feminisation' of swooning in the eighteenth century. But for now, let us return to Troilus' swoon, with Mieszkowski's injunction in mind to attend to it as an indicator of strength of feeling.

The question of Troilus' 'mannes herte' is raised, Mieszkowski contends, in order to nudge Troilus towards making love to Criseyde, rather than in response to his swoon. In other words, the swoon precipitates, rather than undermines, the physical consummation of love: Troilus is suddenly resolved and takes Criseyde in his arms. As I suggested earlier, Mann's notion of an equivalence of social and political equality achieved between lovers through Chaucer's 'proces' of love is perhaps an optimistic or utopic reading. Mieszkowski offers a slightly different version of the kind of parity that might be proposed through the romance tradition. A sort of equality, she suggests, may reside in the linked experience of passivity and suffering by *both sexes* in the face of Love. Medieval romances lavish attention on the subjection of male lovers and how excessively they suffer. The male hero is not feminised by this suffering, because 'passive loving is not gendered female or male in these stories ... Romance men and women suffer equal passivity as lovers.'[58]

We have seen that Troilus' experience of desire is potentially overwhelming and that the strength of his feeling causes him to swoon. How might 'equal passivity' then be understood in relation to Troilus and Criseyde in terms of their respective swoons? Criseyde's swoon is given considerable space in the poem, but has received comparatively little critical attention. Criseyde swoons in Book IV, at some distance from the consummation scene; while Troilus' swoon is a kind of crescendo of his suffering, which precipitates the lovers' consummation, Criseyde's swoon initiates a sequence of post-coital events that mitigates against the lovers being together. To understand how these two swoons are paired and differentiated, we need to turn to Criseyde's response to Troilus's courtship and in particular to the extraordinary images surrounding *her* heart.

When Pandarus first presents Troilus' suit, Criseyde's immediate response is fear: she was, 'wel neigh starf [dead] for feere' (II.449) and she is, we are told, the most fearful of persons. Criseyde's anxiety reflects her precarious situation in Troy. Her father has abandoned the city and defected to the Greek side. Her social position is vulnerable, and the possibility of rape (both in the modern sexual sense and the more ambiguous medieval sense of plunder),[59] is frequently evoked in the poem. On the morning before Pandarus' visit to Criseyde, he is awoken by birdsong:

That swalowe Progine, with a sorowful lay [song],

Whan morwen come, gan make hire waymentynge [lament]

Whi she forshapen was [...]

How Tereus gan forth hire suster take. (II.63–73)

It is with the myth of Procne and Philomela, the Greek tale of rape, revenge and metamorphosis, that Pandarus is roused from his sleep and reminded of his task to seduce Criseyde. This is an unsettling reminder of mythologies of sexual violence at the very start of Troilus and Criseyde's courtship, and it echoes darkly through the narrative. Later, when Troilus discovers that Criseyde is to be taken from Troy, Pandarus proposes that he 'ravysshe' Criseyde, carry her off by force, thereby making known that he is a man (IV.538). This is 'no rape ... ne no vice' (IV.596), Pandarus reasons. But Troilus reminds him that the Trojan war is itself the result of the abduction of women, and refuses any masculine action that involves force and risk of injury to Criseyde. When Troilus and Criseyde are separated, it is the possibility of being raped in an attempt to return to him that she dreads 'moost of alle': 'If in the hondes of some wrecche I falle, / I nam but lost, al be [even though] myn herte trewe' (V.705–706). These are all reminders that the world Criseyde inhabits is one in which she is perpetually vulnerable to rape and plunder.

How might Criseyde negotiate her own desires in such a dangerous context? After Pandarus' first approach, Criseyde reflects on her situation. In a much remarked-upon line, Criseyde tells us that she is self-sufficient: 'I am myn owene womman' (II.750). Why, she questions, would she countenance a relationship with a man, a husband who might 'checkmate' her, who might be jealous, or domineering or philandering? These fears overshadow all her 'brighte thoughtes' until 'for feere almost she gan to falle' (II.770). Criseyde almost faints here at the terrible possibility of being in thrall to a man; she is almost overcome by the thought of being overpowered. And yet, despite these fears, she does finally entertain the thought of Troilus: 'He which that nothing undertaketh, / Nothyng n'acheveth, be hym looth or deere' (II.807–808). Nothing ventured, nothing gained seems to be her resolution on the matter. By the end of that day, the early morning chanteuse of sexual violence, Procne, gives way to a new set of disquieting images of birds. As Criseyde falls asleep, she hears a nightingale sing. This transports us again to the mythical scene of rape, to Philomela overpowered, tongueless, and metamorphosed into a nightingale. Yet, the song of the nightingale is now, 'Peraunter in his briddes wise a lay / Of love' (II.921–922). The ambivalence of the 'Peraunter', or 'perhaps', here, is crucial. There is the possibility for the song to be one of love, not rape; the inverse is also, therefore, still possible. A similarly ambivalent set of images follows as Criseyde is described being violently 'seized' by sleep:

Til at the laste the dede slepe hire hente [seized].

And as she slep, anonright tho hire mette [dream]

How that an egle, fethered whit as bon,

Under hire brest his longe clawes sette,

And out hire heart he rente, and that anon,

And dide his herte into hire brest to gon –

Of which she nought agroos [was frightened], ne nothyng smerte [felt pain] –

And forth he fleigh, with hert left for herte. (II.925–931)

Alan Fletcher has described this dream fragment as combining two traditions that would have been familiar to medieval readers: the trope of the exchange of lovers' hearts, and the connection between the *avis predalis* and the heart. Certain medieval bestiaries reveal the custom of rewarding domestic birds of prey with the hearts of the birds they seize, and the influential fourteenth-century treatise on the seven deadly sins and their remedies, the *Fasciculus morum*, depicts the *avis predalis* as eating nothing from its prey but the heart. This leads Fletcher to conclude that the elements of the dream that are most strange to a modern reader might have been more familiar to the medieval reader; but, '[w]hat is more likely to have been surprising to them is how Chaucer has conflated the two traditions'.[60]

This conflation, of a loving exchange of hearts and the violent consumption of the heart in a predatory relation, is indeed a fascinating and troubling one. What is perhaps even more striking is the fantasy that this 'aquiline operation is painless'. The symbolism of the traditional exchange of hearts is rendered profoundly violent through the admixture of the bird-of-prey imagery, and the tearing of Criseyde's heart from her breast. And yet Criseyde dreams herself without fear or pain; in fact, Fletcher suggests, the 'sensation is implied to be quite otherwise'. The possibility posed by the dream for Criseyde is not an escape from a process of violation through the ideal social equality that Mann seems to imagine. Rather it places her in the extreme position of vulnerability, with the possibility of an anaesthetised pleasure through a process of violence. A rending of the heart that is painless. A penetration that produces no fear. These ambivalences are deeply, unresolvably and pleasurably embedded in the dream imagery. And they are crucial to the developing erotics of the poem. The bird of prey imagery is revived a little further on, at the very point of consummation, placing it alongside the swoon at the structural heart of the poem. When Troilus revives from unconsciousness, he is described as taking Criseyde decisively into his hold. She is the hapless 'larke', grasped by the 'sperhauk' (III.1191–1192). The violence of these metaphors has led some feminist critics to describe the consummation depicted here as tantamount to rape.[61] But another interpretation is that there is a mutual erotic pleasure in assenting to the possibility of being overwhelmed and destroyed. Criseyde has emphatically consented to this hold, and consented in advance: 'Ne hadde I er now [If I hadn't before this], my sweet herte deere, / Ben yolde [Yielded], ywis, I were now nought heere!' (III.1210–1211).

I propose a parallel between this yielding, and the possibility of violence it admits, and Troilus' earlier yielding to the dangerous torment of Love: 'O quike deth, O swete harm so queynte, / How may of the in me swich quantite, / But if that I consente that it be?' (I.411–13). Criseyde's assent to the possibility of a pleasurable violent rending is erotically met by Troilus' propensity to 'swete harm' as the consequence of love, and this, I think, is the mutual erotic grounds for consummation. Their hearts are both compromised by the possibility of violent interference: Criseyde's might be torn from her breast; Troilus' is liable to shut down. And both of them, the text suggests, find erotic pleasure in the shadow of this risk. The post-coital moment for Troilus and Criseyde is described as a mutual relief of fear: Criseyde is like the 'newe abaysed [suddenly startled] nyghtyngale' (III.1233), stopped in her song, but then, relieved of fear, letting her voice ring out stronger; Troilus is like one who knows his death has been decreed ('his deth yshapen, / And dyen mot' (III.1240–1241)), but who is suddenly rescued, and brought from death to safety. Criseyde is briefly given the power of her own voice, in contrast to the mythical end of speech as the consequence of rape in the story of Procne and Philomela; and Troilus is temporarily relieved from sickness and the fear of death. The pleasure of relief here is conditioned by the previously threatened risks to both of them.

What's more, Criseyde's recognition of the fragile quality of Troilus' 'tendre herte' (IV.795) is the precondition for her erotic involvement with him, and is, I think, part of what she finds intoxicating about his knightly masculinity. When Criseyde first hears of Troilus' love for her, she muses on how a woman may receive a man's love: 'For man may love, of possibilitie, / A womman so, his herte may tobreste, / And she naught love ayein [in return], but if hire lest [unless she wants to]' (II.607–609). Criseyde uses particularly violent language here of the male lover's heart shattering into pieces – 'tobreste'. She then watches from her window as Troilus rides back into the city after battle. Troilus is a vision of knightly bravery, a man of battle likened to Mars. So 'weldy', or vigorous, he seemed, that it was 'heven' to look upon him. The details of his appearance after battle are noted: his helmet, we are told, has been 'tohewen', or chopped, into twenty pieces; his shield has been 'todasshed', shattered into pieces, by swords and maces, and embedded with arrows that have 'thirled', or pierced it. Criseyde lets the whole scene soak into her heart, we are told, until she is forced to ask herself, 'Who yaf me drynke?' (II.651). Criesyde's use of 'drink' here is ambiguous: she could be imagining alcohol, or some more affecting potion. But whatever 'drink' is being imagined here, the effects to which she attests are those of intoxication. The intoxication of Troilus' knightly masculinity seems to be, at least in part, due to the possibility this weldy performance connotes of its own violation; the performance of strength depends on the possibility of the knight being shattered, 'tohewen', 'todasshed' and 'thirled'. Masculinity is constructed here in close proximity to danger and physical destruction.

The possibility of Troilus' heart and body being overwhelmed, to the point of death, is crucial to his experience of his passion for Criseyde, and to her acceptance of it. And while I want to argue that both lovers are exposed to risk, which acts as a mutualising erotic ambience, there are also important differences between their respective situations. If Troilus' swoon demonstrates his vulnerability to love – and to death as part of courtly ritual – then Criseyde's swoon demonstrates her vulnerability to a different set of external forces, and the asymmetry of their paired swoons will demonstrate the specific differences of the situations of the two lovers. The swoons in this text, I want to argue, are cruxes of possibility, both at the level of action and at the level of genre. Troilus' swoon allows him to revive into the consummation of his love, creating a moment of courtly union. Criseyde's swoon dramatises the specific threats to which she is subject, and in so doing it functions as a sort of generic hinge, swinging Chaucer's text from romance towards tragedy.

At the point in the poem when Criseyde swoons, we discover that she is to be exchanged with the Greeks for a Trojan prisoner,

Antenor, at the request of her father: the full extent of her vulnerability to being traded as a war-commodity has been realised. When the two lovers next meet, Criseyde asks, in desperation, for Troilus' help; and then, we are told, she 'loste speche' (IV.1151). Criseyde sinks into a swoon; she lies as though dead – she is unresponsive, her limbs cold, her complexion now pallid and greenish. Troilus can find no trace of breath. All the risks that have previously attended Troilus' swoon are here attendant upon Criseyde. During the swoon, Criseyde's 'spirit' is described as flickering above her, before returning again into her woeful heart. The swoon is once again associated with the vital spirit of the heart, and with the possibility of it fatally fleeing. Troilus lays Criseyde out, 'And after this, with sterne cruel herte, / His swerd anon out of his shethe he twighte / Hymself to slen' (IV.1184–1186). Criseyde's swoon, and its potential to trigger a death domino-effect, flashes us forward here to the full tragic possibility of Shakespeare's *Romeo and Juliet*, with Juliet in her 'borrowed likeness of shrunk death',[62] Romeo's quick drugs and the final 'happy dagger' (V.iii.170) left to rust in Juliet's breast.[63] In *Troilus*, however, the hero's suicide is averted at the last possible moment: Criseyde revives from her swoon ('of swough therwith sh'abreyde' (IV.1212)) at the very point when Troilus is poised 'With swerd at herte, al redy for to deye' (IV.1211). The swoon is dramatically positioned as the brink between life and death, with Criseyde (and Troilus) poised at the very cusp.

If Troilus' swoon demonstrates his danger in the face of love, Criseyde's swoon dramatises her own apprehension of her vulnerability to a different risk – to being traded and to being raped – and her swoon shows her proximity to death in the context of war, not love. Both Troilus and Criseyde are depicted as subject to the danger of swooning, then, and their early courtship establishes an erotics based on shared risk and vulnerability. But any parity between the two lovers is tragically brief: their shared vulnerability is an important feature of the courtship that leads to consummation, but after this moment, Criseyde and Troilus are set on different trajectories. Criseyde's swoon is not one that ushers in a romantic union, but rather signals the start of the end.

Recent Chaucer criticism has suggested that the poem's particular focus on Troilus' exquisite suffering could be seen as the apotheosis of an elite, spiritually masochistic masculinity which is offered as a superior alternative to the female experience of suffering. This is perhaps most persuasively argued by Holly Crocker and Tison Pugh,[64] and my description of the asymmetries of the two characters' swoons (Troilus' as the zenith of the text; Criseyde's as the domino-fall towards tragedy) might usefully be read alongside their work. Troilus' suffering, they claim, is given an extraordinarily privileged position within the text, in excess of what might be expected even within the traditions of courtly tribulation. The importance accorded to the suffering of Troilus, they argue, gives him an elevated position within the poem, and his ordeal 'refines even more delicately an elite model of masculinity in which his endurance of pain is identified as a defining experience for the culturally privileged male'.[65] They connect this to the sacrificial poetics of the text: the elevation of the penalised male form is informed by the visual sacralisation of Christ's pain in the late Middle Ages, so that the 'cultural valorization of suffering provides a valuable commentary on masochism's connection to courtly love, for in this rendering of loving sacrifice, it is the bleeding, broken body of the divine that is sublimated'.[66] The cultural privilege afforded to Troilus' masochism is, in their formulation, denied to Criseyde as a woman, and it 'achieves fixity'[67] for an idealised Troilus through a refined masculine identity. In the end, they suggest, it is Troilus' 'self-possession' throughout his suffering that is the source of his masochistic pleasure, and his final ascendance to the celestial realms represents the apotheosis of his refined, and redemptive, masculine suffering.

This discussion of the 'immuration' of Troilus' identity through his suffering has important consequences for how we might think of the swoon in relation to masochism. Is masochism (and any swooning it occasions) actually a kind of hardening or 'fixing' of an identity based on refined suffering, rather than an 'undoing' of the subject, as Bersani (at least in his early work) might have it? To assess Crocker and Pugh's reading of Troilus as 'fixed' by his masochistic trajectory, we might pay attention to the remarkable star-trail of images of Troilus' shattered body through the text, which at first seem to exhibit disintegration and abjection rather than fixity. After discovering that Criseyde is to be removed to the Greek camp, Troilus spirals towards the physical disintegration his love has always threatened: his woe '[o]ut breste [bursts out]' (IV.237) his chest, and he is described as acting like a wild bull pierced through the heart; he flings himself around his chamber, beating his breast with his fists, striking his head against the wall and his body against the floor, 'hymselven to confounde' (IV.245). This is love's operation, he concludes, to prove its 'gerful [unpredictable] violence' (IV.286). When Pandarus visits him, he 'gan bresten out to rore' (IV.286); he roars out his pain, a violently rupturing expression of his grief and the inevitability of his death. Separated from Criseyde and increasingly jealous of her love, Troilus undergoes a rapid physical decline. He thinks his heart is split in two ('Hym thoughte his sorwful herte braste a-two' (V.530)). The modern language of a broken heart is anodyne in comparison to Chaucer's depiction of the heart violently ruptured. When Troilus sleeps, he falls into nightmares that wake him suddenly, and strangely disturb his heart: 'And swich a tremour fele aboute his herte / That of the fere his body sholde quake' (V.255–2556). He feels himself to be steered towards death, like a boat on a dark sea ('Toward my deth with wynd in steere I saille' (V.641)). Troilus becomes physically unrecognisable: he becomes thin and weak and walks with a crutch. He is described as violently confounding himself with his anger ('with his ire he thus hymselve shente' (V.1123)); when asked what pains him, he explains that 'his harm was al aboute his herte' (V.1125). He begins to will his own death, wishing that his heart would, irrevocably, break: 'Ful ofte a day he bad his herte breste' (V.1568).

But of course, however physically 'shattered' Troilus might appear, this description of his disintegration is also 'fixed' at the level of the text: Troilus' suffering for love has been celebrated by readers and critics for centuries as rarefied and tragic. The way that the poem ends certainly brings us back to Crocker and Pugh's conception of Troilus as an elevated, fixed point of masculine religious refinement, a ratification of the erotically shattered subject as ascendant. Troilus is, finally, slain in battle by Achilles. At the point of death his spirit (his 'goost') ascends, just as Criseyde's has in her near-death swoon. But this time the spirit does not return to Troilus' ravaged body: it surpasses the planets, moving up to the heavens, from where it has a total view of the 'erratik sterres' (V.1812) and can look down on '[t]his litel spot of erthe' (V.1815). This is, crucially, the point at which the narrative makes the swoon impossible and death inevitable; and we can see the hardening of certain positions after Criseyde's swoon as producing *Troilus and Criseyde* as 'tragedye'. The end of the poem might then show the failure of the erotics of mutual vulnerability, of that brief, shared sense of mutual exposure to risk, to persist for Troilus and Criseyde. After Criseyde's swoon, she is set on the path of pragmatism needed to secure her survival, and Troilus is set on the path towards an idealised death. Troilus swoons in the genre of romance; Criseyde's swoon ushers in the irreconcilability that belongs to the genre of tragedy.

What then of the potential work of masochism as 'undoing', and the swoon as part of this work? Hugh and Crocker see Troilus' final ascendance as the zenith of rarefied masochism: a straight line between swooning and subsequent ascent. But might it also be possible to think of the laying low of the swoon as a moment of *potential*, which is (tragically) succeeded by an ascendance to something fixed? In Bersani's own later revisions to his ideas on masochism, he comes to see masochistic self-shattering as an unsustainable alternative to other modes of selfhood, in part because of the impossibility of sustaining an 'unmaking' of the self. In his later work, Bersani reflects on his ideas about masochism as a radical practice: '[m]uch of this now seems to me a rather facile, even irresponsible celebration of "self-defeat"', and he goes on to write: Masochism is not a viable alternative to mastery, either practically or theoretically. The defeat of the self belongs to the same relational system, the same relational imagination, as the self's exercise of power; it is merely the transgressive version of that exercise.[68]

The 'self' is resurgent – is not, then, 'shattered' or defeated in masochistic practices in the way that Bersani once thought or hoped. There is always the danger of creating a new fixity, a new orthodoxy of the self, even in seemingly 'transgressive' acts of 'self-defeat'. And perhaps any writing that attempts to represent an 'overwhelming' of the subject also risks conferring a new, fixed version of subjectivity: a celebration of the reified masochistic subject. Adam Phillips describes Bersani's version of masochism as synonymous with mobility and disruption in his early work, but emphasises that the masochistic disruption of the self has a complicated relationship with 'representation': '"The masochistic excitement," Bersani and Ulysse Dutoit write in *The Forms of Violence*, "which perhaps initiates us to sexuality can therefore be exploited not as the goal of representation, but rather as a psychic 'technique' for destabilizing representations and maintaining mobility."'[69] If masochistic 'excitement' becomes the goal of representation (and this would be one way to think about the tribulations of courtly love as represented and enshrined in romance), then the 'mobility' of masochism is itself undone.

What comes after the final swoon in *Troilus and Criseyde* – Criseyde's survivalist pragmatism and the 'immuration' of Troilus' salvific masculine masochistic status – would then be the failure of moments of possibility or mobility within the text. Troilus' movement, 'Up to the holughnesse of the eighthe spere' (V.1809), the ascent of his 'goost' above the suffering body into bliss and a panoptic, regulatory, religious vision of the universe constitutes tragedy as sclerosis: a hardening of a religious perspective that is unnervingly still in comparison with the 'erratik stars' it contemplates. I want to suggest that the swoons of this text dramatise moments of mobility and possibility (including the possibility of failure), before the transcendence of this ending. I see the swoons in Chaucer's text as points at which the subjects of the poem are briefly laid low before any resurgence or resolution or remaking; as crux-points where the direction and genre of the text are at stake. These swoons provide the most thrilling moments of the poem: resolution is held briefly in abeyance, characters – and the affective quality of the text – teeter on the brink of different possibilities; bodies are posed as potentially dangerous, existing a whole world below the panoptic, ascended spirit. Coming round from the swoon into an impossible situation, or finally dying, commutes these moments of possibility into fixed outcomes. But the swoon operates as a crux or a hinge between unrealised potential and certain conclusion; between the chaos of possibility and the coherence of genre; between life and death.

Notes

1 Stephen A. Barney, 'Troilus Bound', *Speculum: A Journal of Mediaeval Studies* 47(3) (1972), 445–458 at 458.
2 Barry Windeatt, in his survey of medieval swooning, describes the way in which a swoon often 'precedes a resolution', suggesting its power to change the course of events: 'The Art of Swooning in Middle English', in Christopher Cannon and Maura Nolan (eds), *Medieval Latin and*

Middle English Literature: Essays in Honour of Jill Mann (Cambridge: D.S. Brewer, 2011), pp. 211–230 at p. 222. All future references will be to this version of the text.

3 All dates attested to either in the *OED* and/or the *Middle English Dictionary* (*MED*; https://quod.lib.umich.edu/m/middle-english-dictionary/dictionary).

4 Windeatt demonstrates that this early form often occurs ambiguously in doublets with 'swounen', telling us that: 'As a cessation of conscious thought, swoons may represent a rehearsal and reminder of a sudden death, and are sometimes mistaken for death: medieval medical writers emphasize the short step that may separate swooning from death' (Windeatt, 'The Art of Swooning in Middle English', p. 212).

5 The *OED* gives the first definition of this word as: 'To make a rushing, rustling, or murmuring sound' (*c.*949); whereas the *Free Dictionary* makes this diminution of sound correspondent to diminution of breath through suffocation: see www.thefreedictionary.com/swoon (accessed August 20, 2013).

6 Judith Weiss summarises these responses, which characterise the swooning Troilus as 'unmanly, even emasculated, impotent, helpless and passive. In other words he is supposedly behaving like a woman, or at least a stereotypical one': Judith Weiss, 'Modern and Medieval Views on Swooning: the Literary Contexts of Fainting in Romance', in Rhiannon Purdie and Michael Cichon (eds), *Medieval Romance, Medieval Contexts* (Cambridge: D.S. Brewer, 2011), pp. 121–134, at p. 121.

7 Gretchen Mieszkowski suggests this in her article 'Revisiting Troilus's Faint', in Tison Pugh and Marcia Smith Marzec (eds), *Men and Masculinities in Chaucer's* Troilus and Criseyde (Cambridge: D.S. Brewer, 2008), pp. 43–57. I elaborate on this process of gender acquisition and the swoon in Chapter 3.

8 Slavoj Žižek, *The Metastases of Enjoyment: Six Essays on Woman and Causality* (London: Verso, 1994), p. 84.

9 All my references are to the line numbers of the version of the text edited by Sherry L. Reames, 'Early South English Legendary Life of Mary Magdalen', in *Middle English Legends of Women Saints* (Kalamazoo, MI: Medieval Institute Publications, 2003 [*c.*1290]), and my translations will be based on the ones provided in the notes thereto.

10 Weiss, 'Modern and Medieval Views on Swooning'.

11 Windeatt, 'The Art of Swooning in Middle English', at 224.

12 Manfred Görlach, who has researched the textual history of the *South English Legendary*, claims that the Mary Magdalene account is possibly a much earlier poem that was inserted 'as an emergency measure of the "L" compiler who, not finding a legend of the important saint in his

defective exemplar, adapted the heterogeneous text to the style of the *SEL* collection' (*The Textual Tradition of the South English Legendary* (Leeds: University of Leeds, 1974), pp. 181–182).

13 The OED gives the earliest use of 'throe' for the pain and struggle of birth as 1250, and its sense as 'death-struggle' as 1300.

14 See Windeatt, 'The Art of Swooning in Middle English', 213.

15 Linda Georgianna, *The Solitary Self: Individuality in the Ancrene Wisse* (London and Cambridge, MA: Harvard University Press, 1981), p. 91 *et seq.*

16 Amy Neff, 'The Pain of *Compassio*: Mary's Labor at the Foot of the Cross', *Art Bulletin* 80 (1980), 254–273 at 265, cited by Weiss.

17 'The Gospel of Nicodemus', Ch. 10, v. 1904, at https://biblehub.com/library/unknown/the_gospel_of_nicodemus_/chapter_10_the_sentence_to.htm.

18 Steve Ely, *I beheld Satan as lightning fall from heauen* (Leicester: New Walk Editions, 2019).

19 In personal correspondence with the author (February 6, 2019).

20 The 'Swoon Hypothesis' – a theologically eccentric account, which emerged towards the end of the eighteenth century, of Christ's resurrection as the recovery from a swoon – is similar to the extent that it places swooning in a pivotal position within the Passion; Christ's swoon is at the heart of the divine plan for suffering and redemption and renewal according to those who think of him as 'unconscious' on the cross rather than dead.

21 The swoon is also during this period often figured as a response to, as well as an approach towards, death: 'The grief and shock of confronting another's death and of mourning over a body is conveyed so frequently through swooning that such body language becomes a stock response' (Windeatt, 'The Art of Swooning in Middle English', 218).

22 To name a couple of the most famous instances of this: William Langland's *The Vision of Piers Plowman* (*c.*1360–87), is a swough of different swoons (Christ swoons on the cross, and Hawkin, the Active Man, swoons over his guilty soul; even Sloth swoons); and *Pearl* (*c.* late fourteenth century) concludes with a swoon. See Windeatt, 'The Art of Swooning in Middle English' and Weiss, 'Modern and Medieval Views on Swooning', for many more examples.

23 Mieszkowski, 'Revisiting Troilus's Faint', at 49. Weiss argues that, '[w]ith the appearance of the *romans antiques* [the twelfth-century northern French romances of antiquity] […] the phenomenon of fainting by both men and women is well-established and is clearly meant to denote an accepted response to strong emotion' (Modern and Medieval Views on Swooning', at 124); but, she suggests, these emotions are initially

connected to grief and not romance. It is with the *Roman d'Enéas* and in the figure of Dido that 'fainting has for the first time a close association with love [...] while continuing its connection death' (at 125).

24 *Troilus and Criseyde* is difficult to classify in terms of genre; Molly A. Martin tells us that despite Chaucer's indebtedness to the romance tradition, his text is not classifiable completely, or even primarily, as a romance, but should rather be seen as a play of different genres ('Troilus's Gaze and the Collapse of Masculinity in Romance', in Pugh and Marzec, *Men and Masculinities*, pp. 132–147).

25 Geoffrey Chaucer, *Troilus and Criseyde* in Larry D. Benson (general ed.), *The Riverside Chaucer*, 3rd edn (Oxford and New York: Oxford University Press, 1988 [*c*.1380]) ('*Troilus*'). All future references will be to this edition.

26 Jill Mann, 'Troilus' Swoon', *The Chaucer Review* 14 (1980), 319–335.

27 Again, this may be due to our post-medieval conceptions of gender: Weiss suggests that criticism has been guilty 'of not taking swoons by women into account: precisely because they are thought an action so characteristic of women, they can be ignored' ('Modern and Medieval Views on Swooning', at 122).

28 See Barry Windeatt's 'Introduction' to his translation of *Troilus and Criseyde* (Oxford and New York: Oxford World's Classic, Oxford University Press, 1998), p. xvi. Here he tells us that *Filostrato* was evidently in front of Chaucer as he worked on *Troilus*, with the structure often matching Boccaccio's stanza for stanza. The narrator of Chaucer's *Troilus* claims that he is the translator of his sources, although the only author mentioned is the mysterious and almost certainly apocryphal 'Lollius' rather than Boccaccio (p. xvii).

29 As noted by Windeatt, 'Introduction', p. xvi.

30 There are 1,117 seven-line stanzas, with the lovers' union occurring at the centre of the total lines of the poem, as Windeatt has pointed out ('Introduction', ix).

31 See, for example, Galen's *On the Affected Parts* (*c*. late second century). I am indebted to Nancy G. Siraisi for her summary of Galenic medicine: *Medieval and Early Renaissance Medicine* (Chicago and London: The University of Chicago Press: 1990).

32 Siraisi, *Medieval and Early Renaissance Medicine*, p. 101.

33 *Ibid.*, p. 107.

34 Holly A. Crocker and Tison Pugh, 'Masochism, Masculinity and the Pleasures of Troilus', in Pugh and Marzec, *Men and Masculinities*, pp. 82–96.

35 Leo Bersani, *The Freudian Body: Psychoanalysis and Art* (New York: Columbia University Press, 1986).
36 Sigmund Freud, *Three Essays on the Theory of Sexuality*, 7:203 and 233, quoted in *The Freudian Body*, pp. 37–38: Freud writes that, for the infant, 'all comparatively intense affective processes, including even terrifying ones [spill over into] sexuality'; and that sexual excitement develops as 'a byproduct [...] of a large number of processes as they reach of a certain degree of intensity, and most especially of any relatively powerful emotion, even though it is of a distressing nature'.
37 Bersani, *The Freudian Body*, p. 38.
38 *Ibid.*, pp. 38–39.
39 *Ibid.*, p. 60.
40 *Ibid.*, p. 38.
41 Bersani, describing in Laplanchian terms his work in *The Freudian Body*, in 'Sociality and Sexuality', in *Is the Rectum a Grave? And Other Essays* (Chicago and London: The University of Chicago Press, [2000] 2010), pp. 102–119, at p. 108.
42 Bersani, 'Is the Rectum a Grave?', in *Is the Rectum a Grave?*, pp. 3–30, at p. 25.
43 'Ye ben to wys to doon so gret folie, / To putte his lif al nyght in jupertie' (IIII.867–8); and then again 'his lif al night in jupertie' (III.876).
44 Windeatt, 'Introduction', xxiv.
45 Marcia Smith Marzec, 'What Makes a Man? Troilus, Hector, and the Masculinities of Courtly Love', in Pugh and Marzec, *Men and Masculinities*, pp. 58–72.
46 Here she cites Charlotte Otten, 'The Love-Sickness of Troilus', in Leigh Arrathoon (ed.), *Chaucer and the Craft of Fiction* (Rochester, MI: Solaris, 1986), pp. 22–33 at 22–23.
47 Weiss argues that Mary Wack's *Love Sickness in the Middle Ages* (Philadelphia: 1990) has been too influential on many critics, who are keen to see the swoon as directly implicated *in amor heros*: 'the symptoms of *amor heros* in these and other medical authors do not include fainting' (Weiss, 'Modern and Medieval Views on Swooning', p. 129). However, these symptoms include changes in the heart, which are key to Chaucer's description of the mechanism of the swoon, so I think the conjunction between the swoon and lovesickness is justified here.
48 Windeatt, 'The Art of Swooning in Middle English', at 227.
49 David Aers, *Community, Gender, and Individual Identity: English Writing, 1360–1430* (London: Routledge, 1988), p. 129.
50 Barry Windeatt, *Oxford Guides to Chaucer: Troilus and Criseyde* (Oxford: Oxford University Press, 1992), pp. 225–226.

51 Edward Condren, 'Transcendent Metaphor or Banal Reality: Three Chaucerian Dilemmas', *PLL* 21(3) (1985), 233–257 at 248 and 252–254.
52 Maud Burnett McInernay, '"Is this a mannes herte?": Unmanning Troilus through Ovidian Allusion', in Peter Beidler (ed.), *Masculinities in Chaucer* (Boydell & Brewer, 1997), pp. 221–235, at pp. 222–225.
53 Gretchen Mieszkowski, 'Revisiting Troilus's Faint', in Tison Pugh and Marcia Smith Marzec (eds), *Men and Masculinities in Chaucer's Troilus and Criseyde* (Cambridge: D.S. Brewer, 2008), pp. 43–57 at 47–48.
54 Ibid., pp. 44, 48.
55 Ibid., p. 50.
56 Ibid., p. 52.
57 Ibid., p. 52.
58 Ibid., pp. 45, 47.
59 Rape can in the medieval period mean plunder and/or sexual assault: the *MED* gives as one definition 'the act of abducting a woman or sexually assaulting her or both'.
60 Alan Fletcher, 'Lost Hearts: Troilus and Criseyde, Book II, lines 925–31', *Notes and Queries* (June 1990), 163–164.
61 Mary Behrman gives an overview of these positions, citing, inter alia, Angela Jane Weisl, who views Criseyde as 'invaded by male power' (*Conquering the Reign of Femeny: Gender and Genre in Chaucer's Romance* (Cambridge: (1995), p. 28); and Catherine Cox, who sees the consummation as tantamount to rape (*Gender and Language in Chaucer* (Gainesville, FL: 1997), p. 45); see Mary Behrman, 'Heroic Criseyde', *The Chaucer Review* 38(4) (2004), 314–336 at 315.
62 William Shakespeare, *Romeo and Juliet*, IV.i, line 104 in *The Riverside Shakespeare* (Boston and New York: Houghton Mifflin Co., [1623] 1997).
63 There has been scattered scholarship on the relationship between Shakespeare's *Romeo and Juliet* and his reading of Chaucer's *Troilus and Criseyde*: see Ann Thompson, who suggests that 'the medieval poem was very much in [Shakespeare's] mind if not actually in front of his eyes when he was working on *Romeo and Juliet*' ('*Troilus and Criseyde* and *Romeo and Juliet*', *The Yearbook of English Studies* 6 (1976), 26–37 at 26). Prior to this M.C. Bradbrook suggested: 'That the author of *Romeo and Juliet* had learned from the author of *Troilus and Criseyde* would seem to be one of those possibilities not to be measured by the number of detectable parallels. A poet learns his trade not from books of rhetoric but from other poets' ('What Shakespeare Did to Chaucer's *Romeo and Juliet*', *Shakespeare Quarterly* 9(3) (1958), 311–319 at 312).

64 Holly A. Crocker and Tison Pugh, 'Masochism, Masculinity and the Pleasures of Troilus', in Pugh and Marzec, *Men and Masculinities*, pp. 82–96.
65 *Ibid.*, p. 83.
66 *Ibid.*, p. 87.
67 *Ibid.*, p. 86.
68 Bersani, 'Sociality and Sexuality', in *Is the Rectum a Grave?*, p. 110.
69 Leo Bersani and Adam Phillips, *Intimacies* (Chicago and London: The University of Chicago Press, 2008), pp. 93–95.

2

'Fall'n into a pit of ink': Shakespearean swoons and unreadable body-texts

> Do not live, Hero, do not ope thine eyes;
>
> [...] why, she, O she is fall'n
>
> Into a pit of ink, that the wide sea
>
> Hath drops too few to wash her clean again,
>
> And salt too little which may season give
>
> To her foul tainted flesh!
>
> (*Much Ado About Nothing*, IV.i.123–144)

The swooning Shakespearean body is mired in expressive complexity. The Shakespearean swoons of interest to me here are abyssal: they stage a fall into the dark depths of a body that is inaccessible to the modes of 'reading' attempted by the characters of the play-world. In this chapter, I focus on pivotal swoons in three plays: *Much Ado About Nothing*, *Julius Caesar* and *Othello*.[1] Falling, fainting and shaking are crucial to the action of these plays, and to the trajectories of their characters. These are also plays in which bodies are initially presented as texts to be read and deciphered, and in which swooning reveals such processes of reading to be highly tendentious, fraught, and/or tragically flawed. In *Much Ado*, for instance, Hero's swooning body is subject to the 'reading' and 'observations' of the Friar, among other characters (IV.i.165); in *Othello*, Desdemona's body is 'fair paper, this most goodly book' (IV.ii.71). In both cases, the female body is being read suspiciously, against accusations of sexual promiscuity: the anxious male characters in these plays desire a legible female body – one that will signify reliably when women's words are not trusted.

But this desire for bodily proof will end in comic disaster, and in tragedy, respectively. Each swoon that I draw into focus here demonstrates that the body cannot be parsed straightforwardly through the signifying systems available within the world of the play. The swoon occurs when the systems by which bodies are made to *mean* something – according to humoral theories of the body and/as character, through constructions of (dis)ability and health, or via narratives of gender and race and religion, for example – break under pressure. And in each of these plays we can see a slightly different system of meaning being brought into critical focus: in *Much Ado*, the female body is being parsed for chastity; in *Julius Caesar*, fitness to rule is being measured by the conspirators against the perceived rectitude of Caesar's body; in *Othello*, racial, religious and gendered norms (the 'politics of plausibility',[2] to borrow Alan Sinfield's phrase) are manipulated by Iago in order to manoeuvre Othello into frenzied, shaking, murderous states. The prostrate bodies in all of these plays become sites of contestation; they elude and complicate attempts at reading. And by paying attention to the faltering, falling bodies of Hero, Caesar and Othello, we can better see the complexities of early modern understandings of the body.

I draw on recent work on disability in Shakespearean scholarship in my approach here, in particular the 'ethical staring' promoted as a mode of analysis by Allison P. Hobgood and David Houston Wood in their work *Recovering Disability in Early Modern England*. Hobgood and Wood suggest paying close attention to the depiction of bodies that are deemed extraordinary or egregious or insufficient in some way, in order to better understand the 'compulsory able-bodiedness that insidiously excludes, stigmatizes, and devalues difference'.[3] I draw on this work, and hope to add to it: Shakespeare's swoons powerfully dramatise the complexities of the different significatory matrices surrounding individual bodies and highlight the contestability of different narratives of bodily health in circulation at this time.

Swooning, silence and sullied bodies in *Much Ado About Nothing* (1598)

In *Much Ado About Nothing*, the action of the play rises towards a spectacular swoon: Hero, arrayed in church in her wedding finery,

Shakespearean swoons and unreadable body-texts 61

3 Alfred Elmore, Depiction of the church scene in *Much Ado about Nothing*, 1846

is about to be married to the young Count Claudio, who has recently returned victorious from battle. But Hero has been the victim of a conspiracy authored by the disgruntled, illegitimate brother of Claudio's commander: falsely accused of promiscuity by Don John, she is publicly jilted at the altar. Humiliated and spurned, accused of a wrongdoing that she cannot fathom, Hero swoons spectacularly. The men who have humiliated her leave the church and her father wishes her dead. In the lines that follow her faint, Hero's swooning body is seen as a text to be read by the other characters in the play, and its meaning is fiercely debated: her unconsciousness is interpreted both as her sinking into her own guilt and sin (she is 'fall'n / Into a pit of ink, that the wide sea / Hath drops too few to wash her clean again' (IV.i.139–141)) and as proof of her innocence (she lies 'guiltless here' (IV.i.169)).

This contest for the meaning of Hero's prostrate body is the climax of a long-running disputation of the reliability of words and/ or physical demonstrations to communicate feeling, thought and intention in the play – especially when it comes to female sexual desire and agency. *Much Ado* opens with a discussion of the 'measure' of masculine feeling: a messenger brings news to Leonato, Hero's father, of Don Pedro's victory in battle, and they discuss the particular honour of 'the young Florentine called Claudio' (I.i.10–11). Leonato asks how Claudio's Uncle, a resident of Messina where the play is set, has received the news of Claudio's worthy conduct in battle:

> Mess. I have already deliver'd him letters, and there appears much joy in him, even so much that joy could not show itself modest enough without a badge of bitterness.
> Leon. Did he break into tears?
> Mess. In great measure.
> Leon. A kind overflow of kindness. There are no faces truer than those that are so wash'd.
>
> (I.i.20–27)

A fitting masculine performance of feeling is being described and venerated here; the joy of the uncle is tempered and made 'modest' through his 'badge of bitterness' (i.e. tears). This 'badge' of tears describes feeling taking a circumscribed, measured, physical form. It is seen as a reliable signifier – an external 'overflow' taken to show the internal measure of the man; to make his face 'true'.

This exemplar of a legible 'badge' of feeling, which is conveyed through words and physical demonstrations that cohere, is in sharp contrast to affective demonstrations that come under scrutiny through other key characters in the play. Don John, for example, Don Pedro's bastard brother and the villain of the piece, is marked out at the very start by communicative dearth: 'I am not of many words' (I.i.157). This admission of taciturnity might have made Don John readable as a melancholic character on the Renaissance stage: Claire McEachern, in her edition of the text, quotes Timothy Bright's *A Treatise of Melancholie* (1586) to tell us that, '[r]eticence was a hallmark of the melancholic, a humoral personality type also noted for being "lean, dry, lank, the face beneath pale, yellowish, swarthy ... enuious and jealous, apt to take occasions in the worse part, and out of measure passionate"'.[4]

Early modern ideas of the melancholic associated this humoral type with unbalanced, uncontrolled and uncontrollable feeling. This seems to be how Hero 'reads' Don John later in the play: 'He is of a very melancholy disposition' (II.i.5). The melancholic's lack of measure in feeling is in stark contrast to the 'modesty' and measure exhibited by Claudio's uncle. Don John's excessive capacity for feeling, and his inability to control it, are remarked upon: 'Why are you thus out of measure sad?' (I.iii.1–2) Conrade, his companion, asks him. 'There is no measure in the occasion that breeds, therefore the sadness is without limit,' (I.iii.3–4) Don John replies. This could be a further reference to melancholy, but his defence of his right to emotional excess also intersects with ideas about Don John's illegitimacy (his *breeding*), and suggests that his circumstances warrant high passion. Don John's response further defends his tendency towards truculent silence as fitting:

> I had rather be a canker in a hedge than a rose in his grace, and it better fits my blood to be disdain'd of all than to fashion a carriage to rob love from any. In this (though I cannot be said to be a flattering honest man) it must not be denied but I am a plain-dealing villain. I am trusted with a muzzle, and enfranchis'd with a clog, therefore I have decreed not to sing in my cage. If I had my mouth, I would bite; if I had my liberty, I would do my liking. In the meantime, let me be that I am, and seek not to alter me. (I.iii.27–37)

Don John will not assume the 'song' of the disciplined, legitimate, male subject, even when it might benefit him. There is something admirable in his 'plain-dealing', this speech tries to suggest: Don John will not 'fashion a carriage' nor dissemble in the way that more supposedly 'flattering honest' man may. He has just been beaten in battle, and has been brought to heel by his brother: he will not perform happy compliance. If feeling is disciplined into seemly external shows, then the caged bird's song becomes a less a reliable marker than the unmuzzled dog's bite. And Don John's conspiracy to implicate Hero could be seen as an attack on the whole system of measured, performative feeling that confers legitimacy through 'exterior shows': he will undermine her assumed innocence, present her 'seeming modesty' as cankerous in order to invalidate the whole rotten show of 'flattering honesty'.

Hero, our slandered, swooning heroine, is also noticeable for her reticence on stage. Hero is present in many scenes early in the play, and is often even directly addressed, while remaining speechless. Her quietness is never noted or discussed by other characters in the manner of Don John's, perhaps because it coheres with notions of feminine 'modesty' in currency at the time of the play's composition. But her reticence becomes extraordinary in contrast to the quick tongue and wit of her cousin, Beatrice, and in the face of extreme provocation from the verbal parries of the men around her. Some striking examples: when Don Pedro's men, including Claudio, return from battle and are entertained by her father, Hero's paternity is debated in jocular fashion:

> D. Pedro ... I think this is your daughter.
> Leon.   Her mother hath many times told me so.
> Bene.   Were you in doubt, sir, that you ask'd her?
> Leon.   Signior Benedick, no, for then you were a child.
> D. Pedro You have it full, Benedick. We may guess by this what you are, being a man. Truly, the lady fathers herself. Be happy, lady, for you are like an honourable father.
> (I.i.104–112)

Don Pedro and Leonato move away at this point, and Benedick continues to extend the joke about Hero's mother's potential infidelity, even though no one is listening – as Beatrice enjoys pointing out to him. But Hero has still not spoken; her appearance has stood in for any verbal contribution to this conversation – and her appearance is the physical proof that is trusted more by these men than feminine speech (her mother's words).

In another long scene in which Hero is on stage but barely speaks, the match between Claudio and Hero is proposed by her father in front of her uncle, Antonio, and her cousin, Beatrice. Antonio addresses Hero directly: '[*To Hero*] Well, niece, I trust you will be rul'd by your father' (II.i.50–52). But Beatrice answers in her stead: 'Yes, faith, it is my cousin's duty to make cur'sy, and say, "Father as it please you." But yet for all that, cousin, let him be a handsome fellow, or else make another cur'sy and say, "Father, as it please me."' (II.i.52–56). Leonato speaks next, and Hero says nothing. A few lines later, she receives this injunction from her father: 'Daughter, remember what I have told you. If the Prince do solicit you in that kind, you know your answer' (II.i.66–8). Another direct address, and yet once again Beatrice speaks next: 'The fault will be in the music, cousin, if you be not woo'd in good time' (II.i.69–70). Hero speaks not a word on the matter of her betrothal.

A final example from later in the same scene: Don Pedro, pretending to be Count Claudio at a masked ball (on account of his ability to take a woman 'hearing prisoner with the force / And strong encounter of my amorous tale' (I.i.324–325); lucky her), has wooed Hero and secured the match.

> *Leon.* Count, take of me my daughter, and with her my fortunes. His grace hath made the match, and all grace say amen to it.
> *Beat.* Speak, Count, 'tis your cue.
> *Clau.* Silence is the perfectest herald of joy; I were but little happy, if I could say how much. Lady, as you are mine, I am yours. I give away myself for you, and dote upon the exchange.
> *Beat.* Speak, cousin, or (if you cannot) stop his mouth with a kiss, and let not him speak neither.
>
> (II.i.302–311)

Claudio responds to Beatrice's incitement to speak, even if it is to affirm the efficaciousness of silence. Language cannot adequately express the joy of love, he counters. Even so, Beatrice rankles at the disparity between expression here: that Claudio speaks while Hero doesn't. If silence really is to be preferred, Beatrice begs Hero to shut her fiancé up. Don Pedro cuts in here, and we do not hear Hero's voice – though we are told that she now whispers into Claudio's ear.

Shakespearean scholar Oliver Morgan has recently proposed a new way of approaching dialogue in terms of speaker-sequencing and turn-taking, which he calls 'dialogical scansion'.[5] His method of analysis focuses 'on patterns of interaction and habits of speech – on figures of dialogue that can be identified in the text with as much confidence as alliteration, chiasmus, or feminine rhyme'.[6] Dialogue scansion, he argues, should be attended to with the same care as prosody. Morgan establishes a normative 'speak-when-you're-spoken-to' rule that operates to establish turn-taking in dialogue on the stage (and off it). But he is especially interested in when and how Shakespearean speech disrupts this normative rule, and shows that paying attention to this can open up new interpretations: 'Which characters select which other characters to speak, who tends to self-select, or to speak only when selected, which characters break these rules to speak when someone else has been selected, why and when they do so – a range of applications comes immediately to mind.'[7] Morgan identifies a number of ways in which turn-taking is established and disrupted; through, 'intervention, blanking, and apostrophe – turns at talk can be shared out, snatched at, or thrust upon the unsuspecting bystander.'[8]

This gives us another useful way to think about Hero's (dis)engagement with dialogue. As we can see from the above examples, Beatrice *intervenes* in conversation in important ways: she answers when Hero is directly addressed about important matters, taking her turn; in the later example, she curates turn-taking, prompting Hero to speak or to use her body to decisively contribute to the conversation when it is her turn (i.e. asking her to shut Claudio up with a kiss). Whether she is speaking over Hero or filling for her (allowing her the space for silence by taking or offering another kind of substitute for her turn) is a matter that the text leaves open to interpretation.

Morgan's work helps us to see that Hero's speech patterns challenge conventions of speech, and the convention *to* speak, in a significant way. It is difficult to know how an early modern audience might have read her quietness. Dympna Callaghan reminds us that in this period women were often injuncted to remain,

> chaste, silent and obedient, which has been dealt with by numerous scholars of the 'woman question' in this period. One example should be sufficient to make the point here: utilising the common metaphor of horse-breaking, Whatley's description of the perfect wife as one who '...submits herself with quietness, cheerfully, even as a well-broken horse ... readily going and standing as he wishes that sits upon his backe'.[9]

This 'common metaphor' of the disciplined animal body might put us in mind of Don John's description of the caged bird singing. A man who is constrained is still expected to speak, or at least to chirrup agreeably, but the cheerful, submissive woman-as-horse doesn't even neigh.

If Hero's quietness, her disruption of 'normative' dialogue patterns, is part of her portrayal as a 'gentle', 'modest' maid ('I will do any modest office, my lord', (II.ii.375) she replies when asked directly by Don Pedro to help in the ploy to match-make Beatrice and Benedick), then it becomes clear as the play develops that her reticence is still not enough to protect her from accusation of unchasteness. The male characters in the play (as in much early modern drama) are preoccupied by the possibility of cuckoldry and female dishonesty to such an extent that her 'seeming' modesty will be construed as an extra injury to Claudio.

The climax of the play is the marriage-to-swoon scene: what should be a moment of public, legal, admissible speech for Hero slides into chaos and unconsciousness. Hero awaits Claudio in the church. When he arrives, the Friar begins the ceremony, but something is already amiss. As Morgan has pointed out, 'Shakespeare is a master of the disrupted formal occasion – of the scene in which a ceremony or a trial or a dramatic performance descends into chaos'.[10] The breakdown of the wedding ceremony begins when Leonato, Hero's father, intervenes in the pre-allocated turn-taking of the wedding vows, to attempt to 'patch up' the ceremony when faced with Claudio's strange answers. But Claudio is intent on entirely de-railing the wedding: he has been led, by Don John, to believe that Hero is unfaithful and is here to publicly expose her supposed dishonesty and licentiousness. He begins the attack by breaking with the pre-allocation of the vows and addressing Leonato. He rejects the gift of Leonato's daughter as a 'rotten orange' (IV.i.32): the orange is a symbol of deception – its thick rind can obscure the quality of the fruit beneath – and the fruit was associated with prostitution.[11] Claudio goes on to rail against Hero's appearance of modesty:

> Behold how like a maid she blushes here!
>
> O, what authority and show of truth
>
> Can cunning sin cover itself withal!
>
> Comes not that blood as modest evidence
>
> To witness simple virtue? Would you not swear,
>
> All that you see her, that she were a maid,
>
> By these exterior shows? But she is none:
>
> She knows the heat of a luxurious bed;
>
> Her blush is guiltiness, not modesty.
>
> (IV.i.34–42)

The signs of the body that are usually taken as evidence, the 'exterior shows' that *stand in* for credible female speech, are maligned as manipulation here. Neither a woman's words nor her body's responses can be believed, if Claudio is to be believed; that which might be taken as an authoritative sign of innocence takes on the glow of guilt if Claudio is in possession of the truth, as he assumes he is. Claudio now reads the book of Hero's body according to his predetermined prejudices.

Hero intervenes in the dialogue later on in this tirade. Claudio, still addressing Leonato, tells him that he only ever showed Hero, 'Bashful sincerity and comely love' (IV.i.54). 'And seem'd I ever otherwise to you?' Hero asks, supplanting someone else's turn to speak at long last. 'Out on thee, seeming! I will write against it', Claudio responds, blasting her appearance of chastity in contrast to her 'savage sensuality'. To this Hero can only respond with incredulity: 'Is my lord well that he doth speak so wide?' (IV.i.62). She is charged with answering the accusation of speaking with another man at night; she does so, honestly, and is not believed. Language is broken in this moment for Hero. Male sexual anxiety has far more power than Hero's speech: the fear of cuckoldry is voiced repeatedly, almost incessantly, through the play, through Benedick's frequent harping on it through to Don John's opportunistic miming of Hero's infidelity. Hero's body becomes plausibly promiscuous because the story of female promiscuity is already long written before Don John intervenes and attempts to pin this narrative to her.

Leonato, believing Claudio over his daughter Hero, wishes for his own death, and then hers. At the point that Leonato asks for a dagger's point, Hero falls. Beatrice attends to her. The accusing men see her faint as proof of her guilt, and leave the scene of their crime: 'These things, come thus to light / Smother her spirits up' (IV.i.111–112). What now follows is an extraordinary discussion of the meaning of Hero's prostrate body. Hero's own speech acts are completely disregarded; it is through her body, now, that the surrounding characters attempt to understand the truth of the matter. Beatrice fears that Hero is dead, and appeals to Leonato for help. Leonato *wishes* his daughter dead. Hero seems to stir, and Leonato is incensed that she looks upwards, towards heaven, a supposed sign of innocence. He sees Hero's swoon as a sign of her irremediable fall into sin:

> ... why, she, O she is fall'n
> Into a pit of ink, that the wide sea
> Hath drops too few to wash her clean again,

> And salt too little which may season give
> To her foul-tainted flesh!
>
> (IV.i.139–143)

That this fall into sinful unconsciousness should be described as one into 'ink' is striking given that Claudio has just claimed he will 'write against' her seeming modesty. Claudio has the power to express himself convincingly and powerfully through words; Hero is drowning in the dark pit of expressive failure. She may notionally have the means of expression, but her fall shows that the tools of language can be a murky obscurant: ink is a dangerous, besmirching substance for the unconscious woman who is written against.

Beatrice defends her cousin, believing her to be 'belied'. And the Friar too comes to Hero's defence, and offers an alternative to Leonato's reading of her body:

> Hear me a little,
> For I have only been silent so long,
> And given way unto this course of fortune,
> By noting of the lady. I have mark'd
> A thousand blushing apparitions
> To start into her face, a thousand innocent shames
> In angel whiteness beat away those blushes,
> And in her eye there hath appear'd a fire
> To burn the errors that these princes hold
> Against her maiden truth. Call me a fool,
> Trust not my reading, nor my observations,
> Which with experimental seal doth warrant
> The tenure of my book; trust not my age,
> My reverence, calling, nor divinity,
> If this sweet lady lie not guiltless here
> Under some biting error.
>
> (IV.i.155–169)

The Friar's act of physiognomy, while offering support for Hero, also reaffirms that masculine writing and reading, his 'marking' of the signs of her body to give a 'reading' of her character, have more credibility than female speech. The swoon demonstrates the absolute impossibility of Hero's communicative position when men rule the process of signification and can make the female body connote whatever they anxiously fear about female desire and dishonesty. '[S]he not denies it', Leonato chides, still unconvinced that the swoon is any proof of innocence (IV.i.173). He believes instead Claudio's words, which have been validated by masculine tears in the same manner as his uncle's at the very start of the play: 'speaking of her foulness / [He] Wash'd it with tears' (IV.i.153–154). But Hero has *passed out* of this discourse in perhaps her most extreme refusal of the expectation that she take her turn in a fundamentally corrupt conversation.

The swoon is the crisis point for female expressivity in the play: it is the symbolic death of Hero ('"Done to death by slanderous tongues / Was the Hero that here lies"' (V.iii.3–4) Claudio later reads over her supposed resting place; and her father, we should remember, threatened to kill her if she should revive from her swoon) and shows that men's words have the potential to overwrite female speech: they 'do' the work of death. But this play does not end in tragedy. The swoon is a crisis point that becomes a pivot point. The Friar suggests that they capitalise on Hero's swoon to publish that she is dead. There are echoes of *Romeo and Juliet* here, but this semblance of death will be successfully used to, '[c]hange slander to remorse' (IV.i.211). Don John's plot to defame Hero is revealed, and Claudio finally marries Hero in a masked ceremony; his belief that he is taking a cousin's hand to make amends is happily revised when she reveals that, 'One Hero died while I was defiled, but I do live, / And surely as I live, I am a maid' (5.4.63–64). Benedick and Beatrice are also joined in matrimony, though they prattle against it until the very last.

Is this the happy resolution of a comedy? Certainly, the play is marked by verbal mischief, and the possible disaster of Hero's death has been averted; the destructive capacity of male conversation to make corpses of women is one element of conversational interaction here, but so too is the amusing 'skirmish' in language produced by the characters of Beatrice and Benedick. Under the rubric of witty exchange, language in the play is subject to proliferation and revision. Words will not stay still, will not denote in one direction: they are constantly shifting and destabilising their referents through word-play. That Beatrice excels in this mode of discourse, which is typical of the young male characters in the play, shows that women can also direct language with creativity and agility.

But the verbal parry in which Beatrice energetically engages has consequences that are different for the male and female characters of the play. The most intense verbal skirmishes are produced by Benedick's analyses of women, by his constant undermining of the appearance of love, by his assertions on the impossibility of ascertaining female chastity. The female body is the most persistent of the indecipherable referents around which language flickers back and forth in the play. The harping fear of the illegibility of sexual desire will eventually drown out female speech; Hero passes out of the conversational modes of the play, and is still made subject to tendentious readings and over-writings of her body. The swoon, I think, continues to cast the shadow of the death-that-might-have-been over the apparently celebratory finale. *Much Ado* has recently been thought of as a problem play,[12] and its conclusion produces the ambivalence that Frederick Samuel Boas thought of as characteristic of these generically complex dramas: 'we move along dim untrodden paths, and at the close our feeling is neither of simple joy nor pain; we are excited, fascinated, perplexed, for the issues raised preclude a completely satisfactory outcome'.[13] The swoon unsettles this drama, darkens its comedy; it demonstrates that Hero has to be publicly in abeyance while the 'truth' of her character continues to be interrogated by the men around her; her word has no weight or meaning in public discourse against any charge made by credible male speakers; there is no 'badge' of character or 'exterior show' that she can convincingly produce.

The swoon is the crux of overlapping enquiries into truth, performance and the (un)reliability of appearances in this drama of miscommunication. The play's playfulness contains a dark threat: the pit into which Hero falls is an inky abyss, the consequence of an expressive act of bukkake which sees Hero's body overwhelmed by the narratives of the men who surround her. The swoon intensifies the generic complexity of the play, and shows the uneven consequences of a system of signification that depends on female bodies being narrated, 'marked' and 'read' only by men.

'We have the falling sickness': Male bodies, sickness and power in *Julius Caesar* (c.1599)

Julius Caesar is a play preoccupied with men falling. The proper exercise of power, the risks of ambition and tyranny, the incendiary suggestibility of 'the people', the reliability of systems of order (fraternal, political, environmental, rhetorical): all of these are explored through a play-long discourse on bodies rising and falling, with a particular focus on bodies falling into disorder – fainting, swooning, shaking, sickening, falling on their own swords. At the heart of the dramatic action is the discussion of Caesar's 'falling sickness' and responses to it; this has led Allison P. Hobgood to read the play as a 'disability narrative' – a narrative that 'takes shape around the epileptic body and considers the complex ways that body signified in late sixteenth and early seventeenth-century England'.[14] Hobgood argues that the play is '[s]ituated at the juncture of myriad disability discourses' and that the presentation of Caesar's epilepsy is 'informed by Hippocratic pathology, medieval marvelousness, Renaissance monstrosity, Galenic humoralism, and seventeenth-century rationalism'.[15]

I want to attend to swooning in this play, and in particular to the ways that other characters *describe* Caesar's falls, to argue that ableist versions of the body – narratives circulating in the play about Caesar's falling that seek to present him as 'unfit' to rule and prize instead masculine 'mettle' and uprightness – are revealed to be highly tendentious, and vertiginous even: the men who construct these narratives will themselves fall from power in a disorderly and violent manner.

The play opens with a bad-tempered exchange between Flavius and Murellus (two tribunes) and some commoners who are discovered unexpectedly abroad celebrating Julius Caesar's return to Rome. Flavius and Murellus determine to vandalise garlanded public images of Caesar, incensed by his rise to glory and fame, and by the impropriety of the celebration of his victory over Pompey (a fellow Roman):

> *Flav.* These growing feathers pluck'd from Caesar's wing
> Will make him fly an ordinary pitch,
> Who else would soar above the view of men,
> And keep us in servile fearfulness.
>
> (I.i.72–75)

The scene for the dramatic action is here set: Julius Caesar is flying too high; they want to bring him down a peg or two. The exchange establishes relative height as the comparison that will inform the conspiracy to come: when one man ascends, others are forced into relative 'servile' lowness. Fears of tyranny overlap undecidably in the play with anxious, envious fears about Caesar's rise.

The next scene introduces the key conspirators. And here the charge against Caesar is intensified and complicated. Cassius relates to Brutus a memory of a swimming contest between himself and Caesar: upon a 'raw and gusty day' (I.ii.100) they take to the Tiber. Caesar finds himself in difficulty: '"Help me, Cassius, or I sink!"' (111). Cassius helps the 'tired' Caesar to the shore, but this physical weakness, this liability to sink, incenses Cassius. Cassius rails against Caesar's repeated shows of physical vulnerability, and in particular his liability to 'shake' and 'fit':

> He had a fever when he was in Spain,
>
> And when the fit was on him, I did mark
>
> How he did shake – 'tis true, this god did shake;
>
> His coward lips did from their color fly,
>
> And that same eye whose bend doth awe the world
>
> Did lose his lustre; I did hear him groan;
>
> Ay, and that tongue of his that bade the Romans
>
> Mark him, and write his speeches in their books,
>
> Alas, it cried, 'Give me some drink, Titinius,'
>
> As a sick girl. Ye gods, it doth amaze me
>
> A man of such feeble temper should

So get the start of the majestic world
And bear the palm alone.

(I.ii.119–131)

Cassius is horrified that a man so 'feeble', rendered in Cassius' imagination as vulnerable and helpless and feminine by sickness, should assume a high position: 'And this man / Is now become a god, and Cassius is / A wretched creature and must bend his body / If Caesar carelessly but nod on him' (I.ii.115–119). The charge here and elsewhere is ostensibly against the overbearing power of one man as tyrant; but there is a swooning-inflection to this objection: Julius Caesar is seen as especially undeserving of his status as a 'Colossus' because he is physically compromised by shaking and falling. Hobgood argues that the seemingly antipathetical terms that constellate around Caesar here ('godlike' and 'feeble') are also at play in characterisations of epilepsy at this time:

> Since antiquity, epilepsy has been characterized in many ways as many things. Divine, demonic, pathological, and geohumoral, philosophers and physicians alike have struggled to determine its nature and significance. Classical traditions understood epilepsy as both sacred and sinful. The term 'seizure,' for example, recalls ancient Babylonian medical notions of epileptics seized by gods or demons (Temkin 20). Often this association with the supernatural gave epilepsy an ominous connotation and encouraged interpretations of the illness as a sign of moral corruption (8–9). The middle ages into the Renaissance saw continued association of epilepsy with depravity but, with increased conversion of the populace to Christianity, epilepsy's connections to divine prophecy (*divinatio*) (150) and ecstatic possession (86) became more pronounced.[16]

Caesar's epilepsy, then, does not necessarily signify straightforwardly to an early modern audience, and the 'falling sickness' could, Hobgood tells us, produce 'sacred wonder' as well as being associated with 'monstrous depravity' and/or 'feebleness'. It is important to note here that Caesar does not swoon on stage within the play. All of his falls and fits are reported and discussed by others. What is at stake, then, is the *meaning* of Caesar's body when it falls. Cassius is shown here attempting to control the narrative: Caesar's body is an affront to the proper exercise of masculine power because it is prone to sinking, fitting, and to disorderly, feminine shows of weakness.

But a range of different interpretations of Caesar's epilepsy would have been available to the audience at this time. Cassius is trying to corral Caesar's body into what we might now recognise as an ableist narrative of unfitness to govern (recent examples of which abound in US politics where the health of candidates is fiercely scrutinised: Hillary Clinton's public 'faint' after the 9/11 memorial service in the run-up to the 2017 presidential elections was widely discussed, for instance, and her body and supposed maladies were 'read' by Donald Trump and his supporters as evidence of her unfitness for office).[17] One effect of Cassius trying to insist on a stigmatising version of Caesar's 'fit' here, when so many overlapping discourses surrounded epilepsy at the time, is to show him as man who is cynically attempting to martial meaning and seize control of events. Jeffrey R. Wilson argues for the importance of the 'figure of stigma' as a way of understanding Shakespearean characters who are marked in the plays in terms of their difference from others: one of the things that 'stigmatised' characters share, he argues, is that despite them being 'quite dissimilar in their differentness ... they never get to present themselves to others (including audiences) for unbiased interpretation'.[18] The interpretation of difference is always at stake with stigmatised characters, and Cassius' vicious narrative of Caesar's epilepsy shows us the process of stigmatisation in action.

Caesar's falls and swoons, by virtue of being off-stage and becoming narrative events, are especially ripe opportunities for stigmatising projection from the conspirators. Later in the play, Casca relates to Brutus how Caesar has been met by the crowds of Rome. Caesar is offered a crown three times, but refuses it. At which, Casca tells us,

> the rabblement howted ... and threw up their sweaty night-caps, and utter'd such a deal of stinking breath because Caesar refus'd the crown, that it had, almost, chok'd Caesar, for he swounded, and fell down at it. (I.ii.244–249)

There's a great deal of disgust expressed here at the bodies of the people in whose interests these men ostensibly act – in the intimate description of their sweaty bed-clothes and the reek of their breath. Hobgood suggests that Casca is relating Caesar's fall through a nascent medical framework that depends on humoral theory:

> Through Casca's language especially, Shakespeare appropriates 'rationalist' perceptions of epilepsy as an abnormal physiological response

'caused by some humor or vapour; suddenly stopping the passage of spirits in the brain, which the brain striving to expel, causeth the Patient to fall down, and commonly foam at the mouth' (Blount). ... Casca rationalizes Caesar's disability through scientific discourse, he associates the uncleanness of the masses with infectious illness and attributes Caesar's epilepsy to contagious 'bad air'.[19]

Cassius takes up this diagnosis and fixates on the fact that Caesar has swooned – that he has fainted and fallen again:

> Cas: But soft I pray you; what, did Caesar swound?
> Casca: He fell down in the market-place, and foam'd at mouth, and was speechless.
> Brut: 'Tis very like, he hath the falling sickness.
> Cas: No, Caesar hath it not; but you, and I,
>   And honest Casca, we have the falling sickness.
> (I.ii.251–255)

Brutus' response seems matter-of-fact here; he is unsurprised, and simply notes Caesar's 'falling sickness'. But the swoon is presented as a shameful affront by Cassius to his ableist notions of vitality and virility. The tarnish of this falling sickness is catching: if they are willing to bend to a falling man, then it is they who are shamefully sick.

There's a telling contrast between the ways Cassius pejoratively characterises Caesar's sinks and swoons and fits and his prizing elsewhere of masculine 'mettle'. When Brutus agrees to a further audience with him, Cassius describes him as 'noble', but admits the possibility that Brutus is less firm than his nobility suggests: 'I see / Thy honourable mettle may be wrought [...] For who so firm that cannot be seduc'd?' (I.iii.308–312). He casts sly judgement over Brutus for entertaining his mutinous talk when Caesar loves Brutus so, and implies that if their situations were reversed, he would resist seduction: 'If I were Brutus now and he were Cassius, / He should not humour me' (314–315). Standing firm is the ultimate test of noble masculinity for Cassius, and no one stands as firm in his own regard as himself. The scene ends with Cassius' ominous threat to 'shake' Caesar from his seat (322), the fitting punishment for a man who has revealed himself to be vulnerable and prone to discombobulation. Cassius' readings of Caesar's swoons lead Hobgood to conclude that 'Caesar's assassination ... is motivated by ableism': when Brutus later rationalises his participation in Caesar's murder, he declares the actors 'purgers, not murders' (II.i.180), making the death a medical intervention, which will 'restore the republic to its paramount health',[20] as well as politically motivated.

The shaking in this play begins to spread, inexorably. In the scene following the discussion of Caesar's swoon, a terrible storm comes to Rome, and 'all the sway of the earth / Shakes like a thing unfirm' (I.iii.3–4). 'Sway' here connotes rule and order: there's an elemental disturbance in Rome that is causing palpitations through all of the bodies of the city and through the body politic in Casca's description of it. Cassius interprets the reports of the storm and other strange occurrences (men burning with fire, ghostly appearances, animals acting unnaturally) as warnings of a 'monstrous state' (I.iii.71). This shaken world is, for Cassius, proof that the state has become disordered; the chaos is a kind of contagion from Caesar's sick body. Casca has previously asked Cicero what he makes of these 'portentous things' (I.iii.31). Cicero's reply is cooler and less shaken than either of the conspirators': 'Indeed, it is a strange-disposed time; / But men may construe things after their fashion, / Clean from the purpose of the things themselves' (I.iii.33–35). Cassius loves to present himself as free from external interference, unmoved by any other man, inviolable and self-sufficient – take this as an example, from slightly later in this scene:

Cassius from bondage will deliver Cassius.

[...]

Nor stony tower, nor walls of beaten brass,

Nor airless dungeon, nor strong links of iron,

Can be retentive to the strength of spirit

[...]

That part of tyranny that I do bear

I can shake off at pleasure.

(I.iii.90–99)

To admit one's spirit might suffer, to be shaken in any fundamental way, is, to Cassius, to be shown 'womanish' (I.iii.84). Cassius is obsessed with the inferior, yielding bodies of other men: with shaking Caesar; with gaining control, part by part, of the yielding body of Brutus (I.iii.15515–6); with the 'hinds' that Roman men have shown themselves to be by becoming feminine quarry to Caesar. Yet Cicero's few 'clean' words show us that Cassius's fantasy of his own able-bodied inviolability is deranged in ways he cannot countenance: he projects his own narrative onto the shaking environment; his sense of his relationship to the world around him is 'construed' by his own interests.

Cassius, then, sees himself as clear-sighted, as perfectly in control of his body and cognitions. Yet, as Nicholas Royle has written, one of the most striking elements of *Julius Caesar* is its 'shaking of distinctions between being awake and being asleep ... its sense of "phantasma"'.[21] For Royle this is not just something that effects the characters within the play – it also pertains to the 'world' of the play, the strange interior that it projects to the reader or audience: 'Shakespeare's play seems to envelop a singularly nightmarish world of its own, rendering to itself a hallucinatory, hideous dreamtime.'[22] The play, then, powerfully dramatises and also produces altered states of consciousness. The dramatisation of altered states might seem obvious when we think of Caesar, who temporarily 'loses himself' through fits ('What said he when he came unto himself?' Brutus asks after the report of Caesar's public swoon (I.ii.262)); or of Brutus, who cannot sleep and exists in a kind of 'phantasm or a hideous dream' after Cassius has persuaded him to murder Caesar (II.i.65). But it is perhaps Cassius' doomed sense of himself as operating outside of the vulnerabilities of other men – vulnerabilities revealed through swoons and falls and shakings – that is at the heart of this tragedy. For Cassius is soon revealed to be every bit as vulnerable to the strange contingencies of the world of the play – to vicissitude, to the 'melting spirits of women' (II.i.113), to physical downfall – as the 'feeble' men he derides.

This vulnerability is gradually, tragically revealed. When discussing the details of the plot against Caesar and whom to enlist, for example, Cassius and Casca's patterns of speech shows them to be highly, comically, changeable:

> Cas. But what of Cicero? Shall we sound him?
>   I think he will stand very strong with us.
> Casca. Let us not leave him out.
>   [...]

Bru.	O, name him not; let us not break with him,
	For he will never follow any thing
	That other men begin.
Cas.	Then leave him out.
Casca.	Indeed he is not fit.

(II.i.141–153)

The inverse symmetry of these exchanges shows how Cassius and Casca bend to and flatter Brutus. The assertion that Cicero will 'stand very strong' rapidly shifts to an admission of unfitness; Cassius' assertion of standing firm is reversed into rhetorical infirmity. 'Sound' is an alternative spelling – and likely an alternative pronunciation – for 'swoon' in this period.[23] When Cassius proposes to 'sound' Cicero, then, there may be a subdued pun here, especially given the proximity to the assertion that he will 'stand very strong'. The two men are inadvertently discussing whether or not to drag Cicero down with them – into the collective swoon that will engulf the conspirators.

And as the plot thickens, Caesar begins to look less and less like the 'feeble' man Cassius has claimed him to be. Cassius' narrative of him is melting. Caesar is made out to be a man who has become susceptible to superstitions, for example. This supposed change of his is derided as, 'Quite apart from the main opinion he once had' (II.i.196). Superstition has compromised Caesar's strength and integrity of thought, in this account. Caesar is also derided as highly susceptible to flattery, to being worked upon by other men (II.i.207–208). This imputed inconstancy is in contrast to Brutus' assertion of what it means to be a 'true' Roman; no oaths are needed from the conspirators, because of their absolute reliability and the 'insuppressive mettle of [their] spirits' (134).

But when the audience next encounter Caesar, in the very next scene, we are shown something quite different: Calpurnia is terrified of the omens she perceives around them – a lioness has whelped in the streets, graves have returned the dead, clouds have 'drizzled blood upon the Capital' (II.ii.20). She begs Caesar not to go out. Caesar initially refuses to yield to her fears; he will not ruminate on the possibility of his downfall for, 'Cowards die many times before their deaths, / The valiant never taste of death but once' (30–31). When he finally agrees to stay at home, it is to humour Calpurnia. Decius Brutus, one of the conspirators, arrives, and quickly persuades Caesar to go to the Capitol to receive a crown. Caesar regrets having been temporarily swayed by Calpurnia: 'How foolish do your fears seem now, Calpurnia! / I am ashamed I did yield to them' (104–105). The irony here is that acceding to ideas of masculine bravery, rather than yielding to feminine fears, will bring Caesar low. He is not superstitious as charged, but might have survived the day's plot if he were as susceptible to portents as Calpurnia.

When he arrives before the Capitol, there is another test of the assertion of Caesar's inconstancy and feebleness. The conspirators petition for a banished man, Cimber. Caesar will not be moved; he rejects 'sweet words' that 'melteth fools' (III.i.42). Caesar instead asserts his absolute immovability in a speech that seems designed to compensate for his public swooning and shaking:

> But I am constant as the northern star,
>
> Of whose true-fix'd and resting quality
>
> There is no fellow in the firmament.
>
> The skies are painted with unnumb'red sparks,
>
> They are all fire, and every one doth shine;
>
> But there's but one in all doth hold his place.
>
> So in the world: 'tis furnish'd well with men,
>
> And men are flesh and blood, and apprehensive;
>
> Yet in the number I do know but one
>
> That unassailable holds on his rank,
>
> Unshak'd of motion; and that I am he ...
>
> (III.i.60–70)

Caesar describes himself as the opposite of the melting, shaken, feeble-bodied man that Cassius narrates and stigmatises; in his own account, he is stellified into the firmament, hardened into place. This speech may seem deeply ironic, perhaps even the apex of hubris, given that the conspirators have orchestrated this interaction and have manoeuvred Caesar into a position where he is about to be murdered. But it allows for a contestation in the play of what immovability might mean, and for an interrogation of its desirability. Caesar asserts his immovability; Cassius also believes himself immovable and detests Caesar's infirmity: both will fall in quick succession. To claim oneself immovable is to attempt to deny the existence of the human body and its inherent infirmity; it is the doomed attempt to be a kind of god or other celestial body.

A mere seven lines after Caesar's description of himself as 'unshak'd', the conspirators orbit around him, kneel before him, stab him to death. In one of the most famous lines in literature, Caesar sees that he has been betrayed by his dearest, most inconstant friend, Brutus, and succumbs to the fall: '*Et tu, Brute?* – Then fall Caesar!' (III.i.77). This moving moment in the play, one of the most quoted lines in Shakespeare, memorialises a willing fall: a giving in to the downwards trajectory of death. This powerful tragic utterance recognises the inconstancy of men, and the concomitant vulnerability of the self. Prefigured by his swoon, Caesar's death shows him succumbing to falling – the question falls away; the line is sheared in two by the apprehension of betrayal – and dramatises the profound contingency of power.

What follows in the play is now an intensified interrogation of the exercise of power, the suggestibility of men, and the rectitude of the noble male body. Caesar's corpse speaks powerfully to Mark Antony, and begs in turn that he must speak on Caesar's behalf: 'Over thy wounds now I do prophesy / (Which like dumb mouths do ope their ruby lips / To beg the voice and utterance of my tongue)' (III.i.259–262). As with Hero's swooning body in *Much Ado*, Caesar's inert form 'speaks'; his entry wounds have become mouths in this macabre image, which speak violence. The inert is reanimated into action and vengeance through Anthony's process of reading, interpreting and speaking; Caesar's body will not remain passive, even and *especially* now that he is dead.

Cassius fears that Mark Antony will speak to 'move' the people, is spooked by the unpredictability of what is to come, and by the possibility that he has triggered a domino-effect; he is become uncertain: 'I do not know what may fall, I like it not' (III.i.243). Shakespeare's use of 'fall' here describes a double anxiety over what may happen (befall) and what or who may be destroyed (fall): the fall is both the temporal progression of tragedy and the bodies it will lay low.

Cassius is right to be so fearful; in a masterpiece of oration, Mark Antony denies his own rhetoric while powerfully directing the people towards revenge:

> I am no orator, as Brutus is.
>
> [...]
>
> For I have neither [wit], nor words, nor worth,
>
> Action, not utterance, nor the power of speech
>
> To stir men's blood; I only speak right on.
>
> I tell you that which you yourselves do know,
>
> Show you sweet Caesar's wounds, poor, poor, dumb mouths,
>
> And bid them speak for me.
>
> (III.ii.217–226)

It is Caesar's body to which Mark Antony returns, to the powerful idea of his speaking wounds, and to the narrative of a fall that will bring down all men if they do not stand against it:

> O, what a fall was there, my countrymen!
>
> Then I, and you, and all of us fell down,
>
> Whilst bloody treason flourish'd over us.
>
> (190–192)

War befalls them: the conspirators flee and are pursued by Mark Antony and his supporters. Brutus is haunted by Caesar, who appears to him in the night. Cassius hears a report that a battle has gone badly for Brutus – that his 'soldiers fell to spoil' (V.iii.7) – and believes that he is 'enclos'd' by Antony. The report of Brutus' downfall is incorrect, but this news is delivered too late for Cassius: unable to bear the thought of being overpowered by other men, the thought of being 'enclosed' by them (this unnervingly tender and intimate phrase is used repeatedly through this scene), Cassius persuades Pindarus to stab him with the sword he used to kill Caesar. Cassius sinks; exsanguinated; red as the setting sun (IV.ii.60). When Brutus arrives and discovers the bloodbath, it is Caesar to whom he speaks: 'O Julius Caesar, thou art mighty yet! / Thy spirit walks abroad, and turns our swords / In our own proper entrails' (V.iii.93–95).

The spectre of Caesar seems now more powerfully upright, more physically mighty, than Cassius would ever have credited him in life. Again, the intimacy of the violence here is shocking: Caesar is described turning Cassius' own sword; he's inside Cassius, making a mess of his entrails. Brutus will finally fall on his own sword, his dying words a plea to his murdered friend: 'Caesar, now be still ...' (V.v.50).

In this play, men are shown impossible in their ideas of themselves; they are powerfully affected by words, by the intimations of others, by superstitions and dreams and ghosts, by falls and shakes and swoons. 'Clean' thought is impossible for any, saving perhaps Cicero (who knows just how suggestible men are). Tragedy comes to those who attempt to present themselves as invulnerable to illness and to falling – to Caesar, whose swooning, shaking, bleeding body speaks more strongly than his declarations of 'constancy'; and to Cassius, whose veneration of able-bodied rectitude drives the downward action of the tragedy. Shakespeare's decision to present the swoons off-stage, as primarily narrative events, shows us again how the swooning body is the crux of contested meaning: in the context of the polyvalent complexities of understandings of epilepsy in this period, the audience might recognise the violent impulses at play in attempts to narrativise Caesar's swoon in only one direction – as insufficiency that legitimates murder. If the epileptic body fails to 'function in a predictably legible manner'[24] in this period, Caesar's off-stage swoons allow Shakespeare to dramatise competing understandings of his illness – and the consequent power grab that is founded on an unsustainable fantasy of the able body.

'I am he that was Othello': Poisoned bodies, altered states and swooning self-estrangement in *Othello* (1604)

If *Julius Caesar* shows us that the 'ableist demand for control over the non-standard body'[25] is a tragically violent one, then *Othello* paints a yet darker picture of the exercise of Venetian male power over vulnerable bodies: specifically, the tendentiously gendered body of Desdemona, and the racially and religiously differentiated body of Othello. Conceptions of race in the early modern period were complex and varied, and differ in important ways from how we might construct race today. Ania Loomba demonstrates in her work that ideas about skin colour, religion and community, 'contact with outsiders' through trade and colonisation, and other systems of difference like gender and rank, all mingled to produce various 'ideologies of "difference"'[26] in early modern England. It is ideologies of gendered and racial difference that I focus on in my discussion of *Othello*, and I sometimes use the terms 'race' and 'racism' to summarise the complex matrix of intersecting ways in which Othello is differentiated from the white Venetians around him.[27]

Iago uses his position as a Venetian insider to manipulate Othello, producing extreme, altered states of consciousness in the Commander – states of trance, swooning, convulsion, and violent fugue, in which others no longer recognise Othello and he becomes a stranger to himself. *Othello* revisits ideas that are explored with a happier outcome in *Much Ado* about the illegibility of female desire; it becomes possible for Iago to manipulate Othello because of a perfidious 'reading' of the book of Desdemona's female, Venetian body, and the production of dubious 'proofs' to substantiate this reading. Much has already been written about *Othello* in terms of colonialism, race and religion, and the convulsions that Iago produces in the Commander's sense of himself. What I seek to suggest here is that Iago is a kind of poisoner: he is a man who seeks to alter the minds and bodies of others through the administration of toxic materials, and his deadly effectiveness is demonstrated by Othello's swooning, fitting reactions in the play.

The idea of being affected by an external substance, of consciousness being played upon and altered, is an anxious trope in the play, frequently explored via fears of poisoning and occult practices. Ironically, it is Othello, the victim of Iago's poison, who is initially accused of being a poisoner – this being the familiar working of the ideology of racism: the victim is accused of the crime, those in danger are made to seem dangerous. Iago's logic, shared by Desdemona's father, has it that Desdemona cannot love Othello except as a result of interference from poison or magic. Othello is repeatedly accused of practising on Desdemona with 'foul charms', with 'drugs or minerals / That weakens motion' (I.ii.73–75), of corrupting her with 'spells and medicines bought of the mountebanks' (I.iii.61). Loomba tells us that Othello, the 'Moor of Venice', 'stands at the complicated crux of contemporary beliefs about black people and Muslims'.[28] Partly at stake in the accusation of Othello drugging Desdemona is his religious difference: if we read Othello as a convert to Christianity, then the completeness, or reliability, of his conversion is cast into doubt here – he is accused of occult practices, and the 'otherness' rendered through these accusations is religious, racial and sexual.

Further on in the play, these accusations are revealed to be poison; they are the alarmist fantasies of minds affected by jealousy, and by racist and sexist narratives of promiscuous Venetian women and 'lusty' Moors. Iago will later reveal that *he* has in fact been worked upon by just this manner of jealous poison:

> I do suspect the lusty Moor
>
> Hath leap'd into my seat; the thought whereof
>
> Doth (like a poisoned mineral) gnaw my inwards.
>
> (II.i.295–297)

Iago's lurid imagining that Othello has slept with his wife, his horror at this prospect and the way that it has poisoned his experience of the world around him, is the initiator of him 'practising' upon Othello. Iago will now practise to rid Othello of the 'peace and quiet' of his own mind (II.ii.310) by pouring 'pestilence into his ear' (356).

Iago's plans are made possible because of another kind of dangerous intoxicant: alcohol. Cassio, Othello's lieutenant, cannot take his drink, he is 'unfortunate in the infirmity' (II.iii.41–42), and is profoundly changed by drink: 'To be now a sensible man, by and by a fool, and presently a Beast! O strange!' (I.iii.305–307). Drink makes Cassio a stranger, even to himself. Iago is able to intoxicate Cassio and manipulate him into a brawl, an activity that is out of character and will make him seem suspiciously unpredictable, even unknowable, to Othello. As people begin to alter in front of Othello's eyes, Iago is able to exploit his 'insider' status: Iago, as a Venetian, can pretend to be able to 'read' Cassio (who is a Florentine, and whose courtly manners and affectionate shows can be misrepresented to Othello) and Desdemona more fluently than Othello can. Iago installs himself as the authority on the meaning of people's bodies and behaviours.

Othello, in the midst of all of this uncertainty, looks for corroborating bodily proofs of inward character. Again, Iago can use this to his advantage. Iago dissimulates a halting delivery in his speech, and is subtle in his performance, seeming to hold back from making direct accusations about Cassio and Desdemona. This engenders trust from Othello:

> Therefore these stops of thine fright me the more;
>
> For such things in a false disloyal knave
>
> Are tricks of custom; but in a man that's just
>
> They're close dilations, working from the heart,
>
> That passion cannot rule.
>
> (III.iii.120–124)

Othello is desperately seeking a reliable system of communication, something that works 'from the heart', as people's spoken accounts of themselves begin to lose credibility for him. This desire to see inside a person quickly takes on shades of violence. Othello becomes increasingly insistent that Iago show his thinking: '[By heaven,] I'll know thy thoughts' (III.iii.162). Iago responds with a bloody and visceral image: that Othello couldn't know his thoughts, even if he rent his body apart: 'You cannot, if my heart were in your hand' (III.iii.163). The search for bodily proofs is revealed here to be an impossible and violent quest: a heart rendered in a fist might be what Othello now desires, but it would not disclose what Othello seeks.

The desire for bodily proof becomes a violent compulsion for Othello. Iago has set up 'dangerous conceit' that now works on Othello like poison:

> ... Trifles light as air
>
> Are to the jealous confirmations strong
>
> As proofs of holy writ; this may do something.
>
> The Moor already changes with my poison;
>
> Dangerous conceits are in their natures poisons,
>
> Which at first are scarce found to distaste,

Shakespearean swoons and unreadable body-texts

But with a little act upon the blood

Burn like mines of sulphur.

(III.iii.322–329)

In the next scene, Othello searches Desdemona's body for signs of her true feelings and action. Feeling her hand to be moist ('Hot, hot and moist' (III.iv.38)), he gives a humoral reading of her character, which suggests her nature is rebellious; she requires castigation and sequestration. The hand that has been given in marriage is now a suspicious signifier of her heart.

Othello begins to be driven to distraction by the poisonous idea of the (in)tangibility of female chastity and honour, and by the ceaseless searching for bodily proofs that this fear requires of him. Othello's concept of his own mind starts to change: 'Farewell the tranquil mind! Farewell content!' (III.ii.348). He speaks 'startingly and rash' (III.iv.78) and becomes almost unrecognisable to those who know him from Venice (III.iv.125). And when Iago claims to have a confession, a verbal and physical proof of Desdemona's infidelity, Othello's speech, and then his body, give way:

Lie with her? Lie on her? We say lie on her,

when they belie her. Lie on her! [Zounds,] that's

fulsome! Handkerchief – confessions – handkerchief!

To confess, and be hang'd for his labor – first to be

hang'd, and then to confess. I tremble at it. Nature

would not invest herself in such shadowing passions

without some instruction. It is not words that shakes

me thus. Pish! Noses, ears, and lips. It's possible?

Confess? Handkerchief? O devil! [*Falls in a trance.*]

(Iv.i.?34–43)

Othello begins to tremble and shake, and his own physical response is interpreted by him as a further proof, or 'instruction'. Finally he falls into a kind of swoon. 'Work on, / My medicine, [work]!' (Iv.i.43–45), Iago declaims over Othello's supine body. Iago is now a master poisoner, using his 'medicine' to incapacitate the great Commander, to make his body shake and fall. Cassio enters the scene, and Iago spins a fresh story about Othello's propensity to fall and fit:

> My lord is fall'n into an epilepsy.
>
> This is his second fit; he had one yesterday.
>
> [...]
>
> The lethargy [coma] must have its quiet course;
>
> If not he foams at the mouth, and by and by
>
> Breaks out to savage madness.
>
> (Iv.i.50–55)

As in *Julius Caesar*, a great man's 'falling sickness' is used in an attempt to discredit him; here, though, Iago takes the ploy one step further, and along racially differentiating lines. The fall is used to suggest proximity between Othello's body and 'savage' disorder. What's more, Iago uses the fall to discredit Othello to *himself*:

> Whilst you were here o'erwhelmed with your grief
>
> (A passion most [unsuiting] such a man),
>
> Cassio came hither, I shifted him away,
>
> And laid good 'scuses upon your ecstasy ...
>
> (Iv.i.76–79)

Othello is shamed by Iago for his swoon; and Iago uses the swoon to estrange Othello further from his sense of himself: he can no longer understand himself to be 'such a man'.

Othello is fatally altered, and othered, by Iago's manipulations, which hinge on this self-estranging swoon. 'Are his wits safe?' other characters now ask. 'Is he not light of brain'? (IV.i.269). Believing Iago's 'proofs', Othello now 'reads' Desdemona's body as a lying book: 'Was this fair paper, this most goodly book, / Made to write 'whore' upon?' (IV.ii 70–71). The female bodies in the play are overwritten by Iago: Desdemona's body is used to produce the story of female guilt that Iago has authored; he accuses his own wife of infidelity; in a later scene, Iago will publicly read Bianca's body (the butt of the men of the play) as showing guilt for the attack on Cassio that he orchestrated: 'Look you pale, mistress? – [...] Behold her well; I pray you look upon her. / Do you see her gentlemen?

Nay, guiltiness will speak, / Though tongues were out of use' (V.i.105–110). This is Iago's successful strategy almost to the end: to make the bodies of others signify along the lines of dominant, 'plausible' narratives of gender and race[29] – narratives that blame poisoning and sexual licentiousness and violence on the very people who are most vulnerable to being manipulated, sexually exploited and murdered.

Iago's promulgation of 'dangerous conceits' proves a fatal poison for Othello. As Desdemona describes his deadly, final approach, she notes his altered appearance and his trembling form: 'Alas, why gnaw you so your nether lip? / Some bloody passion shakes your very frame' (V.ii.43–44). After Desdemona's murder, Othello identifies himself as irrevocably changed, doubled in self-strangeness: 'That's he that was Othello; here I am' (V.ii.284). His famous final speech places him dramatically in the position of 'the other'; he is 'perplexed' beyond self-recognition:

> Speak of me as I am [...]
>
> Of one not easily jealous, but being wrought,
>
> Perplexed in the extreme; of one whose hand
>
> (Like the base [Indian]) threw a pearl away
>
> [...] Set you down this:
>
> And say besides, that in Aleppo once,
>
> Where a malignant and turban'd Turk
>
> Beat a Venetian and traduc'd the state,
>
> I took by th' throat the circumcised dog,
>
> And smote him – thus.
>
> (V.ii.342–356)

Othello's sense of himself has altered so much that he now coincides with the figure of the racially and religiously othered man whom he has murdered: a Turk who is hated by the Venetian state. Othello kills himself in a mime of this killing of the other; or he becomes, again, that symbolic other of the Venetian state, to which he was only temporarily allowed admittance. Othello's swoon is the turning point in this process – he now exists in a kind of trance, playing out the part apportioned to him by Iago's narrative of him as a violent and savage Moor. Loomba argues that the figure of Othello is complex in terms of concepts of race: 'Othello yokes together and reshapes available images of "blackamoors" and Moors, giving us a black Moor who has both a slave past and a noble lineage, a black skin and thick lips as well as great military and rhetorical abilities, a capacity for tenderness as well as a propensity to violence.'[30] It is complexity that Iago attempts to work against in his narratives about the three female characters in the play and about Othello; he seeks to project 'plausible' stereotypes about sexualised, racialised and religious proclivities, to orchestrate lies that are tragically too late in their discovery. Othello's swoon is both a rejection of the things that he is being told (his consciousness cannot admit these ideas and remain intact) and a moment of vulnerability that can be exploited to corroborate these tales (his propensity to wild, unfitting, savage states). *Othello* is a play about poison and toxic states of mind; about alarmist narratives of women being drugged and preyed upon by the occult powers of outsiders; about the effects of jealousy on the male mind; but most of all about 'dangerous conceits' of race, religion and sex that can overwrite individual bodies and make violence tragically inevitable.

*

The swoons of Hero, Caesar and Othello, different as they are, all occur in plays where the reliability of the body as a legible entity is highly contested. These swoons are the result of unbearable pressure brought to bear on individual bodies – Hero's body is subject to tendentious scrutiny and to unanswerable male accusation; Caesar and Othello's bodies are scrutinised and vilified as unseemly and unfit for power. Shakespearean swoons are a rejection of systems of legibility, when these systems coerce bodies into being 'books' with only one supposed meaning: no one character within any of these plays reads the swooning body in a way that we, the audience, can wholly trust. The swooning body's silence is subject to contestation, to projection and misconstruction within these play-worlds, and the action of the swoon dramatises the complexity of systems of bodily signification at the time, as different humoral, religious, sexist and racist narratives of physicality and subjectivity are shown to be in (violent) contention. Subjectivity refuses legibility in these swoons – it is fallen into a 'pit of ink'; the supposed instruments of signification produce the dark obscurity of unconsciousness. Shakespeare shows us that these swoons cannot be straightforwardly parsed through the available systems that attempt to generate meaning from bodies: the swooning body will keep its secrets, even though its heart were rendered bloodily in hand.

Notes

1. I refer to the texts of the plays as collected in *The Riverside Shakespeare*, 2nd edn (Boston; New York: Houghton Mifflin Co., 1997). References throughout will be to 'Through Line Numbers' as established by Charles Hinman in the *Norton Facsimilie: The First Folio of Shakespeare*.
2. Alan Sinfield, *Faultlines: Cultural Materialism and the Politics of Dissident Reading* (Oxford: Clarendon Press, 1992), p. 30.
3. Allison P. Hobgood and David Houston Wood, 'Introduction: Ethical Staring – Disabling the English Renaissance', in *Recovering Disability in Early Modern England*, eds Allison P. Hobgood and David Houston Wood (Columbus, OH: The Ohio State University Press, 2013), pp. 1–22, at p. 3. Hobgood and Wood convincingly argue that the 'notion of early modern disability is not anachronistic because human variation, though conceived of and responded to diversely, has always existed' (p. 7).
4. Claire McEachern (ed.) of William Shakespeare, *Much Ado About Nothing* (revised edn) (London: Bloomsbury, 2015), notes to p. 197.
5. Oliver Morgan, *Turn-Taking in Shakespeare* (Oxford: Oxford University Press, 2019).
6. *Ibid.*, p. 73.
7. *Ibid.*, p. 33.
8. *Ibid.*, p. 49.
9. Dympna Callaghan, *Woman and Gender in Renaissance Tragedy: A Study of King Lear, Othello, The Duchess of Malfi and The White Devil* (London: Harvester Wheatsheaf, 1989), p. 13.
10. Morgan, *Turn-Taking in Shakespeare*, p. 30.
11. McEachern tells us that this was an 'unsavory' enough insult as to be bowdlerised from most productions, from Garrick to the start of the twentieth century (notes to *Much Ado*, p. 296).
12. As noted by Jeffrey R. Wilson, 'The Figure of Stigma in Shakespeare's Drama', *Genre* 51(3) (2018), 237–266, at 261.

13 Frederick Samuel Boas, *Shakespeare and His Predecessors* (New York: Scribner, 1896), quoted by Jeffrey R. Wilson, 'The Figure of Stigma', at 261.
14 Allison P. Hobgood, 'Caesar Hath the Falling Sickness: The Legibility of Early Modern Disability in Shakespearean Drama', *Disability Studies Quarterly* 29(4)(2009), https://dsq-sds.org/article/view/993/1184 (accessed March 5, 2020).
15 *Ibid.*
16 *Ibid.*
17 Prior to her fall, even Clinton's manner of blinking and her head movements had been interpreted by Sean Hannity of *Fox News* as symptomatic of underlying health conditions that compromised her fitness for office (Rachael Revesz, 'Hillary Clinton's "Collapse"', *Independent* (September 11, 2016)). Clinton's 'faint' led to even more intense scrutiny and suspicion over the candidate's health and, by extension, over her 'fitness' for the White House (see Rachael Revesz, 'Hillary Clinton Collapses: Most US Voters do not buy Campaign's Reason for "Fainting" Episode', *Independent* (September 13, 2006)). The presentation of Clinton's faint was a success for Donald Trump's campaign: Trump's supporters successfully authored her body as frail and unfit, in order to bolster a soon-to-be president whose history of 'moving on' women, 'grab[bing]' their bodies, using them for 'anything you want', would shortly become a matter of record.
18 Wilson, 'The Figure of Stigma'.
19 Hobgood, 'Caesar Hath the Falling Sickness'.
20 *Ibid.*
21 Nicholas Royle, *How to Read Shakespeare* (London: Granta, 2005), p. 24.
22 *Ibid.*, p. 37.
23 My thanks to Oliver Morgan for drawing my attention to this possible pun.
24 Hobgood, 'Caesar Hath the Falling Sickness'.
25 *Ibid.*
26 Ania Loomba, *Shakespeare, Race, and Colonialism* (Oxford: Oxford University Press, 2002), p. 7.
27 See Loomba's work on *Othello* for a much more detailed discussion of Othello's skin colour and religious status, as well as concepts of Venetian difference: Loomba, *Shakespeare, Race, and Colonialism*, p. 91 *et seq.*
28 *Ibid.*, p. 92.
29 What Sinfield calls the 'conditions of plausibility', in *Faultlines*, p. 30.
30 Loomba, *Shakespeare, Race, and Colonialism*, p. 92.

3

Feeling too much: The swoon and the (in)sensible woman

In Jane Austen's *Persuasion* (1818), the young Louisa Musgrove, prospective fiancée of Captain Wentworth, develops the habit of throwing herself into the captain's arms from various heights, because she finds the sensation 'delightful'.[1] In one such incident, on the steep steps of the Cobb at Lyme, she insists on running back up the incline to hurl herself at him; she is 'precipitate by half a second' (78), and, missing Wentworth's arms, knocks herself out cold on the pavement. Louisa's sister, seeing her unconscious, sinks into a sympathetic swoon, so that both are 'insensible', and a third woman in their party is thrown into 'hysterical agitations'. News of this spectacle travels:

> [T]he report of the accident had spread among the workmen and boatmen about the Cobb, and many were collected ... to enjoy the sight of a dead young lady, nay, two dead young ladies, for it proved twice as fine as the first report. (79)

The 'fallen and fainted'[2] refined female forms here offer a doubly 'fine' proposition to their male labouring-class audience, and Austen offers us a double lampoon: she satirises the spectacular necrophilic pleasure that the swoon provides the male viewer in regarding a dead, nay two dead, young ladies; and at the same time satirises the performances of fine-feelinged femininity that have produced this hysterical sisterly scene of reciprocal unconsciousness.

By the time Austen was writing, the swoon had, in Gretchen Mieszkowski's phrase, 'acquired gender':[3] it had begun to be seen as a specifically feminine mode of response under the rubric of 'sensibility' – a situation to which Austen shows a keen satirical sensitivity in this scene in *Persuasion*. The 'cult of sensibility', an important aesthetic and cultural trend in the eighteenth century, shares some things in common with the medieval 'cult of tears'[4] (albeit that it arises in a more secular context). Claire Tomalin has connected the emotional valence and demonstrativeness prized in these two periods when she (with deliberate anachronism) posits Chaucer's Troilus as an early 'hero of sensibility'.[5] We can begin to see that a preponderance of literary swooning might coincide with historic moments during which emotional demonstrativeness is highly valued: the literary swoon flourished during the twelfth century alongside an increase in 'approved emotional behaviour',[6] and there is a similar flourish of swoons in eighteenth-century novels under the rubric of sensibility.

The literary swoon has, I will argue, a crucial status in the discourse of sensibility: the swoon is the most dramatic in a long list of textual somatic signs of sensitivity – sighs, blushes, tremblings, flinchings, agitations, palpitations, tears and fevers. These physical responses are also prized in emerging medical discourses in the period; physicians such as George Cheyne and Robert Whytt were producing models of the 'sensitised body' in which the concept of 'sensibility', seen as natural responsivity, was 'the co-ordinating principle of bodily integrity, providing the basis for the overall integration of body function'.[7] But, paradoxically, the swoon pushes high sensibility over into insensibility: it makes the responsive body unresponsive.[8] In this chapter, I read the swoon in sentimental literature as a test of some of the aspirations that emerged through the discourse of sensibility; in particular, the aspiration to produce a communicable, socially useful version of interior feeling through a new rhetoric of the body. As the crux between the sensible and the insensible, the swoon risks functioning as a bathetic[9] version of these aspirations of communicability of feeling; it dramatises the risk that high 'sensibility' might turn in on itself, becoming incommunicable and unconscious; that the speaking body might become sickly and silent, producing insensibility from its own sensitivity. Swooning, then, textually literalises the possible failure of sentimental language. And this swooning failure of communicability is the kind of problem highlighted by Eve Kosofsky Sedgwick in 'Jane Austen and the Masturbating Girl': Sedgwick describes sensibility as a point of 'dangerous overlap' between 'the allo-identifications that were supposed to guarantee the sociable nature of sensibility' and 'solipsism, a somatics of trembling self-absorption'.[10] In the readings that follow, I suggest that the swoon is intimately bound up with the textual depiction of inwardly directed feminine feeling that Sedgwick deems auto-erotic and pornographic in some texts of this period.

In this chapter, the swoon in eighteenth-century literature is read as pivotal for performances of gender. Sentimental scenes of feminine swooning in the popular novels of this period fall back on the pleasures of regarding the inert female form, and I discuss the complex scenography created around pitiable objects. My main referents here are depictions of 'fallen' women, but the swooning scenography I discuss, and the uneasy asymmetries produced by voyeurism and ostensible sympathy, might also pertain to other forms of suffering within sentimental literature, and in particular to depictions of colonialism and slavery.

Focusing on the differences in the depictions of feminine swooning in two novels set apart by forty years – Henry Mackenzie's *The Man of Feeling* (1771)[11] and Jane Austen's *Sense and Sensibility* (1811)[12] – I show that their treatment of the swoon is symptomatic of changing attitudes towards the female body in relation to sensibility. As anxieties about sensibility and its representation in 'feminine' novels[13] deepened towards the end of the eighteenth century and a morbid excessiveness of feminine feeling was linked to different types of falling: to the disastrous tumble of the 'fallen woman', to 'falling ill' and to 'falling into hysterics'. Swooning becomes charged with all the risks of a particularly female susceptibility to seduction, to sickness, and to hysteria. In the readings that follow, Mackenzie is seen to demonstrate the erotic impasse of (in)sensible feminine swooning, while Austen is seen to respond to this, venerating 'exertion' and a Wollstonecraftian notion of vigour, contra swooning.

Sentimental novels, 'fallen women' and *The Man of Feeling*

What does it mean to have feelings? How *much* should one feel, for oneself and for others? Is the limit of feeling to be measured in sympathy, in charity, in radical political action? In pleasure? In being overwhelmed, or in illness, or in shooting oneself in the head? These questions are posed by writers and philosophers concerned with the notion of 'sensibility' as it develops through the eighteenth and into the early nineteenth century, and are of particular interest to the sentimental novels of the same period. 'Sensibility' was originally used in medical parlance to describe the body's response to physical stimuli – to indicate its sensitivity and responsivity. In the early eighteenth century this use was extended to include emotional responsiveness; and later in the eighteenth century, fine-feelinged responsivity became aspirational: 'sensibility' connoted a 'laudable delicacy', and the 'cult of sensibility' was born.

The eighteenth century is the period during which 'feelings', proliferated into the plural noun-form from 'feeling',[14] first come into linguistic being, and the sentimental novel, an unprecedentedly popular literary form,[15] became an important crucible in which these 'feelings' were tested under the rigmarole of readerly sensibility. '"Sentimental"', John Mullan tells us, 'was usually a description of a representation; a person possessed "sensibility"; a text was "sentimental" ... "Sentimental," by becoming a word for a type of text, promised an occasion for fine feeling.'[16] 'Sentimental' was 'so much in vogue among the polite',[17] that its use was extended to all works that wished to attest to the 'refined' sensitivity of their author and to the reader's finer feelings: take for instance Joseph Hanway's *A Sentimental History of Chimney Sweeps* (1785). The *OED* tells us that these early uses of 'sentimental' were strongly approbatory, referring to 'persons, their dispositions and actions: Characterized by sentiment ... Characterized by or exhibiting refined and elevated feeling', and the term was liberally applied as a descriptor of many novels of the time.[18]

Henry Mackenzie's *The Man of Feeling*, a popular sentimental novel of the second half of the eighteenth century,[19] was written and read as one such occasion for refined feeling. In a well-known letter to Sir Walter Scott in 1826, Lady Louise Stuart describes reading the book at the age of 14, and fearing that she 'should not cry enough to gain the credit of proper sensibility'.[20] Mackenzie's novel builds on the popularity of previous novels of sentiment and readers' expectations of the genre: it draws on the weeping men of Samuel Richardson's novels, and its fragmentary style borrows heavily from Laurence Sterne's *A Sentimental Journey Through France and Italy* (1768). The novel consists of discontinuous scraps of narrative, and the reader's attention is focused on the central character, Harley, and on the opportunities for his sensibility to be displayed as he meets a cast of unfortunate characters who share their stories with him.

Harley is both protagonist and exemplary reader of sentimental scenes. His responses to the stories he hears provide examples of his finely tuned sensibility and his responsivity to the narratives of the sufferings of others; the man of feeling is also, then, an exemplar of the reader of sentimental novels. As such, Harley experiences 'the most delicate feelings' (9) and his tears flow in a constant course of pity and sympathy in response to the moving tales he hears.[21] Harley's emotional response is positioned as an emphatically *moral* encounter with the world around him. Harley's fine feelings, for example, are figured as a moral rejection of acquisitive greed: he is informed by others of the interests he should have on behalf of himself in relation to 'power, wealth, or grandeur'; but 'Harley was apt to hear those lectures with indifference' (10). He chooses instead to sympathise with those who have been disadvantaged and dispossessed by the ambitions of the more powerful. The investigation of sentiment as an emotional and moral response is at the heart of literary and philosophical enquiry in the eighteenth century. 'It is no coincidence', John Mullan tells us, 'that the moral philosophers who were the contemporaries of Richardson, Sterne and Mackenzie produced complex analyses of "moral sentiments".'[22] David Hume (1711–76), for instance, rejects a rationalist ethics, arguing that 'morality ... is determined merely by sentiment'.[23] In *A Treatise of Human Nature*, he suggests that moral judgements cannot be made with the same strict rationality as other forms of knowledge and must instead depend on feeling: 'Morality ... is more properly felt than judged of.'[24]

Morality, then, emerges from feeling. And the essential bridge between moral reason and feeling comes through Hume's concept of sympathy: 'No quality of human nature is more remarkable, both in itself and its consequences, than the propensity we have to sympathise with others, and to receive by communication their inclinations and sentiments, however different from, or even contrary to, our own.'[25] This anti-Hobbesian notion of sympathy is extended and elaborated upon in the work of Adam Smith (1723–90), particularly in *The Theory of Moral Sentiments*:

> As we have no immediate experience of what other men feel, we can form no idea of the manner in which they are affected, but by conceiving what we ourselves should feel in the like situation. Though our brother is upon the rack, as long as we ourselves are at our ease, our senses

will never inform us of what he suffers ... it is by the imagination only that we can form any conception of what are his sensations.[26] This philosophical veneration of imaginative suffering positions it as the precursor of sympathy and moral virtue.[27] Markman Ellis describes the reading of sentimental novels as a parallel process that offers the reader the opportunity 'to feel the emotions of the character',[28] reproducing Smith's theory of sympathy in terms of delicacy of sentiment. Mackenzie, in describing his composition of *The Man of Feeling*, relates a similar notion of the efficacy of the sentimental narrative; he describes it as exciting 'both the memory and the affections deeper than mere argument or moral reasoning', and it is for this reason that he thinks of 'introducing a man of sensibility into different scenes where his feelings might be seen in their effects, and his sentiments occasionally delivered without the stiffness of regular deduction'.[29] The opportunity sentimental literature offers for producing morally improving sympathy is crucial to Mackenzie's understanding of his work as a novelist – and, as Mullan has suggested, 'sentiment' in this context means both 'feeling' (we should read the sentimental novel to be 'touched') and 'precept' (we should read the sentimental novel to be morally instructed by the sympathy it produces).[30] But the ethics of sympathy, and particularly of the sentimental as a mode of spectating suffering, are more complex than Mackenzie allows here – as I hope to show in the following discussion of the swooning woman in his work.

Picturesque pathetic objects: The 'fallen woman'

The swooning 'fallen woman' is a frequent feature of sentimental narratives, and she is an exemplary instance of sentimental literature's complex relation to sentimental objects: the pretty, prone woman is displayed for our sympathy and our viewing pleasure. The most dramatic swoons in *The Man of Feeling* are described in the course of the friendship Harley strikes up with Emily, a woman who has 'fallen' into prostitution. Emily, who initially begs from Harley a pint of wine, is described in the narrative as emphatically and literally fallen: her body cannot stay upright. At their first meeting, Emily catches Harley's arm and 'her eye grew fixed, her lip assumed a clayey whiteness, and she fell back lifeless in her chair'; she is a 'dying figure'; Harley later succeeds in catching her to prevent her 'falling to the ground' (49). Harley's desire to visit Emily, following her supplication and faint, is mocked by his friends; they believe him to be 'bubbled by a fine story invented by a whore' (52–53). The possibility of Harley being fooled by a bubble-work of words, 'deluded by bubbles' (53), is in his own mind weighed against the physical prostration of the woman: 'he recalled the languid form of the fainting wretch to his mind; he wept at the recollection of her tears' (53); her faint wins his sympathetic response and he sets out to see her.

The faint is 'proof' for Harley; he sees no possibility of it being a feint. He reads Emily's swoon in accordance with contemporary medical accounts of the nervous system, via which demonstrations of sensibility are seen to function as natural, physical and reliable manifestations of a sensitised body. As previously mentioned, physicians such as George Cheyne and Robert Whytt were producing models of the 'sensitised body' in which the concept of 'sensibility' was 'the co-ordinating principle of bodily integrity, providing the basis for the overall integration of body function'.[31] Christopher Lawrence argues that, to such physicians, the notion of sympathy 'was no more than the communication of feeling between different bodily organs, manifested by functional disturbance of one organ when another was stimulated'.[32] Whytt's suggestion in 1768 that 'by doleful stories or shocking sights delicate people have often been affected with fainting and general convulsion'[33] shows the proximity between a doctrine of physical sympathy and the scene of literary production, with 'stories' and 'sights' affecting the sensitised, sympathetic system. Markman Ellis argues that this is 'enthusiastically articulated in the novels of the sentimental school, who adapted the vocabulary of the scientists' model of the workings of the nerves to communicate a deepened range of emotions and feelings. On these foundations is built a repertoire of conventions associated with the sentimental rhetoric of the body: fainting, weeping, sighing, hand-holding, mute gesture, the beat of a pulse, blushing – and so on.'[34] Emily's faints and swoons, then, are read by Harley as a reliable expression of her 'natural' sensibility within the signifying system of the nervous, sympathetic body.

By paying attention to the swoon of the 'fallen woman' in sentimental novels, I hope to show that this particular response is more frequent and significant than other markers of sensibility in their characterisation (than trembling, weeping or sighing for instance). It has been shown elsewhere how prostitutes became 'sentimentalized subjects' in the eighteenth century, with Richard Steele, among others, writing sympathetic accounts of 'seduced' prostitutes.[35] The swoon's rhetorical shape, I suggest, is as important to these novels as its correspondence with medical accounts of the sensitised body: the swoon is a key component of a sentimental depiction of prostitution that depends on the downward trajectory of the female body, and the subsequent possibility of upwards transformation through repentance. Within these novels, this pattern is usually presented as a moral one; the swoon, after all, shadows the narrative shape of salvation. But sentimental novels also revel in the downward trajectories of female bodies – they erotically elaborate on the prostrate female form.[36] A careful reading of the swoons of 'fallen women' will help to show their importance for the complex, voyeuristic construction of sympathy and of sympathetic subjects produced by sentimental novels.

According to Ellis's pivotal work on *The Politics of Sensibility* (1996), which informs much of the following discussion, the public debate around prostitution reform at this time had two main consequences: first, the possibility that 'unhappy women' might re-establish their social standing through repentance; and second the establishment of benevolent charities for the reformation of prostitutes. The most famous of such establishments was the Magdalen Hospital for the Reception of Penitent Prostitutes, where church services were open to the public by ticket and became fashionable events. Young, 'fallen' women were effectively paraded as a sympathetic spectacle. Horace Walpole records his visit in January 1760, and notes the sympathetic responses of the audience: Walpole listens to a sermon in which the minister 'apostrophized the lost sheep, who sobbed and cried from their souls – so did my Lady Hertford and Fanny Pelham'. Following the sermon, Walpole is 'struck and pleased with the modesty of two of [the penitent prostitutes], who swooned away with the confusion of being stared at'.[37] Walpole's observations exemplify the creation of the prostitute as sentimental object: she is a picturesque, modest, swooning spectacle and Walpole experiences the 'pleasing' sight of her speechless confusion.

The Magdalen Hospital gave rise to a number of sentimentalist narratives and novels, which related histories of exemplary Magdalens to raise money for the charity. These novels, Ellis tells us, translate 'the seduction motif (down and away from domestic respectability to the status of the "fallen woman") into the discourse of repentance (up towards the status of the virtuous penitents)',[38] a narrative shape that we might see redoubled in the narrative pattern of the swoon. Ellis describes Magdalen novels being forced to distinguish themselves from one another by focusing on 'how low the fallen woman can fall, or on the peculiarities of her fall'. These novels elaborate at length on women falling, the swoon of seduction, and begin to risk resembling the libertine erotica they ostensibly vilify. The swoon, I want to suggest, is a metonym of the sentimental depiction of prostitution; the narratives of 'fallen women' that pretend to raise them up also glory in their demise, taking pleasure in the moment of the swoon, the locus of female susceptibility to seduction as well as to spiritual transformation. The complex pleasures of viewing the suffering of others through a sentimental lens here takes on an overtly erotic dimension.

I read Mackenzie's description of swooning Emily in *The Man of Feeling* as a sister account to these novels: it is structured along the supposedly moral downward/upward trajectory of the 'fallen woman', while simultaneously producing prurient readerly pleasure in Emily's fall. Emily relates her history to Harley as one long decline. Importantly, her moral dip begins with aberrant reading: after her mother's death, she gives up reading religious books and instead turns to the 'plays, novels, and those poetical descriptions of the beauty of virtue and honour, which the circulating libraries easily afforded' (55). Mackenzie is corresponding in this description with a contemporary anxiety about the reading habits of women in the context of increased access to literature and especially in relation to the novel. The fear that the sentimental novel might pose a particular danger to women – that it might seduce the imagination, stimulating fantasies of romantic love and therefore weakening the 'prophylactic power of innocence'[39] – was widespread, with even Samuel Richardson censuring the 'indistinct reading' of sentimental novels because it might 'corrupt ... more female hearts than any cause whatsoever'.[40]

Anxiety on behalf of female readers was often expressed in the language of the fear of feminine susceptibility to excessive feeling and seduction. Ellis shows us this in citing a number of prominent figures of the time railing in this vein:[41] the Reverend Edward Barry, for example, described novels as 'incentive to seduction' because the 'main drift of such writing is to interest, to agitate, and convulse the passions, and is but too prone, by a sympathy of sentiment, to lead the mind astray'. Clara Reeve described the effects of the circulating libraries as profoundly ambivalent, providing as they did both 'food and poison' to the young mind. The novel is often associated with intoxication and narcotic effects; or, in Fanny Burney's worst imagining, as a kind of virus in the circulatory system, producing a 'distemper' or 'contagion'. Underlying these fears is a particular anxiety about *female* susceptibility: what might be good for men is poison for women. William Craig, in *The Lounger*, for instance, describes the sentimental novel as potentially civic and virtuous: 'The cold and selfish may be warmed and expanded by the fiction of distress or the eloquence of sentiment.' But the feminising reformation offered by sensibility to gentlemen is dangerous when extended to the 'tender, warm and visionary' minds of the young and *women*, for whom 'the walks of fancy and enthusiasm, or romantic love, or exaggerated sorrow, or trembling sensibility, are very unsafe'.

Sure enough, after she reads the intoxicating material available in the circulating libraries, Mackenzie's young Emily falls in love with a man and 'imputed to his sensibility that silence which was the effect of art and design'; she projects her romanticised notions upon the man and is seduced by him, falling 'prey to his artifices' (58). Emily travels with the man to London and when she discovers that he has no intention of marrying her – that he intends instead to discard her or keep her as a mistress – she is choked by '[s]hame, grief, and indignation ... unable to speak my wrongs, and unable to bear them in silence, I fell in a swoon at his feet' (62). 'What happened in the interval [of swooning] I cannot tell', Emily tells Harley as she relays the story of her life. Emily describes a literalised downward trajectory whereby she has been seduced by a man who abandons her, swoons, and comes to in the arms of an unscrupulous landlady; she suffers a miscarriage and is forced into drudgery, prison and then prostitution.

Emily provides an impassioned call for sympathy following her disastrous swoon and its expressive impasse, and this call is founded on the basis of the conditional possibility of compassion for what is currently unknown and unseen: 'Oh! Did the daughters of virtue know our suffering! Did they see our hearts torn with anguish amidst the affectation of gaiety which our faces are obliged to assume; our bodies tortured by disease, our minds with that consciousness they cannot lose!' (65). This is certainly an advertisement for sympathy, and a striking description of the pain of consciousness, but the narrative has also relayed Emily's seduction in a way that revels in her debasement – from the initial description of her fainting in front of Harley, through to the lurid details of her seduction into prostitution. Eve Kosofsky Sedgwick has described the 'nonaccountable viewer satisfactions' that might be at play in narratives like this: 'sentimental spectatorship seemed to offer coverture for differences in material wealth (the bourgeois weeping over the spectacle of poverty) or sexual entitlement ... [But m]aterial or sexual exploitations ... might even be perpetuated or accelerated by the nonaccountable viewer satisfactions'.[42] In these kinds of sentimental works, Sedgwick suggests, *desire* might be misrepresented as pity, and reading pathetic scenes might 'accelerate', not ameliorate, inequality. I see the swoon of the 'fallen woman' as a dramatic instance of the *mise en scène* of sentimental pathos and these 'unaccountable pleasures': the 'fallen woman' is rendered prone and silent and sexually susceptible for supposedly charitable purposes; but also for our reading pleasure.

The complex pleasures provided by the sentimental swoon return us to philosophical and moral accounts of sensibility, and to question of what kind of relation the novel of feeling has to the ethical and political concerns of its day. This question, especially in relation to slavery, is the focus of much of Ellis's work in the *Politics of Sensibility*. Ellis argues that the sentimental novel moulds the 'feelings' of the reader and attempts to 'reformulate social attitudes to inequality through the development of a new humanitarian sensibility'; writers insert 'matters of political controversy into the text of the novel itself'.[43] Of contemporary examples of inequality, the most egregious was the slave trade. Ellis reads Mackenzie, and particularly his later novel *Julie de Roubigné* (1777), as providing an active opposition to the *conditions* of slavery. He describes the way in which sentimentalists attack the terminologies of racial difference which were fundamental to slavery; Sterne, for example, describes 'typological gradations of complexion as "insensible"',[44] and sentimentalist discussion of slavery accords a priority to the possibility of mutual feeling rather than to 'scopic typologies of complexion and race'.[45] '[A]ffectual equality',[46] a mutual ability to feel, is one sentimentalist ground which could be seen to challenge the racist and dehumanising basis for slavery.

And we might detect a critique of colonial appropriation and slavery operating in *The Man of Feeling* through what I want to call an ethic of shedding. Harley's studied failure to pursue his own material advantage, alongside his copious shedding of tears, demonstrates an anti-accumulative ethos. His shedding accords with Janet Todd's description of the sentimentalist as 'ardently anti-capitalist, despising those who hoard and increase money and dispensing his own wealth liberally and with speed'.[47] Harley's ethic of shedding is an emotional one (his frequent weeping) but it extends into an ostensibly anti-imperialist political stance.[48] This is his view on colonial India for example:

> I cannot ... rejoice at our conquests in India. You tell me of immense territories subject to the English: I cannot think of their possession, without being led to enquire, by what right they possess them ... When shall I see a commander return from India in the pride of honourable poverty? ... they are covered with the blood of the vanquished! ... Could you tell me of some conqueror giving peace and happiness to the conquered? ... [D]id he return with no lace on his coat, no slaves in his retinue, no chariot at his door, and no Burgundy at his table? (102–103)

The acquisitive motive of the British in the East Indies is one of the charges against conquest here, and it is 'feelings' that Harley calls up as the defence against injustice: 'the *feelings* are not yet lost that applaud benevolence, and censure inhumanity. Let us endeavour to strengthen them in ourselves' (p. 104; my italics). Moral justice is, in this account, tightly bound to intensity of feeling; strengthening feeling, exciting passion, is the way to censure inhumanity. And shedding is not just a performance of tears: it must also be a shedding of wealth, of imperialist accumulation, and of people acquired as slaves.

But can we take this literary ethic of shedding to constitute a coherent politicised response to the injustices of colonialism and slavery? The swoon has shown us that there are complex pleasures involved in spectating suffering in sentimental narratives. While these novels might be thought of as 'innovative and forceful ... brave and even radical', they stop short, in Ellis's view, of being meaningfully 'anti-slavery'. Along with the discursive positions 'pro-slavery' and 'anti-slavery', Ellis proposes 'a third position, called ... "amelioration", that argued for the mitigation of the conditions of slavery, but not its abolition'.[49] It is this ameliorative voice that Ellis hears in sentimentalism, and particularly in Mackenzie's work: Mackenzie 'seeks to transform the peculiar asymmetries of power endemic to the slavery economies, but without destroying the ideology or economy of slavery'.[50] The failure to radically address slavery at the ideological level is bound up with the structurally asymmetric aesthetics of suffering that exist and persist in the literary occasion of the sentimental:

> The sentimentalist rhetoric is a one way street: the colonial viewer is distressed by the condition of the slave ... but the slave is not empowered by it, nor given any greater insight into the condition of slavery. The slave remains in the hyperbolically violent underworld of chattel slavery. The slaves are treated as a kind of property within sentimentalism, alongside and equivalent to dead asses, lame lap-dogs, lunatic women, incarcerated starlings, and so.[51]

The sentimentalist approach might be seen to 'advertise' the suffering occasioned by slavery and other situations of inequality, Ellis suggests, but in doing so it is also drawn into a relation of voyeurism with it, and 'runs aground on the shoals of the pathetic and the little – that category of the sentimentally apotropaic which voyeuristically focuses on the powerless resigned to powerlessness'.[52] Because it is structured around this scopic encounter with the powerless, the sentimentalist approach must fail 'to move beyond the depiction of its theme to a critique of that theme's subject, slavery proper'.[53]

Reading the novel of sentiment, then, is an ethically and politically fraught endeavour. John Mullan hints at the murky complexities of the form in his description of the 'cadences of self-satisfaction' sounding through the 'powers of feeling' in sentimental novels;[54] Ellis attributes to the sentimental 'a complex aesthetic logic akin to the sublime, that discovers pleasure in distress and misery'.[55] I want to suggest that sentimental literature involves itself in a complex and potentially sado-masochistic scenography; it advertises pathetic objects for our moral sympathy, but depends on the readerly pleasures of regarding their debasement. And the *type* of sentimental objects focused on in novels, in contrast to those chosen by philosophic discourse, are striking in this respect: the violent examples used to model sympathy by Adam Smith, for instance (the man torn upon the rack; the hanged, dancing corpse; the ulcerated beggar), give way to more picturesque and feminised objects (incarcerated starlings and swooning women) in sentimental literature. Swooning, then, is a paradigmatic case of sentimental literature's complex relation to prettified objects: the prone woman is paraded by sentimental literature for our sympathy *and* our viewing pleasure.

I conclude this discussion of Mackenzie's work with a further consideration of the swoon and feminine speechlessness to show how pitiable objects are given sympathy but are not granted communicative power or agency. Mackenzie's hero, Harley, takes the 'fallen woman', Emily, to see her father. 'Unable to speak [her] wrongs, and unable to bear them in silence', Mackenzie's Emily swoons. The failure of speech to adequately express intensity of feeling is a common idea in the sentimental novel. In this description of Emily's swoon, however, the impasse is intensified: female desire and complaint are impossible to express in an available language. When Emily's father arrives, he demands that she 'speak' to him. But the father's language has already wished Emily dead ('Her death I could have borne! But the death of her honour has added obloquy and shame to that sorrow which bends my gray hairs to the dust' (76)); and the narrative gives her no tenable subject position from which to speak, positioning her, as Ellis described, as the 'paradoxical figure of the seduced but virtuous prostitute'.[56] Emily's body symptomatises the impossibility of her verbal expression in the language of her father, and she mimes the cessation of her verbal expressivity, falling to the ground, and bathing his feet with her tears. The swoon here gestures towards inarticulacy itself, constituting a paradoxical attempt to communicate incommunicability, to make legible the impossibility of sustained female expression and consciousness under these linguistic and narrative circumstances.

But there is another endemic complication to Emily's speechlessness: the novel relies on words to recount this silence; it simultaneously disavows language, yet depends on its own language to make legible the speaking/speechless body. When Harley first hears Emily's story, for instance, he shares a sympathetic connection to her speechless condition: overcome with feeling for her, 'he could not speak, had it been to beg a diadem' (66) and she sees 'his tears' as the demonstration of his sympathy. But Harley determines *to speak for* Emily to her father, just as the novel insists on articulating her swoon as part of its sentimentalist discourse.

Harley's speech on Emily's behalf, whilst urging sympathy, is unable to make an account of female sexual desire without giving way to desire as voyeurism, and then to alarm. The conversation between Harley and Emily's father is addressed to a female readership of sentimental literature; and it is a conversation that takes place between two men, written by a man, which restates the danger of women reading sentimental literature as a progression towards falling into prostitution. Benevolence towards the 'fallen woman' here is an extension of paternal control and protection, that is also prurience. The novel's attempt to render the swoon in language is an exhortation towards sympathy with the downward trajectory of the 'fallen woman', where being 'moved' by her story is to be emotionally affected by her physical instability and the impossibility of her eloquence; yet it produces a language of benevolence as discipline. It privileges silence over the articulation of female complaint and makes of swooning a potential site of licentious voyeurism.[57]

The gendered terms of silence, feeling and falling are clear in the final stages of Mackenzie's novel. The silent and sexually and morally compromised 'fallen' woman is contrasted at the close with the heroically dying man (in a way that might be seen as a parallel to Troilus' post-swoon elevation at the end of Chaucer's poem).[58] Harley is 'seized with a very dangerous fever', the cause of which is suggested to be 'his hopeless love for Miss Walton' (126). Harley feels too much to exist in a 'hard' and 'unfeeling' world: 'There are some feelings which perhaps are too tender to be suffered by the world' (125). Here Harley seems to share with other contemporary men of feeling a propensity towards dramatic death; their dying contrasts the feminine intermittent insensibility of swooning.[59] Harley, succumbing to his fever, 'is gone forever', his corpse 'stretched without sense or feeling' (131). Unlike the swooning woman, there is no impasse of insensibility here; rather Harley's sensibility ascends the body and becomes immortalised. After death, we are told, his 'feelings will subsist' in some 'better modification', where they will 'deserve the name of virtues'. As if to remind us that the woman of feeling collapses into a worldly insensibility, while the man of feeling ascends to immortal sensibility, Harley's beloved swoons on top of him, but is 'recovered'. The insensible man of feeling is resurrected into religious righteousness. When the curate recalls Harley, '[e]very nobler feeling rises within me! Every beat of my heart awakens a virtue!' (133). The insensible woman of feeling is laid temporarily, erotically, low; the insensible man of feeling lies in the valley of fallen heroes, while his sensibility ascends to the highest realms.

Morbid excess and the woman of feeling

By the end of the eighteenth century, the vogue of sensibility had become the 'problem' of sensibility.[60] Lady Louise Stuart's 1826 letter to Scott marks a concomitant change in readers' experiences of novels of sentiment: Stuart, one evening, decides to read *The Man of Feeling* aloud to friends, remembering how her family once shared the book 'with rapture' and fearing that it might 'prove too affecting'; but the audience's response is now quite different: 'Nobody cried, and at some of the passages, the touches I used to think so exquisite – oh dear! they laughed.'[61] The modern pejorative sense of sentimental as '[a]ddicted to indulgence in superficial emotion; apt to be swayed by sentiment',[62] had begun to impinge on the word's earlier approbatory use, such that Raymond Williams describes the word undergoing a change through its association with 'unregulated feeling' which results in it being 'permanently damaged'.[63] We might briefly note here that the 'damage' done to the literary reputation of the sentimental novel is closely bound with its relation to femininity. Ellis describes sensibility as inherently gendered from its inception: '[sensibility] was in some sense a feminine attribute'.[64] Sensibility was *available* to men, but was commonly apostrophised as a feminine figure and was particularly 'associated with the behaviour and experience of women'.[65] George J. Barker-Benfield suggests that sensibility can be thought of as part of a gendered transformation of manners in the eighteenth century, a feminising of social experience and domestic economy and an attempt to socialise male behaviour along supposedly feminine lines.[66] Criticisms of sensibility were often anxiogenic in relation to this process of 'feminisation', and by the end of the eighteenth century, sensibility and its representation in 'feminine' novels of sentiment[67] were subject to new forms of scrutiny.

In many novels that follow in the wake of *The Man of Feeling*, morbidly excessive feminine feeling is shown to precipitate falling – in particular, the disastrous tumble of the 'fallen woman', falling into illness and falling into hysterics – and swooning becomes associated with depictions of feminine susceptibility to seduction, to sickness and to hysteria. Writing in the shadow of the sentimental novel, Austen, like a number of other female writers of the late eighteenth and early nineteenth centuries, is interested in the gendered terms of sensibility, and in the alternatives to them that might now be proposed.[68] In *Sense and Sensibility*, which Jane Austen worked on between 1797 and its publication in 1811, sensibility is explored as a particularly feminine habit. In the reading of her work that follows, I see Austen as valuing feminine sensibility *only* when it is combined with a feminine exertion against what are depicted as its morbid and morally dubious extremes: swooning, seduction and sickness.

The title of Austen's novel has often been read as substituting 'the leading characteristics of [the] principal personages for their names', so that we are presented with the 'sense of Elinor' and 'sensibility (or rather *sensiblerie*) of Marianne'.[69] While this isn't the only way in which we might conceive of the relation between the novel's titular terms, Marianne can usefully be construed as representing the 'survival of the sentimental novel'[70] of the eighteenth century, and she is portrayed in the novel as subject to excessive feeling: 'her sorrows, her joys, could have no moderation', we are told, and Elinor detects 'excess in her sister's sensibility' (5). The novel describes Marianne and her mother reinforcing one another's emotional responses, such that, after the death of Mr Dashwood, they encourage one another,

> in the violence of their affliction. The agony of grief which overpowered them at first was voluntarily renewed, was sought for, was *created* again and again. The gave themselves up wholly to their sorrow, *seeking increase* of wretchedness in every reflection that could afford it, and resolved against ever admitting consolation in future' (5; my italics)

The idea of feeling as a 'natural' response under the rubric of sensibility is being challenged here in the depiction of the women 'creating' and 'seeking increase': emotional agony is becoming a feminine indulgence and performance here. Elinor later describes Marianne 'feeding and encouraging as a duty' (68) her sense of sorrow. Sensibility is being recast and satirised here are as a feminine obligation, and Marianne is portrayed actively producing her overwrought emotional states.

Literary response and taste are important ways in which Marianne's sensibility is demonstrated. She dismisses those people, particularly potential suitors, who have no 'real taste', who are not 'connoisseurs'; it would 'break her heart' to hear a man she loved read with 'little sensibility': 'I could not be happy with a man whose taste did not in every point coincide with my own. He must enter into all my feeling; the same books, the same music, must charm us both' (15). The test for shared feeling is in the correct and sensible response to Cowper and Scott, and in admiring Pope 'no more than is proper' (40). Marianne's poetic sensibility means that she responds to the world with heightened sensitivity. She describes, for instance, the 'transporting sensations' she experiences watching leaves fall from a tree, the refined 'feelings' that the leaves, 'the season, the air, altogether inspired' (77). To which Elinor crisply replies: 'It is not everyone ... who has your passion for dead leaves' (79).

Elinor's responses often sardonically suggest the absurd exaggeration she sees at play in Marianne's literary and aesthetic sensitivities. And her criticisms of Marianne's performances of aesthetic response turn through the novel towards larger questions about the efficacy of sensibility as a system for regulating taste and judgement, particularly judgements of moral propriety. Marianne's sense of her own sensibility means that she believes moral propriety can be worked out through her feelings In her relationship with Willoughby, for instance, she insists to Elinor that she would have been 'sensible of it' had there been any impropriety: 'for we always know when we are acting wrong, and with such a conviction I could have had no pleasure ... I am not sensible of having done anything wrong' (60). But the moral judgements produced by Marianne's sensibility are criticised by Elinor and the narrator as being tendentious in the extreme. In Marianne's dismissal of Colonel Brandon as uninteresting, for instance, Elinor thinks her sister 'undiscerning ... prejudiced and unjust' (44). The narrator agrees and describes 'the injustice to which [Marianne] was often led in her opinion of others, by the irritable refinement of her own mind, and the too great importance placed by her on the delicacies of a strong sensibility and the graces of a polished manner' (174). Marianne's prejudices, here explicitly the prejudices conditioned by the cult of sensibility, mean that she is neither 'reasonable nor candid. She expected from other people the same opinions and feelings as her own, and she judged of their motives by the immediate effect of their actions on herself' (174). Sensibility is figured as a disciplinary code of response,[71] and Marianne's feelings, her supposed 'natural' responsivity, are presented here as conditioned and morally insufficient prejudices. Tolstoy, writing in *War and Peace* (1869), makes an even stronger critique of sensibility when choosing to criticise political hypocrisy through a comparison to morally dubious feminine performances of swooning:

> As it is, we've been playing at war – that's the nasty thing, we act magnanimously and all that. It's like the magnanimity and sensibility of the lady who swoons when she sees a calf slaughtered; she's so kind, she can't bear the sight of blood, but she eats the same calf in sauce with great appetite.[72]

Sense and Sensibility interrogates sensibility as a code of aesthetic and moral response, and finds it similarly wanting.[73] And Marianne's excessive sensibility and the dangers attendant on it are most emphatically marked in the novel through the ways in which Marianne falls, faints and swoons: she falls in the rain, and this 'tumbling down ... tumbling about' (38), is the precursor to her falling in love with Willoughby.[74] At points of extreme feeling she 'falls back' into hysterics (316). The language used to describe Marianne's distress creates a close connection between excessive feeling and illness: Marianne, when suffering from heartbreak, is 'not well'; she is 'indisposed' (172); she is 'much plagued lately with nervous headaches' (191); 'she has had a nervous complaint on her for several weeks' (199); she suffers from a 'a general nervous faintness' (159). These nervous symptoms find full expression in Marianne falling seriously ill: she develops a 'feverish wildness' that threatens to be fatal (276). Marianne describes this illness as the fulfilment of her 'feelings' and the approach she takes to extending them under the rigmarole of sensibility: she has 'courted misery', embracing sleeplessness, tears, fasting and silence. 'Her sensibility was potent enough!' (73) the narrator exclaims; sensibility's power here is seen as a precursor for suffering. Marianne's sensibility is a morbid indulgence: she falls into the abyss of 'self-destruction' (312); she feels too much and almost passes out of the world entirely.

In contrast to this, Elinor stands resolute; her position is staunchly anti-swoon. Elinor ministers to Marianne at crucial moments of faintness, providing remedies and exhorting her to 'exert' herself. When Marianne encounters Willoughby with a fashionable-looking young lady, she turns 'dreadfully white, and unable to stand', sinks onto a chair. Elinor, 'expecting every moment to see her faint', screens Marianne from observation and revives her 'with lavender water' (153), lavender drops being an old remedy for swooning.[75] Later, hartshorn[76] is administered as a smelling salt in an attempt to 'restore' Marianne to herself and to keep her from fainting. Again and again Elinor exhorts the 'faint and giddy' Marianne to avoid swooning – 'Exert yourself, dear Marianne ... exert yourself' (159–160). Elinor is also heroically upright when it comes to her own experience of her potentially overwhelming feelings. When Elinor discovers that the man she hopes to marry is closely acquainted with one Miss Lucy Steele she is in 'silent amazement' and 'though her complexion varied, she *stood firm* in incredulity, and felt in no danger of an hysterical fit or a swoon' (114; my italics). The change in Elinor's complexion marks the intense emotional and physiological pressure she experiences,[77] but she steers clear of the swoon. When the details of a secret engagement between Miss Steele and Edward Ferrars emerge, Elinor is threatened more seriously with sinking: 'for a few moments she was almost overcome – her heart sank within her, and she could hardly stand'; but, crucially, she 'exerts' herself in order to prevent a faint: 'she struggled so resolutely against the oppression of her feelings that her success was speedy, and for the time complete' (120). Elinor's self-command is described as energetic resistance against swooning: she 'did not sink' (117).

In Austen's juvenile work, *Love and Freindship* [sic] (c.1790), the main character is cautioned against fainting: 'beware of swoons, Dear Laura ... Run mad as often as you chuse; but do not faint'.[78] *Love and Freindship* satirises female characters who faint at the slightest provocation, and warns against enfeebling performances of femininity. In Austen's mature work, Elinor successfully produces her own prophylactic practice against passing out.

In *A Vindication of the Rights of Woman* (1792),[79] Mary Wollstonecraft identifies the dangers of a discourse of sensibility that enfeebles women and produces a morbid tendency towards delicacy; and to do so, she uses language that shares much in common with Austen's descriptions of the differences between Elinor and Marianne.[80] The view of feminine delicacy that Wollstonecraft is writing against is typified in Edmund Burke's *On the Sublime and the Beautiful* (1757):

> An air of robustness and strength is very prejudicial to beauty. An appearance of delicacy, and even of fragility, is almost essential to it ... I need here say little of the fair sex, where I believe the point will be easily allowed me. The beauty of women is considerably owing to their weakness or delicacy, and is even enhanced by their timidity, a quality of mind analogous to it.[81]

Wollstonecraft's opposition to the widespread ('easily allowed') approbation of feminine delicacy is set forth in the kind of strident terms that are themselves a denial of the desirability of timidity: she detests the 'weak elegancy of mind, exquisite sensibility, and sweet docility of manners, supposed to be the sexual characteristics of the weaker vessel', because such notions are 'epithets of weakness' that 'soften our slavish dependence' and make of women 'objects of contempt' (73). According to Wollstonecraft, women 'in general', and 'the rich of both sexes' have acquired the vices associated with 'civilized' sensibility and the result is that '[t]heir senses are inflamed, and their understandings neglected; consequently they become the prey of their senses, delicately termed sensibility, and are blown about by every momentary gust of feeling' (130). The language Wollstonecraft uses to describe the ill-effects of sensibility produces a series of images of female physical instability: women are 'blown about', and rendered 'faint', 'unstable', 'wavering', 'exhausted', 'transient'; they exist in 'fits and starts', and lack the stability of 'gravity'. 'Women', she tells us, 'are supposed to possess more sensibility, and even humanity, than men' (277); but the result of this tendentious notion of sensibility is morbidity: it is a 'sickly delicacy' and an 'enervating' indulgence (111).

As an alternative to the 'false descriptions' or 'caricatures' of sensibility, Wollstonecraft proposes the 'vigor of intellect', a 'strengthening' of judgement, and a focus on 'sense': 'it requires sense to turn sensibility into the broad channel of humanity' (261). Here, then, is another way in which we might fruitfully conceive of the terms of Austen's title. Wollstonecraft's version of feminine 'vigour' chimes with Austen's emphasis on 'exertion', and both suggest a redemption of feminine sensibility through its alliance with 'sense'. Both Wollstonecraft and Austen propose models of feminine response that accord with sensibility in terms of a capacity for feeling, but are not sensible to the morbid extent of *insensibility*; that would, in other words, stop short of the inchoate unconsciousness of the swoon.

'Painful exertion': Austen and Wollstonecraft's vigorous women

Sense and Sensibility is not a novel that wishes to dispense entirely with the value of the demonstration of feminine feeling. Elinor is not an unfeeling character; we are told in the opening stages of the novel that she has an 'excellent heart; and her disposition was affectionate, and her feelings were strong' (4). Nor does the novel suggest sensibility's complete usurpation by 'sense'. In fact, Austen repeatedly reinforces the sentimental rhetoric of a body that makes feeling legible through physical display. Language alone, Austen's narrative strategy suggests, fails to be fully expressive: dialogue, for instance, frequently breaks off into the dash of silence at moments of intensity when Austen's characters feel 'too much for speech' (67); changes in 'complexion' (blushing, colouring, crimsoning) are repeatedly deployed as reliable signs of inner emotion, through countenances that 'show' (as demonstrated at length in Mary Ann O'Farrell's work on *Telling Complexions* and the work of Austen);[82] the body 'speaks' for characters when they are unable to do so themselves (when, for instance, the experience of agony affects 'every feature' of a face; or when characters have 'expressive' or 'eloquent' eyes, and 'look' (210) their feelings, as though the oracular could emit emotion, with 'the most speaking tenderness'). In this way the narrator corroborates the narrative physiognomy that is common to sentimental novels: bodies are used to describe inner states through a literary-phantasm of bodily legibility.

However, alongside her use of the body as a site of expressive communication, Austen betrays serious suspicion of descriptions of the female body as the *only* medium of feminine experience and expression. Elinor feels strongly, but she also exerts her sense alongside her feelings; she 'governs' them (4). Following her father's death, for instance, she too is 'affronted', like her sister and mother; 'but still she could struggle, she could exert herself' (5). And when she suffers further disappointments, she is active in procuring consolation for herself, and in aiding others, through 'constant and painful exertion' (231). Elinor struggles against being *all feeling*, and she repeatedly seeks for words to accompany physical demonstration, betraying a mistrust of physiognomy as a master discourse. She is, for instance, anxious for verbal or written corroboration of Willoughby's intentions towards Marianne; she wants 'syllables', and a 'professed declaration' to accompany his imputed somatic declarations of love. Elinor seeks a coincidence of language and bodily expression, an ideal state in which the two forms of communication exist in mutuality and neither need be sacrificed to the other. The novel suggests that when the sensitivities of the body are prized over language, the results, for a woman, are disastrous: she is potentially misled into desire; and, rendered speechless, she falls into swooning insensibility. When Marianne is 'overpowered' by emotion following Willoughby's betrayal of his 'appearance of ... honourable and delicate feeling' (158), it is speech that Elinor recommends for her recovery: 'Elinor encouraged her as much as possible to talk of what she felt' (173). Elinor administers a proleptic 'talking cure' for her sister's 'nervous faintness' and hysterics.

John Mullan has argued that from the time Samuel Richardson was writing up to and including Ann Radcliffe, British novels present us with heroines 'made sick by their sensitivities'.[83] The women in these novels often seem doomed to a perpetual and dangerous falling: into seduction, into hysterics, into illness, into insensibility. Feminine swooning comes to signal the failure of sentimentalism and its promise of communicable feeling as the grounds for sympathy; the silence of the swoon becomes the 'limit' of sentiment – or what John Mullan might term its tragedy: 'the silence of feeling becoming private, visceral, debilitating' (250). In Eve Kosofsky Sedgwick's reading of

Austen and Mullan, the tragic mutability of sensibility's 'sociability' into 'isolation', 'solipsism' or 'hypochondria' can also be interpreted as the intersection 'between alloerotic [eroticism directed towards another] and autoerotic investments'.[84] Sedgwick reads *Sense and Sensibility* in parallel with a text of unknown provenance from 1881, 'Onanism and Nervous Disorders in Two Little Girls'.[85] This text is a fragmented description of the treatment of a female masturbator and it presents pathological, inwardly directed feminine autoeroticism as synonymous with hysteria and swooning:

> The 23rd. She repeats: 'I deserve to be burnt and I will be. I will be brave during the operation, I won't cry.' From ten at night until six in the morning, she has a terrible attack, falling several times into a swoon that lasted about a quarter of an hour. At times she had visual hallucinations. At other times she became delirious, wild eyed, saying: 'Turn the page, who is hitting me, etc.'
>
> The 25th. I apply a hot point to X...'s clitoris. (829)

It is not possible to determine whether this text is a medical case history or a piece of sado-masochistic pornography – that these are substitutable possibilities in terms of plausibility, dramatically demonstrates how swooning is bound up with a voyeurism of the prostrate female form that destabilises the boundaries of different discourses; texts of medicine and of sentimentality alike might turn the female swooning body into pornographic spectacle. And if the swoon here is part of a pathologising account of female autoeroticism – sickly feminine feeling failing to be directed towards the world and instead turning back on itself – then it also reveals the propensity for the sentimental scene to render female feeling in a way that provides 'unaccountable' voyeuristic pleasure for the reader/viewer.

I have attempted here to demonstrate some of the complexities endemic to the gendering of the swoon within sentimental literature during the eighteenth century. The performance of sensibility in sentimental narratives, particularly narratives of 'fallen women', creates an eroticised feminine incapacity and a salacious scenography of the swoon. Jane Austen gives us an arch response to the vogue for female (in)sensibility: her satirical scenes of reciprocal feminine insensibility in *Persuasion* show up the morbidity inherent in feminine delicacy. In *Sense and Sensibility*, she reveals the dangerous insufficiencies of sensibility's rhetoric of the female body. Available language may fail to fully account for feminine feeling and desire; but Austen's work shows us that this doesn't mean the novel is doomed to deliver the female body as a swooning impasse of female silence. Both Austen and Wollstonecraft valorise the female 'exertion' necessary to stay upright against the tendency to swoon, motioning towards a world in which women's bodies might be narrated with their own words – where *to feel* might also be to stay conscious in order to attempt to speak and write.

Notes

1 'In all their walks, he had had to jump her from the stiles; the sensation was delightful to her' (Jane Austen, *Persuasion* (Ware, Hertfordshire: Wordsworth Editions, 1993 [1818]), p. 78. All references will be to this version of the text). The proposition that a woman might 'throw herself' at a man is mordantly literalised here. The OED gives this sense of 'throw' as a peculiarly feminine usage by the end of the eighteenth century: OED, sense 30, b: '*to throw oneself* or *be thrown at* (a man), of a woman, to put herself or be put designedly in the way of, so as to invite the attention of; *to throw oneself into the arms of*, to become the wife or mistress of. [...] 1789'.
2 This is the description given by O'Farrell, *Telling Complexions*, p. 49.
3 Mieszkowski makes this argument via the work of Judith Butler, as discussed in Chapter 1: Mieszkowski, 'Revisiting Troilus's Faint', pp. 43–57.
4 Referred to by Georgianna, *The Solitary Self*, p. 91 *et seq.*
5 Chaucer's swooning Troilus has been described by Claire Tomalin as 'the first hero of sensibility', and his swoon might therefore be seen as a key link to later notions of sensibility: speaking on *In Our Time* (London: BBC Radio 4, January 3, 2002), with Melvyn Bragg, John Mullan and Hermione Lee.
6 Weiss, 'Modern and Medieval Views on Swooning', p. 123.
7 Markman Ellis, *The Politics of Sensibility* (Cambridge: Cambridge University Press, 1996), p. 19.
8 The Old English ancestor of the swoon, '*geswogen*', reveals its influence on its modern progeny in this sense, connoting as it did a *falling* into insensibility. See OED entry for 'swow | swown'.
9 See Chapter 6 for a fuller exploration of Pope's definition of bathos and its relation to swooning.

10 Eve Kosofsky Sedgwick, 'Jane Austen and the Masturbating Girl', *Critical Inquiry* (Summer 1991), 818–837 at 820.
11 Henry Mackenzie, *The Man of Feeling* (London: Oxford University Press, 1967 [1771]). All references will be to this edition.
12 Jane Austen, *Sense and Sensibility* (London: Macmillan & Co., 1926 [1811]). All references will be to this edition.
13 Jane Spencer describes the gendered conception of the novel at the time as follows: 'contemporary commentators on the novel persistently gendered the form as a female one ... the didacticism and sentimentalism that became its standard features were associated particularly with women' (Jane Spencer, 'Women Writers and the Eighteenth-century Novel', in John Richetti (ed.), *The Cambridge Companion to the Eighteenth-Century Novel* (Cambridge: Cambridge University Press, 1996), pp. 212–235, at 215).
14 See *OED*, 'Feeling', entry 4b, which dates the first instance of the 'plural', 'collective' sense of 'Emotions, susceptibilities, sympathies' as 1771.
15 This was the period in which the novel became the dominant literary form, attracting an unprecedented reading audience. See Ellis's description of the rise of the sentimental novel in *The Politics of Sensibility*, p. 2 *et seq.*
16 John Mullan, 'Sentimental Novels', in John Richetti (ed.), *The Cambridge Companion to the Eighteenth-Century Novel* (Cambridge: Cambridge University Press, 1996), p. 238. Others suggest that any rigid distinction is impossible to maintain: see, for instance, Ellis, *The Politics of Sensibility*, p. 6: 'The terms "sensibility" and "sentimental" denote a complex field of meanings and connotations in the late eighteenth century, overlapping and coinciding to such an extent as to offer no obvious distinction. Despite the attempts of some recent critics, it is not possible to legislate between closely allied terms "sensibility" and "sentimental"'.
17 See the *OED* entry for 'sentimental', which gives Lady Bradshaigh's question in 1749 in correspondence with Samuel Richardson as the first written instance: 'What, in your opinion, is the meaning of the word *sentimental*, so much in vogue among the polite [...] Every thing clever and agreeable is comprehended in that word [...] I am frequently astonished to hear such a one is a *sentimental* man; we were a *sentimental* party; I have been taking a *sentimental* walk.'
18 John Mullan describes this liberal use of the term in 'Sentimental Novels', pp. 236–237.
19 Initially published in 1771, *The Man of Feeling* was an immediate success, with its first edition selling out and frequent reprints in

the following years; all references here are to the text of the 2nd edition.
20 Lady Louise Stuart, quoted in Brian Vickers, 'Introduction' to Mackenzie's *The Man of Feeling*.
21 There are so many outbursts of weeping in the novel that the Victorian critic Henry Morley prepared an edition in 1886 with an 'Index to Tears', which contained forty-seven references, despite his decision to exclude 'Chokings, etc.'
22 Mullan, 'Sentimental Novels', p. 248.
23 David Hume writing to Hutcheson in 1740, quoted by Ellis, *The Politics of Sensibility*, p. 12.
24 David Hume, *A Treatise of Human Nature* (Oxford: Clarendon Press, 1978 [1739–40]), III, I, p. 2.
25 Hume, *ibid.*, III, 40, p. 316.
26 Adam Smith, *Theory of Moral Sentiments* (Oxford: Clarendon Press, 1976 [1759]), p. 9.
27 Mullan notes, 'that these philosophers of moral sentiment showed little or no interest in novels, even though it is now clear that it was in novels that the powers of sentiment were being tested' ('Sentimental Novels', p. 248).
28 Ellis, *The Politics of Sensibility*, p. 16.
29 Quoted in Harold W. Thompson, *A Scottish Man of Feeling: Some Account of Henry Mackenzie, Esq. of Edinburgh, and the Golden Age of Burns and Scott* (London and New York: Oxford University Press, 1931), pp. 107–111.
30 Mullan, 'Sentimental Novels', p. 245.
31 Ellis, *The Politics of Sensibility*, p. 19.
32 Christopher Lawrence, 'The Nervous System and Society in the Scottish Enlightenment', in B. Barnes and S. Shapin (eds), *Natural Order: Historical Studies of Scientific Cultures* (London: Sage, 1979), p. 27.
33 Robert Whytt, *The Works* (Edinburgh: 1768), quoted in Lawrence, 'The Nervous System and Society in the Scottish Enlightenment', p. 27.
34 Ellis, *The Politics of Sensibility*, p. 19.
35 I am much indebted to Ellis for his research on this, which informs my discussion here: *The Politics of Sensibility*, p. 62 et seq.
36 Richardson's *Clarissa* (1748) might be an important example to consider here, where the innumerable female faints and fallings seem to build towards the fateful drugged unconsciousness during which Clarissa is raped. In *Pamela*, on the other hand, a different kind of active, struggling form of unconsciousness is a prophylactic against rape: when Mr B., dressed as a maid-servant, attempts to rape Pamela she falls into violent fits, which seem to 'frighten' Mr B. away (Samuel Richardson, *Pamela*;

Or, *Virtue Rewarded* (London: Penguin Books, 1980 [1740]), pp. 242, 273).
37 Horace Walpole, *The Letters of Horace Walpole* (Oxford: Clarendon Press, 1903–25), IV, p. 247.
38 Ellis, *The Politics of Sensibility*, p. 182.
39 *Ibid.*, p. 164.
40 Richardson, quoted by Ellis, *ibid.*, p. 164.
41 For a fuller survey of these responses, see Ellis, *ibid.*, pp. 208–211.
42 Eve Kosofsky Sedgwick, *Epistemology of the Closet* (Berkeley and Los Angeles, CA: University of California Press, 2008 [1990]), p. 151.
43 Ellis, *The Politics of Sensibility*, pp. 49, 2.
44 Ellis quotes much of the correspondence between Sterne and Sancho; *ibid.*, p. 66.
45 *Ibid.* p. 86.
46 *Ibid.*, p. 93.
47 Janet Todd, *Sensibility: An Introduction* (London and New York: Methuen, 1986), quoted by Ellis, *The Politics of Sensibility*, p. 129.
48 Brian Vickers' notes to the second edition tell us that 'Mackenzie's liberalism is ahead of the times'; two years later the first parliamentary report on Indian affairs appeared, which took a neutral attitude towards the situation (Vickers in Mackenzie, *The Man of Feeling*, p. 137).
49 Ellis, *The Politics of Sensibility*, p. 87.
50 *Ibid.*
51 *Ibid.*, p. 123.
52 *Ibid.*, p. 128.
53 *Ibid.*, p. 86.
54 Mullan, 'Sentimental Novels', p. 244.
55 Ellis qualifies this 'sublime' as 'untouched by transcendence': *The Politics of Sensibility*, p. 6.
56 *Ibid.*, p. 165.
57 There is only one male faint in the novel, from an elderly man: Old Edwards falls 'backwards into the arms of the astonished Harley' and is recovered with the assistance of 'some water, and a smelling-bottle' (Mackenzie, *The Man of Feeling*, p. 89).
58 See the final part of Chapter 1 for a detailed discussion of this.
59 Goethe's Young Werther, for instance, feeling too much to carry on living, will shoot himself in the head: Johann Wolfgang von Goethe, *The Sorrows of Young Werther* (Wilder Publications, 2009 [1774]).
60 Ellis, for instance, describes the debate around sensibility accelerating 'into a crisis in the last decades of the century' (*The Politics of Sensibility*, p. 190).

61 Quoted in Vickers, Introduction to Mackenzie, *The Man of Feeling*, p. viii.
62 *OED*, sense 1a.
63 Raymond Williams, *Keywords: A Vocabulary of Culture and Society*, revised edn (London: Fontana, 1983), pp. 281–282.
64 Ellis, *The Politics of Sensibility*, p. 23.
65 Ellis (*ibid.*, p. 24), refers to James Gillray's depiction of 'Sensibility' in the *New Morality* (1798) as a distraught young woman and to George Romney's *Sensibility* (1786), which depicts the famously beautiful prostitute Emma Hart holding a branch of mimosa (the 'sensitive' plant).
66 This is one of the effects of sensibility according to George J. Barker-Benfield, *The Culture of Sensibility: Sex and Society in Eighteenth-Century Britain* (Chicago and London: University of Chicago Press, 1992).
67 Jane Spencer describes the gendered conception of the novel at the time: 'contemporary commentators on the novel persistently gendered the form as a female one ... the didacticism and sentimentalism that became its standard features were associated particularly with women' (Spencer, 'Women Writers and the Eighteenth-century Novel', p. 215).
68 See, for instance, Mary Bruton, *Self-Control* (1811); correspondence between these novelistic explorations and Mary Wollstonecraft's work, discussed later in this chapter.
69 These typical views are expressed by Austin Dobson in his introduction to *Sense and Sensibility*, p. viii.
70 *Ibid.*, p. viii.
71 For a Foucauldian exploration of Austen's bodies – and in particular the blush whereby 'the body is enlisted in the production of legibility in order to serve at surveillance's creation of domesticable bodies, and the novel's use of the blush would be seen as instrumentalizing that service' – see O'Farrell, *Telling Complexions*, pp. 6, 7.
72 Leo Tolstoy, *War and Peace* (London: Penguin, 2007 [1869]), p. 575.
73 Marianne's 'romantic refinements' of mind mean, for instance, that she fantasises Willoughby's character from her literary encounters: 'His person and air were equal to what her fancy had ever drawn for the hero of a favourite story' (41). And this literary romanticisation will prove heartbreaking for Marianne. For a similar warning against the dangers posed to the female romantic imagination by reading, see Gustave Flaubert's later tragic heroine Emma Bovary: *Madame Bovary* (1857); but in contrast to this see Hardy's Tess, who laments her deficient education in terms of novels: 'Ladies know what to fend hands against, because they read novels that tell them of these tricks; but I never had the chance 'o learning in that way, and you did not

help me!' (Thomas Hardy, *Tess of the d'Urbervilles; A Pure Woman* (Ware, Hertfordshire: Wordsworth Editions, 1992 [1891], p. 100).
74 'There, exactly there, on that projective mound, there I fell; and there I first saw W.' (309).
75 See Dobson's introduction, *Sense and Sensibility*, p. viii.
76 Also known as salt of hartshorn or ammonium carbonate.
77 As noted in O'Farrell's *Telling Complexions*.
78 Jane Austen, *Love and Freindship* in Deidre Shauna Lynch and Jack Stillinger (eds), *The Norton Anthology of English Literature* (New York: W.W. Norton & Co., 2006 [c.1790]).
79 Mary Wollstonecraft, *A Vindication of the Rights of Woman* (Oxford: Oxford University Press, 1999 [1792]), *passim*. All references in the text will be to this edition.
80 For more detailed examinations of the relationship between Austen and Wollstonecraft see, inter alia, Lloyd W. Brown, 'Jane Austen and the Feminist Tradition', *Nineteenth-Century Literature* 28(3) (1973), 321–328: 'the textual parallels between *Persuasion* and the *Rights of Woman* suggest that there is a significant connection between Jane Austen and writers like Mary Wollstonecraft on the subject of female "feelings"' (327–328); Claire Tomalin also offers some biographical evidence that Austen may have known Wollstonecraft and her work: *Jane Austen: A Life* (New York: Alfred A. Knopf, 1997), p. 158.
81 Edmund Burke, *On the Sublime and Beautiful* (The Harvard Classics, 1909–14 [1757]), 'On Delicacy'.
82 For much more on blushing and somatic legibility in Austen, see O'Farrell, *Telling Complexions*.
83 This is John Mullan's description of the literary woman of feeling post-Richardson: 'Richardson's Pamela, a resolute heroine who endures suffering triumphantly, also sometimes collapses under the pressure of her feelings. The heroines who follow her up to and including the gothic novels of Ann Radcliffe, are made sick by their sensitivities' (Mullan, 'Sentimental Novels', p. 250).
84 Sedgwick, 'Jane Austen and the Masturbating Girl', pp. 835–836, fn. 22.
85 Demetrius Zambaco, 'Onanism and Nervous Disorders in Two Little Girls', trans. Catherine Duncan, *Semiotext(e)* 4 (1981 [1881]); I quote from Sedgwick's reproduction of the material, which corrects some typographical errors and layout ambiguities.

4

'Dead-born': Shadow resurrections and artistic transformations

> I did not die. But slowly, as one in a swoon
> To whom life creeps back in the form of death,
> With a sense of separation, a blind pain
> Of blank obstruction, and a roar i' the ears
> Of visionary chariots which retreat
> As earth grows clearer ... slowly, by degrees,
> I woke, rose up.
>
> Elizabeth Barrett Browning, *Aurora Leigh* (1856)[1]

To one in a swoon, life creeps back in the form of death. This is the extraordinary formulation used by Elizabeth Barrett Browning in her verse-novel *Aurora Leigh* to describe the transformation of a woman into a poet. For Barrett Browning, the swoon is salvific; it brings death to the old ways and is part of a dark eschatology that looks forward to the arrival of the 'Woman and artist' as inaugurator of a new age. When artists awake from their swoons, Barrett Browning tells us, 'Life calls to us / In some transformed, apocalyptic voice' (I:663–674); the writer is symbolically reborn, into a life that speaks the language of radical transformation as death.

If Jane Austen held the swoon in suspicion, interrogating its function as mannered performance of female incapacity, Barrett Browning does something quite different: she draws on the morbidity of swooning in order to imagine a new age of female poetry, and to darkly rework masculinised narratives of salvation, resurrection and artistic life. I propose in this chapter a series of connections between imagining the task of writing and imagining the swoon, whereby the swoon is offered as a model of artistic transformation and the initiator of visionary experience. The swoon, as we will see, becomes a shadow of dominant narratives of resurrection and rebirth; it is often used to describe a dark and 'death-born' process of revivification. And we find it frequently in the work of nineteenth and early twentieth-century writers who channel representations of feminine morbidity in order to challenge masculinist systems of power. If the swoon was tarnished by associations with feminine incapacity by the end of the eighteenth century, the writers discussed here draw on that association to reject prevailing ideas of health, vitality and virility.

Recent work in the field of disability theory has demonstrated how the formal dimensions of artistic work are often shaped in relation to ideas of the body. Michael Davidson, for example, argues that 'the body becomes thinkable when its totality can no longer be taken for granted, when the social meanings attached to sensory and cognitive values cannot be assumed'[2] – defamiliarisation, that special capacity of art, is strongly connected to experiences of disability in Davidson's account. Tobin Spiers, in his work on *Disability Aesthetics* (2010), 'refuses to recognize the representation of the healthy body – and its definition of harmony, integrity, and beauty – as the sole determination of the aesthetic'.[3] The writers that I focus on in this chapter do something similar in refusing to venerate 'good health' as the starting point for artistic endeavour: all of them prize the swoon as the initiator into a new mode of aesthetics that rejects the vigorous male body as the crucible of art. John Keats, Edgar Allan Poe and James Joyce might initially seem strange swoon-fellows, but I hope to show that they all embrace the possibilities of the swoon as a way into new forms of writing; that they each, in different ways, take up the morbid, dangerous, feminine, auto-erotic connotations of swooning to present their versions of artistic transformation.

John Keats, swooning men and the 'dead-born' artist

Mario Praz, in his famous study *The Romantic Agony* (1933),[4] shows how certain constructions of Romanticism might move all Romantic artists into the denigrated space of the symbolically feminine and the sickly. Praz's argument can be summarised as follows: the roots of Romanticism are typically thought to lie 'in the border between an ancient, hereditary faith which had collapsed and a new faith, the faith in new philosophical and liberal ideals' (xii). To live this new Enlightenment faith, and to believe in the industrialisation, rationalism, colonialism and commodity capitalism that were its corollaries, supposedly required 'courage and a virile attitude'; those who rejected it were therefore stigmatised in terms of their 'feminine, impressionable, sentimental, incoherent, fickle minds' (xii). One name for this rejection would be Romanticism, and if the Romantics could be accused of having 'feminine minds', Praz suggests, then 'it is questionable whether the minds of all artists are not, to a greater or lesser degree, of this [feminine] kind' (xii). The Romantic is often defined in conjunction with the Classic, so that they 'come finally to denote, respectively, "equilibrium" and "interruption of equilibrium"', which comes close to Goethe's formulation *'Classic ist das Gesunde, Romantische das Kranke* [Classic is the healthy, Romantic the sick]' (8). Defined in this way, Praz argues, the terms lose historical specificity; instead they 'indicate the process which goes on universally in every artist' (8). Romanticism, characterised as feminine disequilibrium and sickness, might be generalised to all artistic innovation.

John Keats, that 'poor', 'stripling' poet, is one of the writers who best demonstrates how the imputation of a sickly 'feminine' mind has been used in an attempt to discredit certain artists; and how such attempts might now be seen to confirm the powerful way in which his work breaks with certain ideals of health and masculinity. Nicholas Roe, in his work on Keats and the culture of dissent, describes how Tory journals successfully denigrated the poet: he tells us that in the 'Cockney School' essays published in *Blackwood's Edinburgh Magazine* from 1817 onwards, Keats was ridiculed 'in terms of his youth, his social class, cultural status and gender ... his poetry demonstrated that he was "not capable of understanding", and in this last respect his intellect was shown to be unformed, sickly, and "feminine" in character'.[5] Roe argues that this reviewer discredited Keats by using the terms of the Burkean paradigm of feminine beauty: Keats is afflicted with '"effeminate" incapacity' (11) which is unbecoming of a man.

Yet more virulent attacks on Keats can be found in the 'Fourth Cockney Essay' (1818), which appeared after the publication of his first two volumes, *Poems* (1817) and *Endymion* (1818). Keats is attacked for his youth – he is 'the wavering apprentice'[6] – and is relegated to 'the Grub-street race' of scribbling 'farm-servants and unmarried ladies ... footmen [and] superannuated governess[es]' (16). Finally, the Cockney School poets are dismissed as 'uneducated and flimsy striplings, who are not capable of understanding [... the merits of] other men of power – fanciful dreaming teadrinkers', and Keats as a 'bentling [who] has already learned to lisp sedition' (18). Keats is, according to this account, an illegitimate child who has been taught to versify in a 'lisp', associated with childish or affected 'effeminate' sensibility (205). This criticism aimed to depict Keats in 'the subordinate social position occupied by women' (16), Roe argues, and was successful to the extent that Keats continued through the nineteenth century to be seen as an effeminate poet appealing to feminine tastes. What Roe terms the 'feminization'[7] of Keats is bound up with a long-lasting belief that his poetry has no interest in anything except beauty; it produces a critical obliteration of his poetry's intellectual and political content, a process that Stopford Brookes has called the 'evacuation of Keats'.[8] The stereotypes of childish and effeminate passivity established in the Cockney School essays effectively depoliticised Keats, and Roe claims that for many years his 'intellectual and political presence has been wholly effaced by the supposedly uncerebral category of the aesthetic' (12). An unwillingness to treat Keats as a serious political poet was then partly a result of the success of early reviewers identifying him with stereotypes of feminised passivity, sickness and weakness, and as the antithesis of 'men of power'.

More recent Keats criticism has encouraged readers to consider his failure to be a 'man of power' as part of his political potency. In Keats's own famous conception of artistic creation, 'Negative Capability', a particular kind of passivity is figured as the necessary precondition for literary achievement:

> several things dovetail in my mind, and at once it struck me, what quality went to form a man of Achievement especially in literature and which Shakespeare possessed most enormously – I mean Negative Capability, that is when man is capable of being in uncertainties, Mysteries, doubts, without any irritable reaching after fact and reason.[9]

Much has been written on Keats's Negative Capability as a state of artistic receptivity, and as a rejection of Godwinian philosophical pre-resolution in favour of open uncertainty.[10] Donald Crichlow Goellnicht connects this with Wordsworth's notion of 'wise passivity', and the state of 'calm receptivity' that is venerated in his 'Expostulation and Reply'; but he also insists on the passive quality of Negative Capability more strongly than other critics in suggesting that Keats may have chosen the term 'negative' from the scientific vocabulary of chemistry. Keats trained to be a surgeon, a profession he eventually gave up in order to write, and as a medical student, Goellnicht argues, he would have had a basic understanding of electricity from lectures he is known to have attended. If the 'negative' is an electrical metaphor, then,

> the negative pole becomes the ideal representation of the negatively capable poet: like the negative pole, the poet is *passive, receptive*, and as the negative pole receives the current of electricity from the positive pole, so the poet receives impulses from the world around him, a world that is full of mysteries and doubts that the poet cannot explain, but which in his *passive state of receptivity* he does not feel the need to explain.[11] (My italics)

While this remains a speculative account, it does much to electrify the potential importance of passive receptivity to Keats' account of poetic composition. In making receptivity an inherent part of the quality of achievement for men of literature, notably Shakespeare, Keats privileges symbolically feminine qualities to challenge masculinist accounts of artistic endeavour. And in concluding his musing on Negative Capability, Keats returns to the realm of Beauty:

> This, pursued through Volumes would perhaps take us no further than this, that with a great poet the sense of Beauty overcomes every other consideration, or rather obliterates all consideration.[12]

Roe argues that this foregrounding of the aesthetic is not a retraction from the world of politics; rather, he suggests, the words 'overcome' and 'obliterate' present a combative approach to the power of poetry appropriate to an age of revolutionary struggle. Beauty becomes a challenge 'to the authorised "masculine" discourses of the political and cultural establishment',[13] and this is a challenge that mobilises stigmatised feminine qualities. Roe is one among many recent critics who have set out to reverse the 'evacuation' of Keats' poetry, and who argue for the importance of fervid republicanism and Jacobin intent in his work.[14] These political interests, Roe suggests, are bound up with the receptive, passive principle of Negative Capability, which establishes 'a universal hospitality as the prerogative of poetic genius' (225) and evokes 'a Shakespearean susceptibility to unaccommodated human beings which spoke powerfully for Jacobin aspirations during the 1790s and the Napoleonic period' (236).[15]

I want to add to this work in suggesting that Keats' frequent use of swooning in his poetry can be seen, in the light of his concept of Negative Capability, as a further veneration of a symbolically feminine passivity, placing him markedly at odds with 'men of power'. If swooning was stigmatised by association with feminised debility under the rubric of sensibility, then Keats – a medically trained physician who nursed his brother Tom through tuberculosis, and then suffered himself from its debilitating effects before his early death – powerfully engages with notions of morbidity and debility when he pivots much of his poetry around the figure of the swooning man.

In one of Keats's most famous works, 'Bright Star' (c.1820 – posthumously published in 1838), the poet longs to be as constant as the apostrophised star, or else to 'swoon' forever:

... still stedfast, still unchangeable,

Pillow'd upon my fair love's ripening breast,

To feel for ever its soft swell and fall,

Awake forever in a sweet unrest,

Still, still to hear her tender-taken breath,

And so live ever – or else swoon to death.[16]

Here we find a swooning death positioned as an alternative, *and/ or* an overwhelming correspondence to, eternal life and love. The poet has rejected the immobile viewing position of stellification in the early part of the poem ('*Not* in lone splendour hung aloft the night / And watching, with eternal lids apart'), markedly diverging from the ascendant, panoptic trajectory for the male subject that we witness in the conclusion of Chaucer's *Troilus and Criseyde*, for instance.[17] Keats produces an ending of powerful ambivalence, an ambivalence that has much to do with the strange temporality of 'swoon' here. The swoon might mean the end of life and love; but its position as an alternative for 'live ever' also gives the sense of a continuing after-life in death; or of living now, pillow'd on the lover's breast, as indistinguishable from already having died; *I'm in heaven*, as we might colloquially put it. The poem is written in future conditional, which makes 'or else swoon to death' the temporally unlimited condition of the future; the state of passivity might also, then, be a kind of eschatology, a new continuous beginning. And the pinnacle of masculine brightness in the future is to swooningly engage in modes of passive receptivity (the listener implied by the line, 'Still, still to hear').[18]

In *Endymion*,[19] Keats's longest poem (and the swooniest), Endymion's journey into the realm of the gods begins with a swoon: 'His senses swooned off' (I.398), the poet tells us, and Endymion is left in a trance, to be led away from rustic festivities by his sister. This 'magic sleep ... calms' Endymion 'to life again' (I.453–454): here the swoon's absence of consciousness is restorative in the same way that dying might be restorative, *if* one is subsequently revived. Endymion reveals to his sister that his swooning trance-states are occasioned by the visions he has experienced since he first glimpsed the moon goddess, named here Cynthia.[20] These visions make him 'dizzy and distraught': he has seen wonderful 'colours, wings and bursts of spangly light' and these have become 'more strange, and strange, and dim, / And then were gulfed in tumultuous swim – / And then I fell asleep. Ah, can I tell the enchantment that afterwards befell?' (I.568–574). It is in just such a vision that Endymion first saw the face of Cynthia among the celestial bodies, and when she reached out towards him he thinks he might have 'fainted at the charmèd touch' (I.607); 'I sighed / To faint once more by looking on my bliss' (I.651–652). Endymion's response to Cynthia's beauty is to swoon, or to desire the swoon. And his blissful faint is repeatedly figured as an equivalent of, or a dalliance with, dying ('he a corpse had been / All the long day' (IV.919–920)).

The swoon draws Endymion into close proximity with death; but it is also always the renewal of his life through a strange, self-destroying version of love. When Endymion lovingly approaches Cynthia, for instance, he stages it as an approach to death, which unexpectedly brings life: 'I was distracted; madly did I kiss / The wooing arms which held me, and did give / My eyes at once to death – but 'twas to live' (I.653–655). In one of the most famous passages of the poem, the most intense 'happiness' is described as the product of a potentially deadly 'self-destroying': 'Richer entanglements, enthrallments far / More self-destroying, leading, by degrees, / To the chief intensity: the crown of these / Is made of love and friendship' (I.778–801).

Throughout the poem, new states of being emerge from self-destroying approaches to love and death, with the swoon as a key figuration of such an approach. Finally, Endymion is described progressing towards his end in a 'deathful glee' (IV.945); but his apprehension of the goddess (who has been disguised from him) means that he is 'spiritualized' (IV.944) from his 'mortal state': his openness to dying in love results in a radical transformation of his state of being. This transformation is not transcendence; as Marilyn Butler has argued, while Keats's poetry avoids 'an urban contemporary setting' it is nevertheless 'anything but immaterial'.[21] The transformations that take place in Endymion's form are positioned in relation to the real conditions of a world in which those 'who lord it o'er their fellow-men [...] in empurpled vests, / And crowns, and turbans' (III.1–12), are excoriated. Endymion's material being is radically changed in a manner that invites us to imagine the transformation of other material conditions. In his final union with Cynthia, Endymion swoons into a new existence: he 'knelt adown, / Before his goddess, in a blissful swoon' (IV.988–9), and the couple vanish from sight. The swoon is a crucial part of a poetic process that offers the hope of new forms of being, a process that allows the remarkable possibility that one might become, or perhaps must become, 'dead-born / From the old womb of night' (IV.371–372).

So keen is Keats on swooning, that all sorts of things begin to swoon in his poems alongside people: sounds 'come a-swooning over hollow grounds' (I.286); scenes will come 'swooning vivid through my globèd brain'.[22] In their various forms, Keats's swoons describe the initiating experience of the visionary, and in his later (abandoned) epic poem, *The Fall of Hyperion. A Dream*,[23] the role of poet as visionary is to be tested during a strange journey that begins with a swoon: 'The cloudy swoon came on, and down I sunk' (55). The function of this swoon as a version of dying is made gruesomely evident by the 'shade' who addresses, and tests, the poet when 'sense of life returned' (58): 'Thou hast felt / What 'tis to die and live again' (141), she tells him, later describing him as half rotted.[24] The poet is accused of being 'a dreaming thing, A fever of thyself' (168–169), who 'venoms all his days' (175). But the poet defends himself against the charge, not by denying his connection with morbidity, but by claiming such 'sickness not ignoble' (184). It is fitting that a poet who was a medic and a nurse, who lived so briefly, his poetry blooming into 'posthumous life',[25] should have given us such a strong sense of the swoon as the transformation of the artist, who might 'Die into life'.[26] In Keats's poetry, the swooner is a visionary whose feminine morbidity produces a poetics rich with the possibility of deathly transformation.

Buried alive: Poe's swoon-aesthetics and the 'everlasting faint'

If Keats's swoons figure the possibility of dying into new life, his near contemporary, Edgar Allan Poe (1809–49), gives us the chiasmatic macabre alternative: that the swoon might carry us off, living, into the charnel house. Poe's fictions are famously taphephobic – fearful of being buried alive – and I argue that they amplify anxieties about swoon states in relation to that fear. But, as well as using the swoon to sensationalise certain risks, I want also to suggest that for Poe the idea of a *return* from death is crucial for an understanding of artistic sensibility – for what we might think of as his swoon aesthetics.

The practice of resuscitation is a relatively recent one; Jan Bondeson, in *Buried Alive: The Terrifying History of Our Most Primal Fear*,[27] tells us that it is only at the end of the eighteenth century that medical thinkers established that *apparent* death might sometimes be reversible, that a 'visibly dead' individual might be revived. 'Humane societies' began to appear, encouraging the public to learn resuscitation techniques; and one of the first of these was established in 1767 in Amsterdam, where people frequently drowned in the canals. Alexander Johnson wrote about the society's work in *A collection of authentic cases, proving the practicability of recovering persons visibly dead by drowning, suffocation, stifling, swooning, convulsions, and other accidents* (1775).[28] The swoon, then, is implicated as one form of 'visible' death, a counterfeit which might be mistaken for a fatality. The danger of premature burial was supposedly much feared in the early nineteenth century;[29] and the swoon might become fearful too when it is a potentially deadly precursor to live interment.

Poe's early tales, Bondeson suggests, tap into this taphephobia. Poe's most famous elaboration of the fear of being buried alive is found in 'The Premature Burial' (1844),[30] which details several supposed cases of revival after over-hasty burial. The story also describes various swoon states. When a man opens the door to his family tomb, the skeleton of his dead wife falls into his arms, in a ghastly parody of a romantic swoon. The woman, who had the 'appearance of death', is discovered, three years after burial, to have revived in her coffin. '[C]areful investigation' reveals that the woman then attempted to escape the tomb by the iron door: 'while thus occupied, she probably swooned, or died, through sheer terror; and, in falling, her shroud became entangled in some iron-work which projected interiorly. Thus she remained, and thus she rotted, erect' (259).

Permit me a brief digression here via the slightly later folk tale of the Greenbrier Ghost. This popular American ghost story, the inspiration for stage plays, a recent novel,[31] and featured on BBC Radio 4 series of ghost tales,[32] is based on the remarkable legal case surrounding the death of a young woman, Zona Heaster, in Greenbrier County, West Virginia in 1897. The woman's cause of death was purportedly recorded as 'Everlasting faint', a description that provides an unsettling echo of Poe's rendering of passing out as potentially deathly. Zona's ghost supposedly returned to tell her mother that she had been murdered, and her body was exhumed; her windpipe had been crushed and the court found her husband guilty of murder. The 'everlasting faint' is revealed to be cover story for a man's violence in this popular tale; the imputation of female faintness stands in for strangulation.

Back in Poe's 'The Premature Burial', the narrator reveals that the cause of his own 'all-absorbing' fear of being buried alive is due to a 'positive and personal experience': he suffers from bouts of catatonia, during which he sinks into a condition of 'semi-syncope, or half swoon' (264). These half swoons cause no physical suffering, but 'of moral distress an infinitude': the narrator's fancy grows 'charnel'; he talks of 'worms, of tombs, and epitaphs'; he is lost in reveries of death; 'the idea of premature burial held continual possession of my brain' (264). The narrator's propensity to swoon heightens his preoccupation with live burial: he fears being mistaken for a corpse while unconscious – and then becoming one. But his bouts of unconsciousness also predispose him to the kind of 'charnel' thoughts that saturate the fictions for which Poe is famous; the swoons are a creative stimulus to dark imagining. By the end of the story, the narrator dismisses his 'charnel apprehensions, and with them vanished the cataleptic disorder, of which, perhaps, they had been less the consequence than the cause' (268). The narrator suggests here that morbid fixations may have produced his strange 'half swoon' states of (un)consciousness; the swoon becomes a possible symptom or effect of gruesome fictions, as much as something that might cause or exacerbate their production. In Poe's work, swooning blurs consciousness, as well as the relationship between fearful affect, anxious fictions and morbid physical states.

In her work on death, femininity and the aesthetic, Elisabeth Bronfen describes Poe's writing producing 'risky resemblances'.[33] This might supply us with an apt way to think of the swoon in Poe's work – as a risky resemblance of death. But Bronfen's point is a broader one about repetition and representation. Many of Poe's early fictions feature the apparent death of a female figure, followed by some kind of revival or ghostly return. Focusing on the story of 'Ligeia',[34] in which a dead wife seems to come back to life in the body of her replacement, Bronfen argues that Poe's female characters are always subject to repetition through doubling: live women are doubled by the dead, just as the female body is doubled by its image in Poe's writing. Artists, working under this rubric, come to stand in for mourners, and representation is a kind of returning revenant. The love object, Bronfen suggests along Freudian lines, is always a lost object re-found; for the artist and lover alike, then, the love object is always a repetition.

I want to suggest that the swoon, as a return from death, is another way to think about repetition and representation, and that Poe connects these ideas even more explicitly than Bronfen suggests in his extraordinary disquisition on aesthetic experience and the swoon in 'The Pit and the Pendulum'.[35] This story imagines a scene of highly elaborate torture: the narrator has supposedly been incarcerated as part of the Spanish Inquisition.[36] Condemned to death, the narrator begins to imagine and to long for the 'sweet rest' of the grave; and this thought comes to him with considerable beauty, 'like a rich musical note'. As the thought steals across him, all other sensations begin to be extinguished and he is engulfed by silence and stillness: 'I had swooned' (247). The swoon at the melodious thought of death is not, however, marked as a total absence of experience. Rather, it has a quality akin to dreaming:

> Arousing from the most profound of slumbers, we break the gossamer web of some dream. Yet in a second afterward (so frail may that web have been) we remember not that we have dreamed. In the return to life from the swoon there are two stages; first, that of the sense of mental or spiritual; secondly, that of the sense of physical, existence. It seems probable that if, upon reaching the second stage, we could recall the impressions of the first, we should find these impressions eloquent in memories of the gulf beyond. And that gulf is – what? How at least shall we distinguish its shadows from those of the tomb? But if the impressions of what I have termed the first stage, are not, at will, recalled, yet, after long interval, do they not come unbidden, while we marvel whence they come? He who has never swooned, is not he who finds strange palaces and wildly familiar faces in coals that glow; is not he who beholds floating in mid-air the sad visions that the many may not view; is not he who ponders over the perfume of some novel flower – is not he whose brain grows bewildered with the meaning of some musical cadence which has never before arrested his attention.[37]

This exposition presents the swoon through a series of doubles: First, the swoon doubles death, appearing as a premonitory form through which the narrator imagines himself dying. Second, consciousness takes on a strange secondary nature after the swoon; it is positioned as an after-effect of swooning, an 'afterward'. Consciousness is something 'returned' to: swooning makes future consciousness a condition of return, a coming-back-to. Third, the swoon state *comes back* to haunt the swooner with 'memories of the gulf beyond' consciousness. The 'mental or spiritual' impressions of the swoon/tomb return in all sorts of apprehensions – in vision, in scent, in sound – which give the swooner a sort of extra-sensory sensibility, doubling his conscious apprehension of the world. 'He who has never swooned', is to be pitied; he will not see the beautiful shapes doubling the flames of the fire, nor be struck by the suggestive scent of a flower, nor experience the intensity of music as a derangement. The doubling inherent to aesthetic experience is figured as the return of the experience of the swoon in what I want to call Poe's swoon-aesthetics. He accounts for aesthetic experience here as both a return *from* death and a return *to* death: 'The boundaries which divide Life from Death are at best shadowy and vague',[38] Poe tells us. It is this shadowy area from which Poe's swoon-aesthetics emerge.

Poe's sense of the aesthetic reverberates darkly with Freud's writing on the uncanny. In his famous essay '*Das Unheimliche*',[39] in a seemingly glancing remark, Freud suggests that a superlative source of the uncanny 'feeling' is the fear of premature burial:

> To some people the idea of being buried alive by mistake is the most uncanny thing of all. And yet psychoanalysis has taught us that this terrifying phantasy is only a transformation of another phantasy which had originally nothing terrifying about it at all, but was qualified by a certain lasciviousness – the phantasy, I mean, of intra-uterine existence. (366–367)

Nicholas Royle reads Freud alongside Poe's 'The Premature Burial',[40] and shows that in Freud's original German, the emphasis in the above passage is on the uncanniness of the *appearance of death* ('*schientot*') that might lead to premature burial, rather than internment per se. Royle retranslates Strachey's 'buried alive by mistake' as 'buried because ostensibly dead'. This makes *seeming* to be dead, 'as if in suspended animation' (143), a crucial component of the 'most uncanny thing of all'. Royle suggests that 'suspension, the sense of being, at the same "incomprehensible" time, both dead and alive, neither dead nor alive' (146), is the nub of the uncanny in both Freud's work and Poe's 'The Premature Burial': 'suspension' describes the 'semi swoon', the cataleptic condition from which Poe's narrator suffers. Royle highlights the unnerving substitution that goes on in Freud's thinking on the uncanniness of premature burial, where one fantasy (of live interment) is replaced with another (intra-uterine existence), womb coming to stand for tomb, and tomb for womb. To this rhyming pair, I would like to add a triplicate: swoon. From swoon to tomb to womb. The *schientot* that is central to the uncanny fear of live burial is entwined with Poe's swoon-aesthetics as a deathly return.

And if Poe figures the return to life from swooning as the source of uncanny artistic sensibility, the power of the aesthetic might, in turn, be the return in life of the beautiful thought of the tomb/ womb. Poe's swoon-aesthetics hauntingly coincides with Bronfen's description of the artistic process as the re-finding of a lost object; the artist is always producing a revenant, which is at the same time the birth of something new.

James Joyce and the swooning soul

> His soul was swooning into some new world, fantastic, dim, uncertain as under sea, traversed by cloudy shapes and beings.[41]

This is how James Joyce describes the transformation of the young man, Stephen Dedalus, into the artist in *A Portrait of the Artist as a Young Man* (1914–15). Joyce's description of this soul-swoon – particularly the sibilance of this sentence and the ambiguous, underwater quality of the images it yields – calls to mind Keats's description, a century earlier, of Endymion's visionary swoon: 'more strange, and strange, and dim, / And then were gulfed in tumultuous swim'.[42] I want to suggest that by describing the process of artistic transformation through this soul-swoon, Joyce venerates a partially glimpsed and 'uncertain' world of visions of what could be, preferring this to the fixity of extant frameworks – particularly of contemporary nationalist and religious ideals. But by producing the striking depiction of the *soul* swooning at key moments in his early texts, *Dubliners* (1914) and *A Portrait*, Joyce is also reworking the trope of swooning to complicate the relationship between mind and body – to disturb the received, religious dogma of an immortal soul that will leave the intermittent, swooning body behind. The soul-swoon, I argue, becomes an important part of Joyce's exploration of what it means to be an artist – and to his related sense of the importance of embodied, physical experience. I will argue that a compound of spiritual and physical experience, of high and low, of embodied and disembodied dimensions, is produced in the notion of a swooning soul, and that this compound is fundamental to what John S. Rickard's describes as Joyce's new and profane version of the aesthetics of 'the human animal'.[43]

At the end of Joyce's groundbreaking first work, *Dubliners* (1914),[44] he uses a strikingly sibilant soul-swoon to bring his collection of stories to a close, and in so doing creates one of the most memorable final passages in twentieth-century literature:

> It had begun to snow again. He watched sleepily the flakes, silver and dark, falling obliquely against the lamplight ... Yes, the newspapers were right: snow was general, all over Ireland. It was falling on every part of the dark central plain, on the treeless hills, falling softly upon the Bog of Allen and farther, westward, softly falling into the dark mutinous Shannon waves. It was falling, too, upon every part of the churchyard on the hill where Michael Furey lay buried. It lay thickly drifted on the crooked crosses and headstones, on the spears of the little gate, on the barren thorns. His soul swooned slowly as he heard the snow falling faintly through the universe and faintly falling, like the descent of their last end, upon all the living and the dead. (225)

Joyce's 'The Dead' is the final story of the collection in which Joyce hoped to record 'a chapter in the moral history of my country',[45] that chapter having 'hemiplegia or paralysis'[46] in the face of colonial and papal subjugation as one of its targets. This is to be no work of tourism, Joyce insists; instead he will give the Irish 'one good look at themselves in my nicely polished looking-glass' (64). What it might mean to be Irish, and what it might mean *to write* about that national identity, is therefore at stake throughout these stories. That the final sentence of this collection should have as its animating verbs *swooning* and *falling* is, I suggest, an indication of the way in which certain identificatory, binary subject positions (i.e. nationalist/traitor; naturalist/romantic) are set up and then destabilised through 'The Dead' – these positions giving way to more oblique modes of identification in the final stages of the collection. I read 'The Dead' in light of this ending to suggest that Joyce's description of the snowy soul-swoon dramatises a merging of different identities and literary modes presented in the collection, rather than a veneration of any one of the particular versions of Irish identity and/or writing modelled by and through individual characters.

Gabriel Conroy, the main protagonist of 'The Dead', is a man tormented by his own social distinction: the sense both of his own elevated standing, and of his separation from others. He arrives at his aunts' annual Christmas dance with the task of giving a speech weighing heavily upon him. He listens to the sounds of men dancing in the hall above him, and the 'shuffling of their soles reminded him that their grade of culture differed from his' (179). He is afflicted by the feeling that he will fail in his attempts at social intercourse, and that by quoting Browning in his speech he will 'only make himself ridiculous ... They would think that he was airing his superior education ... His whole speech was a mistake from first to last, an utter failure' (179). Gabriel experiences himself as catastrophically differentiated from those around him. This horror of individual distinction seems to be heightened by the situation of public speaking. Joyce described the stories in *Dubliners* being presented under four aspects: 'childhood, adolescence, maturity and public life. The stories are arranged in this order.'[47] If we are to see 'The Dead' as, in part, an examination of public life, then we might also see that Gabriel's status as a public figure, much lauded by his aunts and other revellers, is a source of anxiety and even humiliation for Gabriel himself.

This humiliation is perhaps most acutely communicated in the exchange about national identity that Gabriel has with Miss Ivors, his friend of many years' standing and erstwhile teaching colleague. We might expect Gabriel to feel an affinity with her, but, during his dance with her, he finds himself marked out again; to add to his sense of class and educational distinction, he now also faces the accusation that he has separated himself from his compatriots through political treachery to the Irish nationalist cause. Miss Ivors has discovered him as an anonymous literary reviewer for *The Daily Express*, a Dublin newspaper with Conservative and Unionist sympathies. 'Now, aren't you ashamed of yourself?' she chastises. 'I didn't think you were a West Briton' (188). She continues to tease him, focusing on his decision to holiday on the Continent, rather than within Ireland: '[H]aven't you your own language to keep in touch with – Irish? ... And haven't you your own land to visit ... that you know nothing of, your own people, and your own country?' (188–189). Gabriel at first meets Miss Ivors' charges with perplexity. He wishes to say that 'literature [is] above politics' (188), to refuse the categories of affiliation being projected as his only options. But he decides against risking a 'grandiose phrase' and instead opts to murmur 'lamely that he saw nothing political in writing reviews of books' (188). Gabriel seems unconvinced himself that there is 'nothing political' in the act of writing. But he is not persuaded that Miss

Ivors is in the right either; Gabriel views her as a heckler, and her notion of national identity as 'propagandism' (192). Her exhortation to embrace the culture that is his 'own' ('own' being repeated by her over and over in a kind of incantation of propriety) makes Gabriel respond with a disavowal of national affiliation: 'I'm sick of my own country, sick of it!' (190).

When the time comes to make his speech, Gabriel sees it as an opportunity to respond to Miss Ivors' idea of national identity. He chooses to do so through the concept of hospitality: 'our country has no tradition which does it so much honour and which it should guard so jealously' (203). We might see a Keatsian mode of thinking at work in the concept of hospitality here; Roe describes Negative Capability as valuing the idea of universal hospitality – Negative Capability renders 'universal hospitality as the prerogative of poetic genius'.[48] What Gabriel values in a sense of Irish national identity, he suggests, is, paradoxically, the welcoming of friends and strangers. At the heart of his concept of Ireland's value is its openness, its admission of others.

But these claims for the virtues of openness are provocative in the context of English colonial domination. One might read Gabriel's panegyric to hospitality as tacit complicity with English power, as the critic Bonnie Roos does. She suggests that Gabriel demonstrates a socially embedded attitude toward hospitality and generosity that is, in Vincent Pecora's words, 'a codified expression of the myth of self-sacrifice, of grateful oppression, lying at the heart of Joyce's Dublin'.[49] This would make Gabriel's position on nationalism in the story a deflection of the reality of colonial oppression, an accommodation of domination, which is set up, according to Roos, to be critically challenged rather than assented to. To demonstrate what she sees as the insufficiency of Gabriel's position in the text, Roos draws on a connection between 'The Dead' and another work of snowy swooning: the American novelist Bret Harte's *Gabriel Conroy* (1876). I will explore this connection in some detail here, and Roos's reading of it, in order to contextualise the controversies of national identity and modes of literary representation that precede and produce the final soul-swoon of 'The Dead'.

Joyce names his character after Harte's eponymous Conroy, making a link between the works explicit, and Joyce's use of the novel as a source has been noted in previous Joyce scholarship.[50]

The resemblance between the snowy opening scene of Harte's work and the ending of 'The Dead' is striking. Harte's novel opens as follows:

> Snow. Everywhere. As far as the eye could reach – fifty miles, looking southward from the highest white peak, – filling ravines and gulches, and dropping from the walls of canons in white shroud-like drifts; fashioning the dividing ridge into the likeness of a monstrous grave, hiding the bases of giant pines, and completely covering young trees and larches; rimming with porcelain the bowl-like edges of still, cold lakes, and undulating in motionless white billows to the edge of the distant horizon. Snow lying everywhere over the California Sierras on the 15th day of March, 1848, and still falling.[51]

Alongside this snowy similarity, Roos sees the most significant connection between 'The Dead' and *Gabriel Conroy* as their mutual exploration of the relationship between national identity and starvation. Harte's novel begins with the predicament of a group of pioneers stranded in the snowy Sierra mountains, slowly starving to death. Despite his novels often being sentimental, Harte stands out from his contemporary American writers, according to Roos, in his refusal to 'mythologize the space of the American West. Harte generally uses some of the most gritty, ugly historical events of American Western emigration to expose the depredation often glossed over in more typical romances.'[52] And the most shocking of these 'historical events' is alluded to in a key moment in *Gabriel Conroy*. The party have long been fantasising about the food they might eat, obsessively imagining 'beefsteak' and 'sassage' and 'taters'. They are involved in a repetitive process of substituting real food for the imaginary. This 'inadequate replacement', as Roos terms it, culminates in Gabriel observing a horrific scene at the camp, which the novel stops short of describing explicitly. Roos claims that the scene is decipherable from parallels between Harte's story and newspaper accounts of an infamous story of Western expansionism of the time:

> In the winter of 1846–47 – a time coincidentally parallel to the beginning of the Irish Famine – a group of emigrants known as the Donner Party crossed the Sierras and were trapped in the mountains by an early snowstorm. Many of the party starved to death, and those who survived did so by eating the flesh of their dead comrades.[53]

The 'horror that cannot speak its name' in Harte's story is the cannibalism that succeeds the inadequate substitutions 'sustained by the deluded, idealist hope that salvation might arrive in time'.[54] For Roos, starvation and the concomitant spectre of cannibalism are key to Harte's de-romanticisation of the American West. And it is 'the will to deromanticize nationalist mythologies and the focus on the issue of starvation' that she believes 'appealed to Joyce'.[55]

Roos's reading of Joyce, then, situates 'The Dead' in relation to Ireland's own starvation story, that of the Great Famine. She reminds us that, at the time Joyce was writing, Ireland's population stood at less than half of its pre-famine level: 700,000 people – almost 30 per cent of the population in some counties – had died as a direct result of the famine, many more were visited by epidemics related to the famine, and, between 1846 and 1851, over a million people had emigrated.[56] She also recalls some of the horrific stories of starvation passed on by those who survived, including tales of infants eating their dead mothers. For Roos, Joyce's most lavish and extraordinary feast, the dinner at the Misses Morkan's Christmas party, is a powerful reminder of recent starvation – and its sister spectre, cannibalism. In a detailed reading of the symbolism of the dishes presented at the Christmas feast, Roos argues that Irish foodstuffs are displaced by English foods, or by more exotic foods made available to the bourgeois family through British imperialism:

> This Anglophilic display, coextensive with the dehumanization of the Irish by the Irish, brings to mind Kinealy's claim that 'the ships that left Ireland laden with food during the Famine were doing so largely for the financial benefit of Irish merchants and traders ...' ... The table confirms that the Morkan sisters are complicit in their own colonization, which historically led to the deprivation of Ireland's future. In light of this symbolic cannibalism – worse, the eating of one's own – it is significant that Molly Ivors, the true Irish nationalist, will not stay to eat even a little morsel before heading on her way.[57]

Roos posits the symbolic representation of cannibalism as part of Joyce's de-romanticisation of Irish national ideals, just as Harte's exposure of cannibalism is seen as de-romanticising the American West. Harte's *Gabriel Conroy* demonstrates the insufficiency of fantasies to compensate for severe lack, suggesting that rather than being a comfort such fantasies might 'exacerbate the difficulties faced'. This, Roos claims, is also Joyce's critique of Irish romanticism. She compares 'miserable emigrants who imagine a feast they cannot eat' to 'Irish romantic writers telling hopeful stories that cannot correspond to harsh realities of Ireland's present'.[58] In particular, she sees the national myth of self-sacrifice, common to the Revival movement, being rebuked in Joyce's story. The debilitating effects of the famine, she reminds us, hampered Ireland's ability to resist the British Empire. The Irish could be characterised by the English as enduring the famine with 'docility' and 'passivity', 'qualities that were perpetuated by the religious ideals of living for the hereafter rather than the present, of giving *hospitality* to even those who deserved it least, and in the glory of self-sacrifice'[59] (my italics).

In reading 'The Dead' in relation to recent Irish history, and in particular the famine, Roos suggests that Gabriel reveals himself to be complicit in colonial subjugation, and that the story also critiques romantic modes of substitution that are inadequate for telling the complicated truth of colonial subjugation. For Roos this story registers failure: a failure to find an adequate mode of narration for the suffering of the famine, and Gabriel's own failure (which is also the story's failure) to sustain a 'realist' mode of truth-telling about Irish cannibalism (literary and figurative). 'The Dead', she concludes, 'serves as testimony to how pervasive the traumatic effects of the Famine were, when even a writer of Joyce's calibre, with conscious determination to articulate the unspeakable, remains unsuccessful in expressing the truth' (124).

Roos's rich and instructive interpretation of this story invites us to read different modes of literary representation presented in competition with each other (romanticism/naturalism/historical realism), with all of them finally failing to live up to the task of telling the story of Ireland's recent history. Roos's is a very particular version of failure: it designates the creation of one of the most memorable and influential works of short fiction in the twentieth century as missing the mark. I want to offer a slightly different reading by moving our attention to the final epiphanic swoon of the story – a crucial component of an ending that is often lauded as one of the greatest achievements in the short story form. If 'The Dead' interrogates its characters' relationships to national identity, and to romanticised modes of story-telling, then the final soul-swoon of this story can be read as a significant intervention in terms of literary genre. The precursor to this closing swoon is Gretta's story of a young man, Michael Furey, whom she thinks may have died for love of her when she was a girl. Furey, more than any other character, might be thought of as typifying the myth of 'heroic self-sacrifice' that Roos sees as a 'romantic' and 'sentimentalized notion of Irish national identity'.[60]

Furey's demise is linked to the 'romantic' disease of TB and to lovesickness. Gabriel has been 'humiliated' by Gretta's story of Furey's love, after which a 'shameful consciousness of his own person assailed him. He saw himself a ludicrous figure' (221). He catches an uncanny glimpse of himself in the mirror, made strange to himself, a 'pitiable, fatuous fellow' (221). He is made absurd by a process of individuation that opposes and compares him to Furey, a figure of romanticised Irish self-sacrifice. He is alienated by an apprehension of 'his own person', as he has been by the sense of himself as humiliatingly different from everyone at the party. But this sense of differentiation from Furey is altered by the encroachment of a snowy swoon. Gabriel lies beside his sleeping wife, with the growing sense that 'one by one they were all becoming shades' (224). 'All' is non-specific and total here, obliterating the singularity of 'his own person'. 'All' share in the same movement towards the ghostly. When Gabriel looks out of his hotel window, he thinks for a moment that he can see the figure of a young man 'standing under a dripping tree' (224), ghosting the consumptive, lovesick figure of Furey. He imagines other forms drawing near, and then feels the 'wayward flickering' of his own existence: 'His own identity was fading out into a grey impalpable world' (225).

Gabriel, in the various ways he has experienced himself as individually differentiated, now begins to feel himself dispersed into the 'world' around him. And as the old awareness of himself fades, Gabriel grows imaginatively closer to Furey, and experiences a swooning sense of shared generality: 'Yes, the newspapers were right: snow was general, all over Ireland … His soul swooned slowly as he heard the snow falling faintly through the universe and faintly falling, like the descent of their last end, upon all the living and the dead' (225). This is the sense of being that succeeds Gabriel's humiliating individuation: the snow covers distinct forms; Joyce's treeless hills recall Harte's snowy Sierras; there is a slow swooning towards all who have come before, and specifically towards the romanticised, sacrificial figure of Furey.

Roos sees this ending as the proof that 'Gabriel's realism is fleeting'; that he 'reverts to his tendency to offer up inadequate substitutions, feeding off ... the dead'.[61] The ending is Joyce's tragic failure of vision, his reversion to romanticised tropes. But I want to suggest that this final, memorable paragraph of 'The Dead' doesn't offer a 'reversion' to one literary mode or another, nor does it constitue the failure of one vision over another; this ending doesn't, I think, offer a resolution to the antipathetical positions that Roos suggests are interrogated in the earlier stages of the story – rather it produces a palimpsestic accretion of different locations, identities and literary topos. The effect is one of accumulation and transformation of the generic tropes being summoned through the story, rather than the triumph or failure of any single literary mode. Accretion is produced in Joyce's writing here in a number of striking ways. The imagination of the story draws multiple locations on to and into the city of Dublin, creating a snow-covered palimpsest of Ireland (the dark central plain, the Bog of Allen, farther westward on to Shannon, as well as the churchyard on the hill where Michel Furey lies buried). The alliterative sibilance of the final sentence (soul/ swooned/ slowly/ snow / falling /faintly/ faintly/ falling) creates an accretion of sound, a literary sensorium of building repetitions. In the lyricism of this final paragraph, we find echoes of the beautiful voice of Furey, the singing figure of Irish Romanticism, as well as of Harte's description of the treacherous, snowy Sierras. This lyrical multi-directionality doesn't obliterate naturalism so much as over-expose it. Joyce vividly produces particular places through the weird negativity of this snow-scene, illuminating the very locations that are supposedly disappearing from sight. And finally, the 'swoon' of Gabriel's soul resonates backwards with the figure of the dying man in Romantic and Revivalist literature, but also changes it – the soul rather than the body is swooning here, the nature of sacrifice is changed. I don't see this as a 'cannibalism of other literatures'[62] that registers the failure of new modes of expression, as Roos does; rather, I think the soul-swoon draws on the history of depictions of swooning (romantic and religious), and creates something newly heterotopic.

By describing the soul rather than the body swooning – by drawing on romantic descriptions of passing out, but fundamentally changing that description – Joyce is re-presenting the aesthetic in light of his developing ideas on the relations between body and mind. The significance of this is reflected in the fact that Joyce returns to the idea of the swooning soul in several important places in *A Portrait of the Artist as a Young Man* (1914–15), the text that Joyce was working on in the interim before *Dubliners* was published. *A Portrait* is often thought of as Joyce's semi-autobiographical *Künstlerroman*; a work in the mould of the 'artist-novel' of the German Romantic tradition, a genre of coming-of-age stories focused on an artist's education, development and artistic self-realisation. In *A Portrait*, Joyce is developing and also critiquing different approaches to aesthetics; this occurs in the text in direct ways (through, for instance, dialogue and direct discussion between Stephen and other college students of poetry and philosophy and theories of beauty), but also through the ways in which Stephen is depicted as embodied – as *feeling* his way into new modes and thinking, being and creating. Joyce's unusual proposition at the end of 'The Dead', that the character's soul is swooning, is repeated at a number of key points in this text. I want to conclude this chapter by showing how this notion reworks ideas of the soul and body to create a new sense of the aesthetic as embodied-physical-rhythmical experience.

Heightened physical experiences are, in the early stages of *A Portrait*, associated with sin, disgust and shame (including sexual desire and masturbation); but by the end of the text, the swooning of Stephen's soul, occasioned by intense sensory experience, becomes the catalyst for a new version of aesthetic life. In the early sections of *A Portrait*, the young protagonist, Stephen Dedalus, is sent to school and takes exception to the nationalistic and religious identities that he is encouraged to adopt. He finds he prefers the 'intangible phantoms' and 'irresolution' of his imagination to the exhortations from his father and his masters 'to be a gentleman' and 'a good catholic'; their voices sound hollow, as do the ones bidding him 'to be true to his country and to help raise up her fallen language and tradition' as part of the 'movement towards national revival' (88–89). There is a strong echo of Miss Ivors' cant on national identity in the conversations and opposing positions that are offered here. Towards the end of the text, Irish nationality, language and religion are described by Stephen as 'nets', aimed at preventing the soul from 'flight'. Stephen does not renounce Irishness per se; rather, his sense of himself is as constitutively Irish, such that everything about him can be understood as Irish, even his renunciation of nationalistic orthodoxy: 'This race and this country and this life produced me, he said. I shall express myself as I am' (220). Stephen argues that those who sacrifice their bodies to nationalist and religious ideals become the victims of hypocrisy:

> – No honourable and sincere man, said Stephen, has given up to you his life and his youth and his affections from the days of Tone to those of Parnell, but you sold him to the enemy or failed him in need or reviled him and left him for another. (220)

Parnell's fate, an important recurring tragedy in the text, has been sealed, Stephen suggests, by the hypocrisy of nationalist-religious strictures of bodily propriety and renunciation; men's bodies are sacrificed to the cause and then abandoned by it.

Alongside the political and religious positions in which Stephen is being educated (and which he will finally reject), the young Stephen is described as experiencing himself in physically intense states, developing a private sensorium that is at odds with religious aspirations to a state of disembodied perfection and physical renunciation. As a young man, he is frequently described as trembling, shivering and flushing – as subject to intense affective states in which his thoughts and experiences affect his body. These states might be seen as early indications of the auto-eroticism explored in the text. Colin Gillis has argued that masturbation is an important, and dangerous, theme of the novel, and that while, 'Stephen's masturbatory habit is never portrayed directly ... recurring patterns of imagery indicate clearly that his auto-erotic life forms an integral part of his growth as an artist'.[63] This is dangerous, Gillis suggests, because masturbation – and depicting masturbation – went against 'rigid norms governing sexuality and masculinity in early-twentieth-century Irish culture'.[64] I want to suggest that the text is auto-erotic both in this direct sense of exploring to Stephen's onanism, but also in a more extended sense of depicting him beginning to *feel* himself; of Stephen working out what it is to feel things physically and that feeling the rhythms of the body might be fundamental to profound aesthetic experience; of Stephen refusing the mortification and sacrifice of the male body that are required by religious and national discourses of masculinity.

In the early stages of the text, Stephen experiences an intensely shaming relationship to sexual desire and to encounters with the body. He confesses to a 'wretched habit', to 'fierce longings of his heart', to 'shameful details of secret riots' in his thoughts (105). The religious instruction he receives lavishes a sadistic lexicon on damnation: a preacher, for instance, details at length the eternal physical and spiritual punishment incurred in hell for mortal sin, and the great remorse that will be engendered by the 'putrefaction' of the soul. The body, then, is the potential source of impurity, shame and eternal punishment in Stephen's early encounters with it. Stephen attempts to purify himself from thoughts of the body and from its desires. But in early adulthood, he continues to be drawn towards 'mortal sin' by the orgiastic riot of his night-time thoughts:

> He wanted to sin with another of his kind, to force another being to sin with him and to exult with her in sin. He felt some dark presence moving irresistibly upon him from the darkness ... He stretched out his arms to hold fast the frail swooning form that eluded him and incited him; and the cry that he had strangled for so long in his throat issued up from his lips ... a cry which was but the echo of an obscene scrawl which he had read on the oozing wall of a urinal. (106)

It is a swooning presence that 'incites' Stephen away from a matrix of purified religious and nationalistic versions of the soul here. And when he acts upon the obscene impulses he describes, finding a girl and going with her to a room, her kiss is described as 'darker than the swoon of sin' (108). Sin and the erotic are mutual dark swoons in Stephen's thinking of them. Stephen takes to regularly visiting women, and gives up on the idea of prayer: '[W]hat did it avail to pray when he knew that his soul lusted after its own destruction?' (111) The swoon of eroticism, then, is an almost Keatsian 'self-destroying' here; a falling that is desirous of damnation, a giving way to the desires of the body that is figured as a giving way *of* the body. This version of swooning also shadows the evocations of dark, feminine figures associated with swooning in the work of the French symbolists (for instance, the work of Paul Verlaine – whose early poems, collected and translated into English, were reviewed in the *Oxonian* as 'A Single Immense Swoon').[65]

Stephen is intermittently gripped by religious fervour and sets out on a course of repentance; finally taking confession, he repents of his sins. God, he feels, has pardoned him, and his soul feels lighter. He begins to aspire to swooning in a very different direction. His repentant soul is repeatedly described as feminine ('her'), and as a woman faint before her masculine God: 'The attitude of rapture in sacred art, the raised and parted hands, the parted lips and eyes as of one about to swoon, became for him an image of the soul in prayer, humiliated and faint before her creator' (162). Stephen, now experiencing desire for the vertigo of the mystical swoon, sets out to mortify his senses and physical body, to reconstitute himself as a feminine soul. He even considers the calling of the priesthood. The image of the female mystic about to swoon overwrites Stephen's own riotous body in this spiritual re-imagining; this is a 'clean' version of the swoon, purged of the shivering, trembling, orgasmic experiences Stephen has felt in the 'swoon' of sin. This is an ideal of the swoon triggered by looking upwards to heaven – like the iconised image of St Teresa – rather than conceptualised as a falling downwards into the desires of the body.

The swoon seems to work in opposing directions in Stephen's imagining here, but in both instances it is made to stand in for a spiritual and affective transformation: the 'swoon of sin' is a giving way to sensual pleasure that is also the descent into damnation; the 'rapture' of sacred art is a renunciation of the body leading to ecstasy and religious ascendance of the soul. In both versions, the swoon is a gateway to a different reconstitution of the body in the realms of eternity – either the everlasting tortures of hell, or the bliss of salvation. The swoon, then, is important both for Stephen's understanding of the darkest sensuality of sin and of the rigours of physical mortification. The French philosopher Georges Bataille's theorisations of swooning in relation to erotic experience might help us to think further about this strange coincidence. In Bataille's extended essay *Eroticism*, '[t]he longed-for swoon [*la défaillance*] ... the desire to fall, to fail, to faint and to squander all one's reserves until there is no firm ground beneath one's feet ... a moment of disequilibrium',[66] is presented as the ultimate vertiginous prize of erotic experience in all its various forms. Eroticism is figured by Bataille in a distinct manner, which doesn't just connote sexuality: he sees eroticism as a violence towards the self that carries the threat of fatality. One form of eroticism is sexuality, or 'physical eroticism' as Bataille terms it, and he sees this as a violation which is 'bordering on death ... The whole business of eroticism is to destroy the self-contained character of the participators as they are in their normal lives.'[67]

In Bataille's thought, all of the seemingly contradictory forms of human sexual activity 'harmonise in the nostalgia for a moment of disequilibrium'.[68] But physical eroticism is, for Bataille, just one means of striving for continuity; he detects a similar desire expressed in the mystical element of religion, for example.[69] In Bataille's thinking, the swoon becomes the apogee of eroticism; it is the ultimate falling away of the identity of the individual while she is still alive: 'The longed-for swoon [la défaillance] is ... the salient feature not only of man's sensuality but also of the experience of the mystics'.[70] In Mary Dalwood's translation of Bataille's work, the English word 'swoon' is used for the French 'la défaillance', which can refer to both a faint and/or to failure. Bataille's work privileges the moment of swooning inundation as the meeting place of mystical and sexual experience: the erotic, whether understood as sexual experience or mysticism, produces an intensity through which an individual's isolated sense of herself is obliterated; it is the failure of the fiction of the individual.

The swoon, then, is the moment in which individual identity is overwhelmed, a feint towards the continuity of death, and the beginning of a new way of understanding and experiencing life in Bataille's work. If we return to Joyce's work, we might draw out some parallels in the way that Stephen conceptualises the swooning sensuality of sin and the transcendent possibility of the mystical swoon: both destroy the individual body into different spiritual experiences (damnation/salvation). But as Joyce/Stephen develop their ideas, they move away from the idea that the destruction of the body is something necessary or desirable. As we might expect from the alter-ego of the writer who will go on to create *Ulysses*, that famous 'epic of the human body',[71] Stephen will come to renounce the renunciation of the body; he will eventually reject the process of the mortification of the senses, and the self-sacrificing religious and nationalist versions of his body that surround him. And he does so in a way that insists on the perpetual inevitability of falling:

> His destiny was to be elusive of social or religious orders ... The snares of the world were its ways of sin. He would fall. He had not yet fallen, but he would fall silently, in an instant. Not to fall was too hard, too hard: and he felt the silent lapse of his soul, as it would be at some instant to come, falling, falling but not yet fallen, still unfallen but about to fall. (175)

The repeated 'falling, falling' in this passage echoes the 'falling faintly ... faintly falling' of the swooning close of *Dubliners*, and the desire 'to fall, to fail, to faint' that Bataille sees in the longed-for swoon. Stephen, while ever he is working within the strictures of religion, even if unfallen, will be perpetually looking forward to his lapse. He rejects the renunciation of the flesh that 'not falling' requires, and this opens up for Stephen a glorious new appreciation of physical beauty and sensation – and of the possibilities of an art that does not renounce the physical plane. At the end of Book IV, Stephen is about to enter the university, realising that he will now escape the 'sentries who had stood as guardians of his boyhood and had sought to keep him among them' (178). He turns 'seaward'; he speaks a quotation to himself ('A day of dappled seaborne clouds' (180)) and weighs up his love of 'the rhythmic rise and fall of words' as well as the 'contemplation of an inner world of individual emotions mirrored perfectly in a lucid supple periodic prose' (180–181). He is beginning to embrace an experience of language that is modelled on the physical and the auto-erotic; on patterns of rhythm, and a precious inner world translated into a prose which is lauded in terms of a physical quality – its 'suppleness'. Stephen encounters a 'squad of Christian brothers' and remembers 'in what dread he stood in the mystery of his own body' (182). But when they call to him – 'Stephanos Dedalos!' – he feels his own name resonate newly as a 'prophecy'; his vocation, Stephen thinks, is foretold in his name: 'Dedalus' doubles Daedalus, the name of skilled craftsman and artisan in Greek mythology. Stephen sees a winged form rising above the waves, and wonders if it is 'a symbol of the artist forging anew in his workshop out of the sluggish matter of the earth a new soaring impalpable imperishable being?' (183). The work of art might be figured here as something that transcends the body in being imperishable, but it is rooted in the 'matter of the earth'. The 'fear' and 'shame' that have previously 'abased' Stephen are now given the status of 'cerements, the linens of the grave', which he will discard.

At this point Joyce employs a remarkable metaphor for Stephen's artistic transformation. Joyce describes a shadow resurrection:

> His soul had arisen from the grave of boyhood, spurning her graveclothes. Yes! Yes! Yes! He would create proudly out of the freedom and power of his soul, as the great artificer whose name he bore, a living thing new and soaring and beautiful, impalpable, imperishable. (184)

The beginning of Dedalus' writing career is figured, then, as the aesthetic return from death, from the 'grave of boyhood' – but this is to be a return to life *in* the body, rather than a resurrection of the soul out of it. After this vision, Stephen records feeling the sensations of his body with an even greater intensity: '[h]e felt his cheeks aflame and his throat throbbing with song'; he is 'near to the wild heart of life' (184–185). Joyce creates here a vital sense of embodiment as the initiator of art, which Rickard refers to as his production of a new version of 'the human animal'; Joyce celebrates the physical senses through Stephen's artistic epiphany, and the soul now appears to be physically integrated, rather than as a transcendent essence. At this point in the narrative Stephen encounters a girl gazing out to sea, whom he likens to 'beautiful seabird' (185). He describes his 'soul' calling out 'Heavenly God!', 'in an outburst of profane joy' (186). His body is trembling in the wake of his vision of her, and he describes her image passing 'into his soul for ever'. Joyce then describes a remarkable soul-swoon:

> He closed his eyes in the languor of sleep. His eyelids trembled as if they felt the vast cyclic movement of the earth and her watchers, trembled as if they felt the strange light of some new world. His soul was swooning into some new world, fantastic, dim, uncertain as under sea, traversed by cloudy shapes and beings. (187)

Throughout this rapturous description of the emergence of artistic vision, the physical and the spiritual form a new accretion: the soaring glory of the soul is now attendant on the most intense physical encounters, and on the trembling body. The body is not a source of sin and shame to be overcome, but the apparatus for apprehensions that enter the soul 'forever'. And the soul is made into something new in this process: something that can swoon, something that shares the movements and rhythms of the body. The soul becomes an organ of physical perception, which senses and mimics the 'glimmering and trembling' quality of the world (187) with its own swooning intermittence.

We might read the soul-swoon, then, as one of the key ways in which Joyce overwrites Cartesian dualism to produce a new materialism; and this would be to agree with Eugene O'Brien who suggests that 'despite Stephen's initial swerve towards the intellectualisation of the apprehension of beauty ... Joyce's more developed aesthetic theory is, in fact, a deconstruction of the mind/body duality, and acts as a call for the primacy of bodily sensations in the aesthetic as a whole'.[72] The binary swoons into sin and transcendence that were offered to Stephen through religious versions of the body as fallen *or* ascended are now replaced by this vision of a body both fallen *and* ascended, low and high, both 'profane' and 'soaring', which is achieved through the notion of a soul that can swoon. Intense sensory experience, experience that is undecidably auto-erotic throughout *A Portrait*, is no longer associated with sickness or debility or sin in any shameful sense; instead, the soul-swoon symptomatises physical experience as an overwhelming effect of 'profane joy' and the beginning of a new sense of what it is to be alive.

Notes

1 Elizabeth Barrett Browning, *Aurora Leigh* (Oxford: Oxford University Press, 1993[1856]), I:559–565.
2 Michael Davidson, *Concerto for the Left Hand: Disability and the Defamiliar Body* (Ann Arbor: University of Michigan Press, 2008), p. 1.
3 Tobin Siebers, *Disability Aesthetics* (Ann Arbor: University of Michigan Press, 2010), p. 3.
4 Mario Praz, *The Romantic Agony*, trans. Angus Davidson (London, New York and Toronto: Oxford University Press, 1954 [1933]), 2nd edn, p. xii. All references in the text are to this edition.
5 Nicholas Roe, *John Keats and the Culture of Dissent* (Oxford: Clarendon Press, 1997), pp. 10–11. All referenced in the text are to this edition.
6 Quoted by Roe, *ibid.*, p. 15.
7 'The feminizing of Keats during the nineteenth century ... has been analysed in detail by Susan Wolfson, who shows how during this period Keats was "deemed to have particular appeal to women"; his poetry was marketed in particular "to female audiences". This was one way of assimilating Keats's threat to prevailing codes of masculinity.' Roe, *John Keats and the Culture of Dissent*, p. 229.
8 Cited by Roe, *ibid.*, p. 12.
9 John Keats, letter to his brothers (1817): *The Letters of John Keats, 1814–1821*, ed. Hyder Edward Rollins (Cambridge, MA: Harvard University Press, 1958), i., pp. 191–194.
10 For a more detailed exploration of Keats's relation to William Godwin's *Political Justice* (1793), see Roe: 'Negative Capability was (among other things) a response to the rationalistic version of eighteenth-century

mechanistic psychology which informed *Political Justice*. Godwin had been proved wrong, but Shakespearean sympathy might offer a boundless yet human means for social renovation – the negatively capable aspect, as it were, of the over confident and at times irritable belief in revolution as change which dated from the early 1790s' (Roe, *John Keats and the Culture of Dissent*, p. 247).

11 Donald Crichlow Goellnicht, 'Negative Capability and Wise Passiveness' (1976), Open Access Dissertations and Theses. Paper 4675, pp. 12–13.
12 Keats, letter to his brothers (1817), *The Letters of John Keats*, pp. 191–194.
13 Roe, *John Keats and the Culture of Dissent*, p. 225.
14 Roe (*ibid.*, p. 4), provides a list of many useful references for other scholars engaged in this work.
15 Roe, *John Keats and the Culture of Dissent*, pp. 225, 236.
16 John Keats, 'Bright Star', in *The Complete Poems* (London: Penguin Books, 1988 [c.1838]).
17 Keats engages directly with the story of *Troilus and Criseyde* in 'Endymion', where he describes 'The woes of Troy' fading 'Into some backward corner of the brain' compared to the intensity of what we feel for 'Troilus and Cressid' (in *The Complete Poems*, II.8–14).
18 The title of the Keats biopic, *Bright Star* (dir. Jane Campion, BBC Films, Screen Australia, UK Film Council, New South Wales Film and Television Office, 2009) makes the biographical figure of Keats synonymous in the contemporary popular imagination with the swooning lover of this poem.
19 Keats, 'Endymion', in *The Complete Poems*, 1988 [1818]), I.398.
20 In the Greek myth on which this poem is based, the goddess is named Selene.
21 Marilyn Butler, *Romantics, Rebels and Reactionaries: English Literature and its Background 1760–1830* (Oxford: Oxford University Press, 1981), p. 124.
22 Keats, 'The Fall of Hyperion. A Dream', in *The Complete Poems*, 244–245. Keats is one of the early proponents of this extension of swooning; from the beginning of the nineteenth century, all sorts of things start to swoon alongside people: the 'languid air' swoons in Alfred Tennyson, 'Lotus-eaters' (1832); 'the landscape' swoons in Henry Wadsworth Longfellow's 'Amalfi' (1845); ears swoon in Elizabeth Barrett Browning's *Sonnets from the Portuguese* (1850); sense swoons in George Meredith's 'Modern Love XXXV: It Is No Vulgar Nature' (1862).
23 Keats, 'The Fall of Hyperion. A Dream'.
24 Moneta describes others perishing 'on the pavement where thou rotted'st half' (153).

25 Andrew Bennett refers to Keats's posthumous life of writing in the title of his work on the poet: *Keats, Narrative and Audience: The Posthumous Life of Writing* (Cambridge: Cambridge University Press, 1994).
26 Keats, 'Hyperion. A Fragment', in *The Complete Poems*, III.130.
27 See Jan Bondeson, *Buried Alive: The Terrifying History of Our Most Primal Fear* (New York and London: W.W. Norton Co., 2001), for a fuller account of the historical development of this fear.
28 Alexander Johnson, *A collection of authentic cases, proving the practicability of recovering persons visibly dead by drowning, suffocation, stifling, swooning, convulsions, and other accidents* (Andover: Gale ECCO, Print Editions, 2010 [1775]).
29 As argued by Bondeson, *Buried Alive*, p. 156.
30 Edgar Allan Poe, 'The Premature Burial', in *The Complete Tales and Poems of Edgar Allan Poe* (London: Penguin Books, 1982), p. 258 et seq.
31 See Sharyn McCrumb, *The Unquiet Grave* (New York: Atria Books, 2017).
32 Kirsty Logan, 'The Tell-Tale Ghost,', in *A History of Ghosts* (BBC Radio 4, first broadcast October 23, 2020).
33 See Elisabeth Bronfen, *Over Her Dead Body: Death, Femininity and the Aesthetic* (Manchester: Manchester University Press, 1992), p. 324.
34 Poe, 'Ligeia', in *The Complete Tales*, pp. 654.
35 Poe, 'The Pit and the Pendulum', in *The Complete Tales*, p. 246 et seq.
36 Although the ritualised torments he faces bear no relation to any historical account of the Inquisition.
37 Poe, 'The Pit and the Pendulum', p. 246 et seq.
38 Poe, 'The Premature Burial', p. 258.
39 Sigmund Freud, 'The Uncanny', trans. James Strachey, in *Pelican Freud Library* (Harmondsworth: Penguin, 1985 [1919]), Vol. 14, pp. 339–376.
40 Nicholas Royle, *The Uncanny* (Manchester: Manchester University Press, 2003).
41 James Joyce, *A Portrait of the Artist as a Young Man* (London: Penguin, 2000 [1914–15]), p. 187. All references in the text will be to this edition.
42 Keats, 'Endymion', I.568–574.
43 John S. Rickard, 'A Portrait of the Animal as a Young Artist: Animality, Instinct, and Cognition in Joyce's Early Prose', *Humanities* 6(3) (2017), 56.
44 James Joyce, 'The Dead', in *Dubliners* (London: Penguin Books, 1992 [1914]). All references in the text will be to this edition.

45 Joyce's letter to Grant Richards of May 5, 1996 in *Letters of James Joyce*, ed. Richard Ellmann (London: Faber & Faber, 1966), Vol. II, p. 134.
46 Joyce's letter to Constantine P. Curran of 1904 in *Letters of James Joyce*, ed. Stuart Gilbert (London: Faber & Faber, 1966), Vol. I, p. 55.
47 Joyce, letter to Grant Richards of May 5, 1906, p. 134.
48 Roe, *John Keats and the Culture of Dissent*, p. 225.
49 Bonnie Roos, 'James Joyce's "The Dead" and Bret Harte's *Gabriel Conroy*: The Nature of the Feast', *The Yale Journal of Literary Criticism* 15(1) (Spring 2002), 99–126 at 119, quoting Vincent Pecora.
50 See, for instance, Gerhard Friedrich, 'Bret Harte as a Source for James Joyce's "The Dead"', *Philological Quarterly* 33(4) (1954), 443–444.
51 Bret Harte, *Gabriel Conroy* (London: Chatto & Windus, 1881), p. 1.
52 Roos, 'James Joyce's "The Dead" and Bret Harte's *Gabriel Conroy*', 105.
53 *Ibid.*, p. 111.
54 *Ibid.*
55 *Ibid.*, pp. 105–106.
56 Roos cites Christine Kinealy, *A Death-Dealing Famine: The Great Hunger in Ireland* (Chicago: Pluto Press, 1997), p. 151.
57 Roos, 'James Joyce's "The Dead" and Bret Harte's *Gabriel Conroy*', 117–118.
58 *Ibid.*, 110–111.
59 *Ibid.*, 101.
60 Roos opens her article with the figure of Furey and the 'romantic ideal of heroic self-sacrifice [he] embodies', suggesting that through his 'romantic' disease (TB compacted with lovesickness), he personifies a 'sentimentalised notion of Irish national identity predicated on starvation' (*ibid.*, 99).
61 *Ibid.*, 121.
62 *Ibid.*, 122.
63 Colin Gillis, 'James Joyce and the Masturbating Boy', *James Joyce Quarterly*, 50(3), (Spring 2013), 611–634, at 616.
64 *Ibid.*, 612.
65 Caroline Ardrey, 'A Single Immense Swoon', *The Oxonion Review* 16(4) (2011), www.oxonianreview.org/wp/a-single-immense-swoon/.
66 Georges Bataille, *Eroticism*, trans. Mary Dalwood (London: Penguin Books, 2001 [1957]), p. 240. All references in the text will be to this edition.
67 *Ibid.*, p. 17.
68 *Ibid.*, p. 240.

69 'The bond between life and death has many aspects. It can be felt equally in sexual and mystical experiences' (*ibid.*, p. 230).
70 *Ibid.*, p. 240.
71 Joyce's description of the work in dialogue with his friend Frank Budgen, as quoted by Rickard, 'A Portrait of the Animal as a Young Artist', 2.
72 Eugene O'Brien, '"Can excrement be art if not, why not?" Joyce's Aesthetic Theory and the Flux of Consciousness', in *Eco-Joyce: The Environmental Imagination of James Joyce*, ed. Robert Brazeau and Derek Gladwin (Cork: Cork University Press, 2014), pp. 197–212 at 201, quoted by Rickard, 'A Portrait of the Animal as a Young Artist', 13.

5

Vampiric swoons and other dark ecologies

'Dark ecology' is the term recently coined by critic Timothy Morton to describe our profoundly interconnected coexistence in a world poised on the brink of environmental catastrophe.[1] Morton's vision of 'nature' as morbid, enmeshed modes of being has more in common, he tells us, 'with the undead than with life',[2] and his thinking might provide a new sense of the gothic as a genre full of dark environmental resonance.

In this chapter, I want to think about the affective excess of vampire tales with Morton's notion of dark ecology in mind. Swooning is endemic to vampire narratives, which depend on the depiction of a subject being overwhelmed in the encounter with the vampire. The critic Kimberly O'Donnell, in her work on 'Feeling Other(s): *Dracula* and the Ethics of Unmanageable Affect' focuses on the swoons and faints in the text as dramatisations of 'automatic, affective response'; of forces impacting on the body at a 'non-conscious' level. In these moments of swooning, she argues, the strangeness of the body is highlighted, as well as an 'openness and responsiveness to the other'.[3] For O'Donnell, the vampire swoon is an encounter with alterity that makes the ethical demand that we accept 'the unknowability of the other – and the other at the heart of the self'.[4] In the readings that follow, I also want to highlight the strangeness of the swooning body as a challenge to the idea of the individual as isolated entity, but I suggest that vampire narratives anxiously – and erotically – present catastrophic entanglements and interconnections between the human and non-human others. In the frequent swoons of vampire victims, human consciousness is reconfigured in ways that are darkly ecological – that connect the vampire victim to networks of predation, telepathy, environmental degradation, contagion, and to the zoonotic transmission of disease (a newly intense fear, perhaps, for those of us reading in the COVID-era, but one which we can trace back to historical outbreaks of plague and other contagions).

The most famous vampire text, *Dracula* (1897), coincides with the early development of psychoanalysis; its swoon-states express deep anxieties about interference and thought transference, anxieties that also dogged the development of psychoanalysis and Freud's treatment of swooning hysterics. I propose a set of correspondences between the vampiric swoon-states of *Dracula*, the early hypnotic treatment of hysteria, and psychoanalysis's anxious relation to telepathy and occult modes of thinking. I argue that the swoon iconises a pleasurable softening into receptivity that allows incursions of one body into another, and different minds into each other; that it produces a mesmerised, ecological continuity between victim, vampire/analyst, and world.

The vampire has been a ubiquitous figure in contemporary popular culture in the early twenty-first century and the focus of much critical exploration. I might risk here adding to an excess of criticism. But being attentive to the swoons in vampire narratives has led me to revisit some of the most common critical approaches to vampirism with new questions about the entanglement of the individual in networks of violence: where the vampire has been theorised as a figuration of the force of capital,[5] for instance, the swoon will cause us to consider the psychological powers at work in the capitulation of the victim; where the vampire has been conceptualised as the spread of disease, the victim's swoon invites us to think about the dark ecologies of infection. I view all of the vampiric interrelations I discuss in relation to swooning here – telepathic, pathogenic, metamorphic, capitalist – as darkly ecological and the vampire genre as one that stages interconnection as both violent and eroticised. In the final stages of this chapter, I return more explicitly to Morton's ideas about the environment to read Sheridan Le Fanu's queer vampire tale, 'Carmilla' (1872). Carmilla is a vampire who denatures the very concept of 'Nature', who argues that what we have historically attempted to exclude from 'nature' – queer desire, communicable disease, the 'more-than-human' – must be incorporated into an expanded vision of nature as darkly ecological. And she leaves a trail of swoons in her wake, dramatising the violent, deadly, and morbidly beautiful forms of interrelation that are at the heart of gothic fiction.

A short history of vampiric swoons

Vampire fiction refuses to die. Its literary popularity was inaugurated in the early nineteenth century, rising to a peak with Bram Stoker's *Dracula* (1897).[6] At the start of the twenty-first century, the ubiquity of vampires in popular fiction, TV series and blockbuster film franchises caused some critics to refer to a vampire 'revival'.[7] Christopher Frayling has described the ever-expanding plethora of literary-critical approaches to vampirism since the 1970s as 'shape-shifting' beyond all recognition: *Dracula* has been related to 'civilisation and its discontents, the return of the repressed, sex from the neck-up, homoeroticism, bisexuality and gender bending; reverse colonialism ... hysteria, the empowerment of women, the disempowerment of women ... And so on.'[8] Frayling's indexical approach suggests that we might be somewhat oversupplied with analyses of the vampire – but one important element of the tradition not yet given extensive consideration is the swoon. And the swoon has been crucial to the English-language vampire tradition from its beginnings: fascination and immobility are key components of the literary depiction of vampirism, as I show in the readings of vampire tales that follow.

John Polidori's 'The Vampyre' (1819) is often cited as the founding text of the modern tradition of vampire fiction in English, though it draws on an older lineage of East European folk beliefs. Polidori's tale is the first sustained fictional treatment of vampirism in English,[9] and it introduced certain elements into the mythology that would have a profound impact on the vampire literature that followed, setting in motion the 'glorious career of the *aristocratic* vampire'.[10] The close relation between this tale and the figure of Lord Byron is well-known: 'The Vampyre' was written as part of that famous creative-writing exercise by Lake Geneva in the summer of 1816, when Polidori was travelling with Byron as his companion. When the story was received in 1818 and published in 1819 by the *London New Monthly Magazine*, it was initially attributed to Byron, a canny and perhaps disingenuous speculation by the magazine to generate maximum publicity. The history of 'The Vampyre' therefore attests to the power of that so-called 'first modern celebrity':[11] not only was Byron's reputation used to establish its popularity, but the story is now often read as an account of Polidori's tie to Byron and the dangerous thrall of his seductive charisma.

The tale recounts the arrival of 'a nobleman', Lord Ruthven, in London. Ruthven is notable for his social magnetism and even those suffering the most profound ennui desire his company; he is, we are told, able to 'engag[e] their attention'.[12] He particularly fascinates a young man named Aubrey, a naïf with 'that high romantic feeling of honour and candor, which daily ruins so many milliners' apprentices' (3). Aubrey sets out to travel on the Continent with Ruthven, despite his guardians' protestations about the danger of Ruthven's 'possession of irresistible powers of seduction' (7). When Aubrey sees this seduction in action, and Ruthven's 'ruin' of a young lady in Italy, he balks and leaves for Greece. Here, he is captivated by a young Greek girl who tells him tales of a 'living vampyre, who had passed years amidst his friends, and dearest ties, forced every year, by feeding upon the life of a lovely female to prolong his existence for the ensuing months' (9). Aubrey refuses to believe these tales, and strays into a forest he has been warned away from by the local people; he witnesses the girl he loves being attacked by a vampyre. Aubrey is thrown to the ground by a creature with superhuman strength and is left 'incapable of moving' (12). The dead girl, discovered with bloodied neck and breast, is described as having 'a stillness about her face that seemed almost as attaching as the life that once dwelt there' (12). The vampire fits the description of Ruthven to a tee, and Aubrey is seized by a 'most violent fever, and was often delirious' (13).

The tale concludes back in London, with Ruthven, who has appeared to die earlier in the tale, reappearing to marry Aubrey's sister. Aubrey is rendered helpless, unable to intervene in the proceedings owing to a promise he made to Ruthven not to speak of him for a year. He lies prostrate for days and 'again sank into a state' from which no one could rouse him (20). When he finally comes to, it is too late: 'Lord Ruthven had disappeared, and Aubrey's sister glutted the thirst of a VAMPYRE!' (23). Alongside instituting the trope of the aristocratic vampire, this tale is paradigmatic in describing the fascination and concomitant immobility that the vampire produces.

The vampire's charisma is his power to compel, and then to render prone and immobile; to produce a languorous, seduced helplessness which will find fuller expression in the swoons of later vampire accounts.

Before we think about these later vampires, I want to return to the claim that Polidori's is the 'first' aristocratic vampire, removing the 'blood sucker from the village cowshed to the salons of high society and the resorts of international tourism'.[13] While Polidori's is the first sustained fiction of an aristocrat vampire in English, there is a long European history of folkloric vampires who can be read as figurations of the bloodsucking economic practices of the privileged classes. Christopher Frayling catalogues many instances of this type of vampire: Voltaire's supplement to the *Dictionnaire Philosophique* (XX) (1765), for instance, describes the 'true vampyres' as 'the churchmen who eat at the expense of both the king *and* the people'.[14] Rousseau takes up the trope in a more extended form: in a draft of the fourth book of *Émile* (1758–59), he tells us that, '[f]or some time now, the public news has been concerned with nothing but vampires'. The interesting question for Rousseau is not the issue of 'proof' for these tales, but rather 'why the vampire (or miracle) should have become such an important article of popular belief in the first place'. For Rousseau, the power of the vampire is as a symbol of the ways in which man has become carnivorous (and then cannibalistic) under the rubric of 'civilisation'. For every one of us living under these conditions, Rousseau, tells us, 'Le vampire, c'est les autres.'[15] In Russia, Nikolai Gogol, Alexis Tolstoy and Ivan Turgenev all wrote folkloric vampire tales under tsarist censorship, using the vampire figure as a means to criticise the privilege of the cossacks or landlords.[16]

A particularly excoriating version of the capitalist vampire arrives in the work of Karl Marx. In *Das Kapital*,[17] Marx deploys a series of figures to describe the attributes of capital; these figures have the consumption of blood as a common characteristic. 'Capital is dead labour', he writes, 'that, vampire-like, only lives by sucking living labour, and lives the more, the more labour it sucks' (160). He refers to the 'were-wolf's hunger for surplus labour' (165), and to the fact that 'the prolongation of the working day quenches only in a slight degree the vampire thirst for the living blood of labour' (172). Sharpening the importance of the vampire-as-cannibal for an understanding of Marx's work, Keston Sutherland describes *Das Kapital* as an 'aggressively satiric' attack on wage labour 'as the fundamental savagery leading to compulsory everyday cannibalism'.[18] *Das Kapital* describes this 'everyday cannibalism' being practised through the consumption of *Gallerte*, a common German meat product available at the end of the nineteenth century. *Gallerte* might not be a familiar substance to Marx's English readers, Sutherland tells us, because it is replaced in the English translations of *Capital* with 'congelation'; thus, we have the misdirecting translation that through the commodity, 'human labour in the abstract' becomes 'a mere congelation of homogenous human labour'.

Gallerte differs from congelation in being a 'semisolid, tremulous mass gained from cooling a concentrated glue substance'; an animal product that would have been regularly bought and eaten by Marx's German readers. For Sutherland, understanding the composition of this *Gallerte* is crucial for understanding Marx's satirical (rather than merely conceptual) work in *Capital*. *Gallerte* is the 'living hands, brains, muscles and nerves of the wage labourer ... mere "animal substances", ingredients for the feast of the capitalist. The capitalist in turn is the great devourer of this undifferentiated human labour'; and it is in this sense that capital is the 'vampire thirst for the living blood of labour'.[19] Sutherland refocuses our attention on *Gallerte* and the figure of the vampire in order to show that the object of Marx's satire is not the human labourer reduced to 'a condiment', but the bourgeois consumer 'who eats him for breakfast'[20] (47). So when Marx tells us that the capitalist 'vampire will not lose its hold on [the worker] "so long as there is a muscle, a nerve, a drop of blood to be exploited"',[21] we should not, Sutherland cautions us, take Marx's imputation of the existence of the vampire as a joke. Rather, the vampire's existence must be taken seriously as the basis for revolution: 'Marx says in the *Communist Manifesto*, the point is that the vampire is not yet impossible, and it remains the task of revolution to see to it that he is "made impossible".'[22]

In Sutherland's reading, the vampire is not Rousseau's 'other', but is *us* – if 'we' are understood to be *Capital*'s bourgeois readers. We may attempt to be the 'Olympian diagnosticians' of Marx's work ('theorists of the sign, psychoanalysts, ethnographers, moralists'), but we are in fact the focus of Marx's satirical hailing: 'we are instead the person, like the infant vampire who licks clean the cauldron of Gallerte, sucking the blood off his milk teeth, who is real by negative virtue of not yet being impossible'.[23] We, Marx's readers, are entrenched in our cannibalistic vampirism, eating 'human beings transubstantiated by industrial reduction into the base of *Gallerte* in every single commodity on the market'.[24]

Queer dreams, erotophobic swoons and *Dracula*

The suggestive and satiric significance of the vampire to critique the violence of economic interrelation and inequality is well-attested to then, before Polidori's *Vampyre* and after him. What I would now like to turn to is the importance of the swoony immobility of the vampire victim to the developing literary genre of vampire fiction. Attending to this might extend our thinking about eroticised complicity in/with capitalist and other potentially violent modes of interrelation.

The fascinating and mesmeric aspects of the power of the literary vampire are perhaps most evident in that more famous epicure of blood: Bram Stoker's *Dracula* (1897).[25] When the first narrator of *Dracula*, Jonathon Harker, is making his journey east to visit the Count – to 'one of the wildest and least known portions of Europe', the gothic sublime landscape of the Carpathian mountains – he does not 'sleep well ... for [he] had all sorts of queer dreams' (8). Harker initially blames the paprika in the local food, but these disturbances foreshadow the queer dream-state that the novel produces. Once Harker is imprisoned in Dracula's castle, pleasure and terror commingle as we watch Harker slide into the 'paralysis of fear' (19) produced by the vampire. Harker describes himself in thrall to the Count, existing in a strange sleep-deprived state in which he often wonders if he is dreaming. He falls asleep in a room in the castle he has been warned away from, and what follows is an exquisite description of the erotic pleasures of immobility. Three finely dressed young women appear before Harker, with 'brilliant white teeth, that shone like pearls against the ruby of their voluptuous lips' (45). Harker feels for them an uneasy 'longing' that is 'at the same time some deadly fear'. And he confesses to feeling in his heart 'a wicked, burning desire that they would kiss [him] with those red lips' (45).

The 'wickedness' he self-diagnoses here is not just the desire for women other than his betrothed, the virtuous Mina; it is also the interdicted desire for passivity, to become the sexual quarry of three women. Harker describes himself 'looking out under [his] eyelashes in an agony of delightful anticipation' as the women advance upon him. As the fairest approaches, he can smell on her 'sweet breath' an 'offensiveness, as one smells in blood'; he's aware of the 'super-sensitive skin of my throat, and the hard dents of two sharp teeth, just touching and pausing there. I closed my eyes in a languorous ecstasy and waited – waited with beating heart' (46). The count intervenes at this point, claiming Harker for himself and depriving him and the female vampire of their consummation. Harker is overwhelmed by what he has experienced – 'the horror overcame me, and I sank down unconscious' (47) – leaving the Count to carry him to bed. The sinking man here is subject to a decidedly queer fall; his sinking shadows his earlier desire to be erotically overwhelmed, to be made passive by the vital, predatory vampires.

When Van Helsing, a model of vigorous masculine endeavour in the novel, storms Dracula's castle and encounters these same sleeping female vampires, he records the same languorous effects of their 'voluptuous beauty'; he describes them producing a desire for, 'delay, till the mere beauty and fascination of the wanton Un-Dead have hypnotize[d] ... man is weak ... I was moved to a yearning for delay which seemed to paralyse my faculties and to clog my very soul' (393). Van Helsing feels a 'strange oppression' beginning to 'overcome' him: 'Certain it was that I was lapsing into sleep, the open-eyed sleep of one who yields to a sweet fascination' (393). A swoony, waking dream/nightmare of languorous immobility, threatens to overwhelm Van Helsing, the upright scientist, too. And the figure of the vampire renders the male characters of the novel prone to all sorts of queer sinkings in other places in the novel: to faints, coyly termed 'falls';[26] to hysterics;[27] and, most frequently, to the desire for a yielding, erotic immobility. The 'lunatic' Renfield, the male character drawn into closest relation to his 'Master', Dracula, 'falls' spectacularly into paroxysms, which exhaust him until he 'swooned into a sort of coma' (118).

This late nineteenth-century vampire, then, makes men subject to the kind of languorous immobility which often characterised feminine forms of pathology in the novels of the previous century.

Timothy Morton describes erotophobia as 'the fear of and fascination with a feminized state';[28] by this definition, *Dracula*, through the male swoons it narrates, produces a lurid erotophobia. The narrative is an alarmist account of the vampiric overwhelming of male subjects, which revels in long descriptions of the temptation towards 'delay'. The possibility of passive (feminised) masculine states here is a source of terror, which nevertheless betrays fascination. Dracula threatens *all* of his victims with the desire to be immobile, to be subject to 'a languorous ecstasy' which comes dangerously close to desiring a feminised state; the queerest of dreams.

The erotic, paralysing effects of the vampire that symbolically threaten men with feminine states of passivity are, as we might expect, exhibited in exemplary form by Dracula's female victims, and the term 'swoon' is frequently used to denote his female victims' states of sickly, languorous ecstasy. When Mina discovers her somnambulant friend Lucy on the Whitby clifftops at night, she describes her in a swoon-like repose: 'There was undoubtedly something, long and black, bending over the half-reclining white figure [of Lucy]' (101). Lucy is described as 'still asleep' as she reclines, and her breathing is ecstatic, coming in 'long, heavy gasp[s]'. The unsettling quality of these scenes is partly the sense they impart of Lucy being lulled into enjoying her mesmerised excursions, her own swooning predation. After this, Lucy begins to suffer from a range of drowsy conditions. Mina discovers her leaning out of their bedroom window, towards a bat; but Mina cannot rouse her – she is in 'a faint' (106). That Lucy is simultaneously described as 'fainting' and 'leaning' here reveals the strange way in which her body's ability to move with volition is being affected. Lucy becomes paler and paler, and expert help is sought in the form of Dr Seward and his old mentor, Van Helsing. After unsuccessfully attempting to keep the vampire away, they discover Lucy 'on the bed, seemingly in a swoon … more horribly white and wan-looking than ever' (137). They administer morphia to her, and 'the faint seemed to merge subtly into the narcotic sleep' (138).

These dreamy, narcotic states culminate in a mass female unconsciousness event: the next morning Van Helsing arrives to find the housemaids all knocked out by laudanum, Lucy's mother dead in Lucy's bed, and Lucy laid out beside her, deathly white. When revived, Lucy recounts waking in the night to see wolves at her bedroom window. The window smashes; the wolves enter. Her mother, who had a 'weak' heart, has been literally frightened to death. Lucy describes trying 'to stir, but there was some spell on me ... I remembered no more for a while' (163). The somnambulant, swooning spell cast on the beautiful Lucy and her household has something of the necrophilic quality of female unconsciousness in fairy tales – the languorous Sleeping Beauty, and the dead-still Snow White – and also of the disturbing modern phenomenon of 'sleepy' pornography; unconscious women posed helplessly, invitingly.

When Mina hears of what has happened to Lucy, through the 'forked metal' of the modern phonograph, she describes herself lying back in her chair 'powerless. Fortunately I am not of a fainting disposition' (238). But, of course, Dracula will prove *everyone* to be of a fainting disposition. Mina is effectively confined to the house for her own protection, while the men set out to hunt the vampire. Ironically, this 'protective' confinement places Mina in the perfect position for vampiric predation. Mina begins to sleep heavily and wakes as though from bad dreams; the reader comes to see that Dracula has a nocturnal relationship with Mina, of which she is not yet conscious. The others finally discover Dracula in the Harkers' bedroom: Jonathon is found 'in a stupor such as we know the Vampire can produce' (300), while Mina, with the tell-tale puncture marks on her neck, is being forced to drink blood from Dracula's breast. Mina later describes how this moment felt: 'I was bewildered, and, strangely enough, I did not want to hinder him. I suppose it is a part of the horrible curse that such is, when his touch is on his victim ... He placed his reeking lips upon my throat ... I felt my strength fading away, and I was in a half swoon' (306). The half swoon described here is a yielding to violence, a pleasurable cessation of hindrance.

The importance of this dreamy, swooning state to depictions of vampiric interference opens up an additional, weird dimension if we return to the idea of the vampire as an exploration of the power dynamics of violent economic interrelation under capitalism. For while Marxist accounts of 'Dracula' reference the violent blood-sucking forces of the privileged classes, we might see in the swoon an exploration of the psychological power of capital to compel its victims. This is the sort of distinction Norman O. Brown makes when elaborating Marx's early formulations of alienation: 'The alienated consciousness', Brown tells us, 'is correlative with a money economy' in Marx's thinking.[29] Focusing, however, on Marx and Engel's *Kleine ökonomische Schriften*,[30] Brown argues that Marx's thinking of alienation mistakes force, a material reality, with power, a psychological category, as the progenitor and sustainer of capitalism:

> Marx comes close to recognizing alienated (compulsive) work as an inner psychological necessity [...] But the psychological implications of this line of thought are too bewildering; and Marx withdraws to the position that the primary datum is the domination of man over man [...] The ultimate category [for Marx] is presumably force, the force which appropriates another man's labour [...] If the cause of the trouble were force, to 'expropriate the expropriators' would be enough [...] The ultimate category of economics is power; but power is not an economic category. Marx fills up the emergent gap in his theory with the concept of force (violence) – i.e., by conceiving power as a material category ... this is a crucial mistake; power is in essence a psychological category. (241–251)

The altered, swooning states of Bram Stoker's vampire victims vividly attest to the psychological power wielded over the weakening individual, who comes to strangely enjoy his or her own exsanguination. The vampiric swoon might, then, dramatise the spellbinding quality of power, and vampiric swoon-states might cause us to think again about the idea of 'free choice' under the conditions of capital; Morton reminds us that the idea that 'our consciousness floats, with free choice, among various ideas that can be selected at will, like so many different bottles of shampoo, or magazines – is itself the ideology of consumer capitalism'.[31] If we read the vampire as a figure of the power of capital, then this becomes clearer: the victims of Dracula cannot choose in any straightforward way; their strength is fading; their consciousness is blurred into their bodies, smudged into narcotic, swoon states that prevent them from resisting their own predation. The gothic renders swooning as a profoundly unsettling, uncanny, feminised and eroticised relation to power.

Oceanic, telepathic swoons and occult psychoanalytic anxieties

Appearing eighty years after the publication of *Dracula*, Ann Rice's *Interview with a Vampire* (1976)[32] is often seen as an initiatory text for the glut of twenty-first-century literary vampires. In Rice's series of novels, swoon states remain crucial. Louis, the central character, describes himself being 'spellbound' by the vampire Lestat, who provides him with 'the most overwhelming experience' (27).[33] When Lestat drinks from him, Louis becomes 'weak to paralysis', characterised by 'helplessness' (22). Powerful vampires put their victims under a 'spell' (225); they 'hypnotise'; they have an 'eerie magnetism' (249); they put victims in a 'trance' (226); they are 'like the sea drawing something into itself from the land' (206). '[T]races of vampirism are to be found in most cultures', Frayling tells us. 'The vampire is as old as the world. Blood tastes of the sea – where we all come from.'[34]

The vampire figured as a return to the ocean, by both Rice and Frayling, calls to mind Freud's discussion of the 'oceanic' feeling: the feeling of 'something limitless, unbounded' that his correspondent Romain Rolland suggests is the cause of continued religious feeling, even in those who reject religious belief.[35] Freud does not recognise this feeling in himself, but speculates on it as a possible residual sense of infantile connection to the world: 'The new-born child does not at first separate his ego from an outside world that is the source of the feelings flowing towards him … the ego is originally all-inclusive.'[36] 'The role of the oceanic feeling', might then be to 'restore unlimited narcissism' and this would 'suggest connections with many obscure psychical states such as trance and ecstasy'.[37] Although Freud goes on to downplay the importance of oceanic feeling as the origin of religiosity,[38] his discussion highlights the pull of an infantile feeling of connection and 'belonging to the whole of the world outside oneself'.[39] This state, he suggests, is often re-found at 'the height of erotic passion' when 'the borderline between ego and object is in danger of becoming blurred' and, '[a]gainst all the evidence of the senses, the person in love asserts that "I" and "you" are one and is ready to behave as if this were so'. A similar abolition of separation, Freud cautions, might also be seen in certain 'morbid processes'.[40]

The morbid, swoony attraction of the vampire, metaphorised as the pull of the ocean, as 'the sea drawing something into itself',[41] feels like an apt evocation of this (ecological) oceanic feeling, and the oceanic pull of certain obliterating experiences of violence and sexuality. In *Interview*, the vampire victim is repeatedly described as being pulled irresistibly towards a sense of unlimited connectedness.

And the delicious giving-in of the victim to this feeling finds its fullest expression in the swoon. Louis describes, for example, a beautiful victim at the Parisian Théâtre des Vampires: 'She was languid ... her yearning towards him ... her dying now ... her swoon ... She was giving herself over' (204). In the swoon, the victim spectacularly lets herself go in the vampire's arms: 'he was lifting her, her back arching as her naked breasts touched his buttons, her pale arms enfolded his neck ... He lifted her off the boards as he drank, her throat gleaming against his white cheek ... displaying her, her head falling back as he gave her over' (204). In *Interview*, this swooning state is not just the experience of the victim; it is also the experience of the drinking vampire, the agent of violence. Louis tells us that his first suck 'mesmerised [him]' (31) and that killing produces in him a 'near swoon' (37). When he gives in to his own desire to drink blood, he describes something 'glimmer[ing] in my swoon' (177). Mind and body extend themselves in unlimited directions in this violent swoony vampiric experience. Lestat, for instance, describes his body *becoming* his mind in moments of trance (37), and also suggests that he can feel the thoughts of potent vampires, 'as if they were palpable in the air like smoke' (215). This is a telepathic plane in which the oceanic meets the material; all experiences, even thoughts, might be swooningly shared in this vampiric, polymeric reconfiguration of body, mind and world.

There is grave danger for both the victim and the vampire in Rice's vision of this shared swoon. The victim's risks are obvious enough, but if the vampire carries on drinking until the victim is dead, he too will be drawn down into mortality. Louis describes himself in the attempt to transform a victim into a vampire, 'trying desperately to break my swoon; and then I felt her powerful pull' (244). When the 'swoon is strongest' (243), he can feel the beat of the victim's heart like a drum through his own undead veins. Victim and vampire are locked together in a swooning embrace, drawn into an oceanic connection that also risks pulling them both into the death of the other.

Vampiric swooning is presented here as a treacherous, potentially deadly form of mutual interference and merging of minds. I want to return briefly to *Dracula*, appearing as it does during the 'golden age' of hysteria[42] and during the early stages of the development of psychoanalysis, in order to think about emerging theories of mind in relation to vampirism: specifically, to think about Freud's early use of hypnosis to treat swooning hysterics as another potentially treacherous form of mutual interference. Elisabeth Bronfen suggests that Dracula's victims exhibit a split consciousness (daytime lucidity/ nocturnal semi-conscious irrationality) that mirrors the patterning of the hysteric's 'double conscience' (315) in Freud and Breuer's early formulations. A 'proclivity towards semi-consciousness', so common, as we have seen, in swooning vampire victims, is, Bronfen tells us, a 'descriptive trait' of the hysteric character for early psychoanalysis, alongside other altered states, such as 'hypnoid conditions, somnambulism, hallucinations and amnesia' (315). These labile states of mind, the 'fluidity between various states of self' (316), meant that the hysteric was thought of as being particularly susceptible to '"suggestibility" as an acceptance and acting out of the desires others have induced in hypnosis' (315).

I want to propose a set of interrelations between the vampiric swoon-states of *Dracula*, the early hypnotic treatment of hysteria, and psychoanalysis's anxious relation to telepathy. In *Dracula*, swoon and trance states make excursions into other minds possible through vampiric telepathy and 'medical' hypnosis, respectively. By making Mina drink his blood while she is in a trance, Dracula claims control of Mina's mind: 'now you shall come to my call. When my brain says "Come!" to you, you shall cross land or sea to do my bidding' (307). But Van Helsing is able to exploit this connection of minds through his own art of telepathy: hypnosis. Placed in a 'hypnotic trance' by Van Helsing (229), Mina is also able to enter the Count's mind, which is the place of death: 'I am still – oh, so still. It is like death!' (333). Hypnosis is, in the novel, figured as the facilitator of Mina's telepathy with Dracula; but it is also figured as an intrinsically telepathic trance-state itself. Van Helsing discusses his belief in the practices of telepathy and hypnosis with the sceptical Dr Seward, chiding Seward for his lack of belief in 'the reading of thought. No? Nor [do you believe] in hypnotism' (204). At this point Seward interrupts Van Helsing to protest that he does believe in hypnotism, since it has been proved 'pretty well' (204) by Dr Charcot. Some critics have suggested Stoker's possible familiarity with Freud's early use of hypnosis in treating hysterical patients;[43] while this remains a speculative claim, we have clear evidence in the novel of Stoker's engagement with Freud's most

Vampiric swoons and other dark ecologies 171

4 Pierre André Brouillet, *Une leçon clinique à la Salpêtrière* (A Clinical Lesson at the Salpêtrière), 1887

influential teacher, Jean-Martin Charcot. Bram Stoker was personally acquainted with Charcot, the famous French neurologist who exhibited his 'hysterical' patients in hypnotic trances in his 'Tuesday Lectures'.[44] The best-known image of these lectures is the painting by Pierre André Brouillet, *A Clinical Lesson at the Salpêtrière* (1887), which depicts Charcot lecturing to a room full of men with a female hysteric swooning at his side, supported by one of his students.

These shows have been scrutinised by some as fakery – and the swoon as part of the theatre of hysteria; Zambreno, for instance, writes that 'Charcot would stage his pretty nubile hysterics in a series of posed seizures in his photographs, sometimes through hypnotic suggestion. (They were so suggestive).'[45] As one of Charcot's students himself, Freud was so profoundly influenced by these lectures that *A Clinical Lesson* hung above the couch in his consulting room.[46] We might go on to suggest, as Frayling does,[47] that Charcot, a major influence on Freud, is also a major source of Stoker's interest in trance-states; the mesmeric power of the vampire is drawn into close correspondence with the mesmeric possibility of hypnosis.[48] The swoon of the vampire victim, the swoon of Charcot's hysteric, and the depiction of that swoon on Freud's wall, all seem to connote a similar mesmerised softening into receptivity for incursions of one mind into another.

As depictions of various states of receptivity, then, these swoons (Brouillet's and Bram Stoker's) also iconise the hypnotised woman's vulnerability to influence from the male figure of authority (*They were so suggestive/ible*), an anxiety that dogged the early studies of hysteria.[49] This risk was theorised and ostensibly accounted for in the psychoanalytic concepts of transference and counter-transference. Carl Jung, for example, claimed that objections to hypnosis were reducible to the fear of transference, which was no bar to useful analysis per se: 'What has disgusted you in hypnotism is at bottom nothing but the so-called "transference" to the doctor'.[50] But he later describes the jeopardy of uncontrolled transference for psychoanalysis through an image of both analyst and analysand falling into unconsciousness – a psychoanalytic mass unconsciousness event: in 'cases of counter-transference when the analyst really cannot let go of the patient ... both fall into the same dark hole of unconsciousness'.[51] There remains the danger, then, that transference might be profoundly 'unresolved and *unresolvable*', that psychoanalysis, in its excursions into the unconscious mind, might profoundly blur consciousness.[52]

Freud was also interested in 'thought transference' and described himself falling into the sin of believing in telepathy.[53] Freud's method of analysis, keen as he is to present it as a science, makes thought and consciousness begin to appear as weird, uncanny, occult phenomenon. Freud is troubled by his own falls: as well as his 'fall' into telepathic belief, Freud experienced fainting spells in Jung's presence.[54] He attempts to analyse these swoons in letters to Ernest Jones, seeing 'an unruly homosexual feeling' at the 'root of the matter'.[55] Nicholas Royle gives a dizzying reading of these swoons and Freud's attempt to determine them: 'Can there be a self-analysis of a fainting-fit?' Royle asks, before demonstrating that Freud is embroiled in 'interminable hetero-thanato-analysis' over his faints, which includes a consideration of 'homosexual feeling', death wishes, 'somatic' factors, and literature – starting with Dostoyevsky and Freud's reading of Dostoyevsky's 'death-like' attacks or 'so-called epilepsy'.[56] Freud, the diagnostician of hysterical falls, is profoundly vulnerable to falling: he is prone to the occult possibility of telepathy; he is overwhelmed in Jung's presence. His work profoundly unsettles the very structures of mind that he is attempting to verify.

I want to suggest that *Dracula*, with its different strands of hypnotic and telepathic influence, can be read as a proleptic exploration of psychoanalytic transference and counter-transference; of uncontrolled psychic influence. Stoker's version of the hypnotic mind-doctor, Van Helsing, suggests that telepathy and hypnosis cannot be kept separate; Charcot, he tells us, moves his mind 'into the very soul of the patient that he influence[s]': as a 'student of the brain' one cannot 'accept the hypnotism and reject the thought-reading' (204). Van Helsing seems to be a fictional forerunner of Freud when he falls into a belief in telepathy, suggesting as he does that an admission of Charcot's method might also lead to a dangerous admission of the possibility of 'thought-reading' (204). Telepathy in *Dracula* is never a one-way street: telepathic interference is met by counter-interference. The influence that Dracula claims over Mina's mind is also a symbiosis that allows her to enter *his* mind. As a result of this, the party are able to trace the Count's whereabouts, tracking and eventually destroying him. The swooning merging of mind opened up between Count Dracula, Mina and Van Helsing makes for a dangerously unresolvable network of influence: if the hypnotised/vampiric swooner is made vulnerable to telepathic incursions, her counter-telepathy might travel in the most unexpected directions. And this might in turn tell us something about the early diagnoses of hysteria: if the hysteric is seen as constitutionally open to influence, quite where hysteria begins or ends becomes impossible to account for. Hysteria, that most feminine malady,[57] might stem from the male doctor's direction and influence. And the great doctor might find himself counter-influenced by a feminine flow; might become prone to falling (into hysterics; into faints; into a belief in telepathy), 'just as a woman does'.[58]

Blood relations and dis-ease

The telepathic transference possible in the vampiric swoon means that the swooner is never entirely, or singly, herself; and that the vampire or doctor also risks incursions into his mind and body. The vampiric drinking of blood and the telepathic swoon it produces are, I have suggested, the main ways in which interrelation and interference are explored in vampire narratives. But there are other ways that vampire fictions render a sense of dark, ecological connections. In *Dracula*, the blood transfusions given to Lucy to treat anaemia provide a shared network of blood between the ostensibly non-vampiric characters in the text. Arthur, Lucy's betrothed, has given her his blood for this purpose, and feels that, even though her premature death has prevented an actual marriage ceremony, the mingling of their blood has made her 'his wife in the sight of god' (185). At this suggestion, Van Helsing's face grows 'white and purple by turns' (185); the Professor's intermittent floridity and blanching here reveals his dis-ease at this blood-tie version of marriage. All of the strong young men in the novel (who have also mostly been in love with Lucy), have donated their blood to her, unbeknown to Arthur. And this blood promiscuity means that all the men are now married to the polyandrous Lucy – and, by blood-mingling extension, to each other, to Mina, to Jonathon Harker, and to Count Dracula.

The medical blood-letting that has made even the most virile among them feel 'faint' (138) has also bound them all together in an erotic mass-transfusion. This is the kind of pan-erotic connection that Frayling refers to as 'haemosexuality',[59] working from Maurice Richardson's description of the characters in Dracula constituting one big incestuous family: a 'kind of ... necrophilius, oral-anal-sadistic all-in wrestling match'.[60] In Richardson's account, the 'morbid dread' of the vampire stands in, following Freud's dictum, 'for repressed sexual desire' and the desire suggested here is for a multilateral, sexual overwhelming in undifferentiated heamosexuality.

The dis-ease with which Van Helsing, the medical professional, greets the idea of erotic blood-sharing is, I suggest, also intimately connected with the imagining of illness. There have long been anthropological accounts of vampire stories that link their appearances to outbreaks of disease. Frayling tells us that when vampire epidemics were reported across Eastern and Central Europe between 1672 and 1772, the Age of Reason and Enlightenment thinking adduced medical explanations that might correspond with contemporaneous scientific ideas: some suggested food poisonings might be responsible for the belief in vampires (too much paprika?); or that communities were embroiled in a collective nightmare following opium use ('It all seemed like a horrible nightmare to me' (22)). But it has also been suggested that plague was being re-imagined as vampirism:

> the symptoms of the victim – pallor, listlessness, fever, nightmare – were thought to be those of the plague. The transmission of the 'vampire's curse' from predator to victim, who then became predator in turn, was a graphic way of explaining the rapid spread of plague germs. Vampires and rats tended to be close companions in European folklore from an early stage, and there was an epidemic of the plague in East Prussia in 1710 [coinciding with a reported vampire epidemic].[61]

Vampirism has also been seen as a way to account for rabies outbreaks and the zoonotic transmission of disease, and Frayling reports that most recent folklorist analyses of the reported vampire outbreaks of 1731–32 have concluded that the 'manifestations' represent, at least in part, 'attempts by preliterate communities to make sense of what we would today call "contagion"'.[62] Ernest Jones, in *On the Nightmare*, makes the same argument: 'In the Middle Ages there was a close correlation between visitation of the Black Death and outbreaks of vampirism, and even as late as 1855 the terrible cholera epidemic in Dantsic revived such a widespread belief in the dead returning as vampires to claim the living that, according to medical opinion, the fears of the people greatly increased the mortality from the disease.'[63]

The vampiric *swoon* might in this context represent an unsettling and eroticised version of succumbing to disease. It is intriguing that Jones mentions cholera here, given the accounts of cholera epidemics in Ireland that Bram Stoker's mother provided in her letters to him. She describes to Stoker the disease's 'bitter strange kiss' and people being buried alive, 'stultified from opium'.[64] The term 'pathology' once referred to the study of feeling[65] as well as to the study and manifestations of disease; this double meaning resonates in Stoker's mother's account of cholera, which gives it the pathological, sensual charge of a deadly kiss.[66] The dangerous vampire embrace and its resultant narcotic, swooning states might then be in close correspondence with accounts of disease that describe it as a kind of seduction and affective overwhelming. And this might take us back round to bubonic plague, and to Daniel Defoe's description of some sufferers dying in a dream-like, affectively overwhelmed swoon: '[They] often went about indifferent easy until a little before they died. Such would be taken suddenly very sick ... and there sit down, grow faint, and die. This kind of dying was much the same as it was with those of common mortifications, who die swooning, and, as it were, go away in a dream.'[67]

Writing in the midst of the world's most recent pandemic, these descriptions can't help but put me in mind of some of the unsettling accounts of states of altered consciousness produced by COVID-19. Reports of 'happy hypoxia' (or 'silent hypoxia') have described coronavirus sufferers with very low oxygen rates – rates that would usually result in unconsciousness and signs of extreme illness – remaining conscious and seemingly unperturbed. The *Guardian* described the phenomenon as follows: 'It is a mystery that has left doctors questioning the basic tenets of biology: Covid-19 patients who are talking and apparently not in distress, but who have oxygen levels low enough to typically cause unconsciousness or even death.'[68] The disturbing element of this report is the absence of an expected faint: those who are gravely ill remain upright. *Not* swooning in this situation feels uncanny. Consciousness, rather than unconsciousness, becomes weird in this account of it; the idea that a person may be gravely ill and oxygen deficient while 'happily' speaking, that as a result they may delay treatment, is an unsettling inversion of the idea of 'stultified' cholera sufferers being buried alive. An anaesthetist in the report tells us how dangerous 'happy hypoxia' can be: '"I have had a few patients like this," the doctor said. "Sadly, their outcomes tend to be bad in my experience."' Descriptions of the 'kiss' of cholera, the 'swoon' of plague, and the 'happy hypoxia' produced by coronavirus, all present advanced states of illness that affect consciousness, with a seductive, dreamy or ecstatic inflection, respectively; these are descriptions that show illness affecting our sense of the body such that illness isn't perceived as such by the sufferer (illness instead becomes an embrace, or a dream-state, or 'happiness'). In these accounts of pathology as the *feeling* of illness, passing out/not passing produces an uncanny sense of narcotic (un)consciousness.

'[Q]uite incompatible with a masculine system in a state of health': Erotic contagion and the host organism

The final vampire tale I want to read here was published two decades before *Dracula* and was written by another Irish writer, Sheridan Le Fanu, who had lived through cholera outbreaks as well as witnessing horrific sights of starvation during the Great Famine.[69] Le Fanu's 'Carmilla' (1872)[70] first appeared as part of his popular *In a Glass Darkly* collection, which ostensibly presented the posthumous papers of an occult detective. This particular case is narrated by its central character, Laura, who recounts a visit she and her father received in their 'lonely' forest mansion in Styria[71] from a beautiful, refined young woman, who is unexpectedly placed in their care.

The two young women, Laura and Carmilla, seem instantly to remember one another other. Carmilla claims to share a traumatic 'dream' that Laura had as a young child, in which a beautiful woman caressed her: she 'lay down beside me on the bed, and drew me towards her, smiling; I felt immediately delightfully soothed, and fell asleep again. I was wakened by a sensation as if two needles ran into my breast very deep at the same moment, and I cried loudly' (90). The two girls begin to share a reciprocal trance-like attraction: 'I wonder whether you feel as strangely drawn towards me as I do to you?' Carmilla asks Laura. 'Now the truth is, I felt rather unaccountably towards the beautiful stranger', Laura tells us. 'I did feel, as she said, "drawn towards her", but there was also something of repulsion. In this ambiguous feeling, however, the sense of attraction immensely prevailed. She interested me and won me, she was so beautiful and indescribably *engaging*' (101). The mesmeric fascination common to the vampire experience is shared by Laura here. And this sense of captivated immobility is deepened and inflected through the repeated use of the term 'languor'. Carmilla's 'bodily languor' is often remarked upon and becomes part of her attractiveness to Laura: 'Her beauty was, I think, enhanced by that graceful languor that was peculiar to her' (123).

Susan Sontag, in her work on illness and metaphor, describes the nineteenth-century vogue for looking consumptive as part of a veneration of the quality of languor; 'romantic agony', she tells us, was during this period directed into a glamorisation of specific kinds of debilitation and was transformed into the desirable state of 'languor'.[72] We might recognise in this version of glamour an echo of the kind of delicacy prized within sensibility (as discussed in Chapter 3); through the notion of 'languor', the cult of sensibility extends in gothic directions with an even more explicitly morbid version of feminine refinement.[73] When Carmilla's attentions to Laura become particularly ardent, she briefly wonders, in a Shakespearean turn of mind, if Carmilla might be a man dressed as a woman, come to woo her. But, she decides, this is implausible: 'I could boast of no little attentions such as masculine gallantry delights to offer ... there was always a languor about her, quite incompatible with a masculine system in a state of health' (105). Carmilla's attractiveness is bound to her languor and the exquisite feminine illness it connotes to Laura.

This languor seems catching – Laura begins to experience it herself, and it becomes fused with both erotic connection and contagion. Laura describes Carmilla's embraces becoming 'foolish', that is, over-intimate, and wishes to extricate herself from them. But her energies seem 'to fail' her and she describes Carmilla's murmured words sounding 'like a lullaby in my ear ... sooth[ing] my resistance into a trance' (104). Young girls in the surrounding area begin to die. Young women report seeing a ghost, or a figure that seizes them by the throat, and the process of their decline is repeatedly described as 'sinking' (109). Laura's father thinks they are in the midst of an epidemic fever, and both girls wear charms as an 'antidote against the malaria' (118). But it soon becomes clear that Laura is suffering from this mysterious illness. Every morning she feels an increased 'lassitude and languor', and believes that she is darkly transforming: 'I feel myself a changed girl'.

Her apprehension of 'illness' arrives in the form of a seductive 'sinking':

> an idea that I was slowly sinking took gentle, and, somehow, not unwelcome possession of me ... Without knowing it, I was now in a pretty advanced state of the strangest illness under which mortal ever suffered. There was an unaccountable fascination in its earlier symptoms that more than reconciled me to the incapacitating effect of that stage of the malady. (118)

The erotic immobility of the vampire/contagion victim is attested to in Laura's nightly dreams, in which strange sensations visit her, intensifying to become 'a sense of strangulation ... a dreadful convulsion, in which my sense left me, and I became unconscious' (119). Sexual ecstasy and horror in the midst of disease/predation climax here in a swoon. And Laura refuses medical help for her dreadful/ecstatic complaint, she tells us, because of the 'narcotic' influence that is acting upon her.

Carmilla *is* the contagion. She admits that she has herself 'suffered from this very illness'. Discussing the spread of the fever with Laura's father she tells him that the 'disease that invades the country is natural. Nature. All things spring from Nature – don't they? All things in the heaven, in the earth, and under the earth, act and live as Nature ordains? I think so' (109). Vampirism, contagion, *is* nature in Carmilla's account of it. Carmilla's philosophy of the natural involves a version of the erotic that is at once a disintegrative and deadly fusion of the lovers *and* their transformation into other organic forms: '[Y]ou shall die', she murmurs to Laura, who is immobilised in her embrace, 'die, sweetly die – into [my life]. I cannot help it; as I draw near you, you, in your turn, will draw near to others, and learn the rapture of that cruelty, which yet is love.' And she kisses her.

The idea of the girls' lives and deaths merging echoes the depiction of swooning, telepathic connection and mass-transfusion in *Dracula*. We might also see the evidence here for Ernest Jones's sense of vampirism as a fantasy of the continued relation between the living and the dead, a reunion which transforms individuals into conjoined organisms. For Jones, vampiric conjoining corresponds with the desire of lovers to die together that is commonly expressed in art, and in particular in Wagner's Liebestod in *Tristan and Isolde*: 'our being we might blend / in love without an end'.[74] Later, Carmilla extols to Laura the virtues of the opportunity 'to die as lovers may – to die together, so that they may live together. Girls are caterpillars while they live in the world, to be finally butterflies when the summer comes; but in the meantime there are grubs and larva, don't you see – each with their peculiar propensities, necessities and structure' (110).

This vision of erotic death as the propensity towards merger and metamorphosis is followed by a striking description of the vampire as an 'amphibious existence' (147). The vampire is both at once: it is symbiotically doubled rather than single; it is an ever-changing 'existence' rather than a solitary life form. In Le Fanu's imagining of the vampire as amphibian, as the contagious metamorphosis that *is* nature, I want to suggest that there is a vision of ecology at play that has much in common with what Timothy Morton has lately termed 'dark ecology'. In *Ecology Without Nature*, Morton calls for a re-estimation of 'nature', demonstrating that 'the term collapses into impermanence and history – two ways of saying the same thing. Life-forms are constantly coming and going, mutating and becoming extinct'.[75] 'Nature' as a static, independent entity, as the 'force of law, a norm against which deviation is measured',[76] deconstructs under the pressure of its own deviating impermanence. Those 'unnatural' terms against which it might seem to stand, for instance 'disease', might instead be drawn into its purview, as Carmilla insists: 'disease ... is natural. Nature. All things spring from Nature – don't they?' (109). Rather than venerating nature as a single, identifiable 'sadistic fetish object', then, Morton encourages us to see the world as ecology in motion; as a multiplying series interconnections. The Latin 'ambo', 'in both sides', infuses Morton's account of how aesthetics might be rethought along ecological lines, in particular through the ideas of ambiguity and ambience: 'Ecological writing shuffles subject and object back and forth so that we may think they have dissolved into each other, though what we normally end up with is a blur this book calls ambience'.[77] Vampire fiction, I suggest, presents us with what we might think of as 'ambient' swooning, as individuals and world merge into one another. An ecological 'rethinking' of aesthetics is bound up for Morton with an ethical imperative to value and protect the marginal, the ambivalent, and in particular the *amphibious*:

> Margin (French *marge*) denotes a border or an edge, hence 'seashore.' Indeed, if current industrial policies remain unchecked, these very spaces, such as coral reefs, and liminal spaces (Latin, *limen*, boundary) such as *amphibians*, will be increasingly at risk of being wiped out ... I mean here to support these margins. As a matter of urgency, we just cannot go on thinking of them as in 'between'. We must choose to include them on this side of human social practices, to factor them into our political and ethical decisions. As Bruno Latour states, 'Political philosophy ... finds itself confronted with the obligation to internalise the environment that it had viewed up to now as another world.'[78]

The amphibian must, for Morton, be brought into our view of what it means to be human, just as in *Carmilla* the amphibious vampire is the spread of disease; which is nature; which is metamorphosis; which is all of us and all other existences. To see this, to undo the habitual conceptual distinction between nature and ourselves, is, for Morton, to provide a working model for dissolving the difference between subject and object, the dualism that he posits as the 'fundamental philosophical reason for human beings' destruction of the environment'.[79]

The concepts of 'hosting' and 'hospitality' take us further into vampiric/ecological/deconstructive symbiosis. The risk of contagion in *Carmilla* simultaneously operates through the body as host (of fever, of 'malaria', of 'the strangest illness' – that is vampirism); and through home that hosts the self-replicating vampire. Hosting and hospitality have long played an important part in vampire mythology,[80] with vampires often needing to be invited across the threshold, needing symbolic consent for predation and infection. In the case of *Carmilla*, the vampire is handed over into the care of various aristocratic homes and thanks each host heartily for their 'hospitality' (114); she is a 'perfidious and beautiful guest' (145). In 'The Limits of Pluralism III: The Critic as Host',[81] J. Hillis Miller provides a powerful deconstructive reading of the terms 'parasite' and 'host'. 'Parasite' originally had a positive meaning, Hillis Miller tells us, referring to 'a fellow guest, someone sharing the food with you, there with you beside [para] the grain' (442). But the meaning of the term 'parasite' modulates towards predation:

> The host and the somewhat sinister or subversive parasite are fellow guests beside the food, sharing it. On the other hand, the host is himself the food, his substance consumed without recompense, as when one says, 'He is eating me out of house and home.'[82]

This sense also echoes through the use of 'host' to refer to the Eucharist bread: the host as sacrifice, or symbolic victim. But if the host is both the eater and the eaten, he also contains in himself 'the double antithetical relation of host and guest, guest in the bifold sense of friendly presence and alien invader', because host and ghost share the same etymological root:

> *ghos-ti*, stranger, guest, host, properly; someone with whom one has reciprocal duties of hospitality ... A host is a guest, and a guest is a

host. A host is a host. The relation of ... host and parasite in the original sense of 'fellow guest,' is inclosed within the word 'host' itself. A host in the sense of a guest, moreover, is both a friendly visitor in the house and at the same time an alien presence.[83]

Working through these terms as an example of deconstruction, Hillis Miller suggests that there is always already an alien guest in the home of the *text*; every reading of a poem contains 'its enemy within itself, is itself both host and parasite'.[84] Deconstruction is, then, itself bound up with the strange logic of the welcomed parasite; 'deconstruction', Derrida famously remarked, 'is just visiting'.[85] Hillis Miller describes deconstruction as an instance of the *inherence* of 'figure, narrative and concept *in one another*'.[86] Deconstruction *is* ecological symbiosis: it performs interrelation and symbiotic interdependence; it deconstructs the individual. Morton reinforces this idea, arguing that life forms cannot be said to differ in a 'rigorous' way from texts; both exist as series of non-unitary *interrelations*, as ecology and deconstruction simultaneously demonstrate. To develop an ecological culture, Morton suggests, we would benefit from 'concepts that ruthlessly denature and de-essentialise: they are called deconstruction'.[87]

Deconstructing the notion of 'nature' out of its 'naturalness', Morton's 'dark ecology' performs the same kind of 'queer' and 'contingent'[88] re-imagining of nature-as-ecology that is exemplified in Carmilla's queer notion of the 'natural' vampire. 'Queer reworlding', Donna Haraway has recently argued, 'depends on reorienting the human'.[89] Haraway is one of a number of critics who have recently highlighted the ways in which the disruptive energies of queer theory might intersect with an ecological disruption of species categorisation. In Haraway's account, '[q]ueering has the job of undoing "normal" categories, and none is more critical than the human/nonhuman'.[90] If queering necessarily extends in ecological directions, challenging the conceptual integrity of the 'natural' and the 'human', alongside the heteronormative and anthronormative[91] apparatus these categories have often supported, it is no surprise that some recent queer and ecologically informed criticism has focused on the vampire as 'a kind of queer nature that refuses the binary opposition between the natural and the unnatural, especially in terms of the sexual'.[92]

In Le Fanu's and Morton's work, dying is imaginatively posited as the high-point of collapse and interconnection: for Morton, 'dying is becoming the environment';[93] for Carmilla, dying is entering into new vampiric life, the girlish larvae metamorphosed into the undead butterfly. The ecological thought, Morton tells us, as 'the thinking of interconnectedness', has a lingering darkness that has nothing to do with 'a hippy aesthetic of life over death, or a sadistic-sentimental Bambification of sentient beings'; it has more in common with the 'goth assertion of the contingent and necessarily queer idea that we want to *stay* in a dying world: dark ecology'.[94] Thinking about the swoon, I suggest, is also thinking about *staying with* the process of dying, in life. 'Lingering' with death, with something 'painful, disgusting, grief-striking' is, Morton tells us, 'exactly what we need right now, ecologically speaking'.[95] We have already entered the sixth mass extinction event, Morton argues, and must imaginatively accept, while staying in the world, that we are already dead.[96] We should, then 'be finding ways to stick around with the sticky mess that we're in and that we are, making thinking dirtier, identifying with ugliness, practicing "hauntology" (Derrida's phrase)'.[97] In his most explicitly vampiric formulation Morton tells us that: 'The task is not to bury the dead but to join them, to be bitten by the undead and become them.'[98] Our entanglements are necessary but dangerous – we are the undead, the happily hypoxic, the carriers of zoonotic viruses – and vampire literature shows us this in its weird, alarmist, erotic ecology of swoons.

Notes

1 See, for example, Timothy Morton, *Dark Ecology: For a Future of Coexistence* (New York: Columbia University Press, 2016).
2 Timothy Morton, *Ecology Without Nature: Rethinking Environmental Aesthetics* (Cambridge, MA and London: Harvard University Press, 2009), p. 201.
3 Kimberly O'Donnell, 'Feeling Other(s): *Dracula* and the Ethics of Unmanageable Affect', in S. Ahern (ed), *Affect Theory and Literary Critical Practice* (Basingstoke and New York: Palgrave Macmillan, 2019), pp. 139–157 at p. 141.
4 O'Donnell, 'Feeling Other(s)', p. 142.

5 Franco Moretti's classic Marxist essay the 'The Dialectic of Fear', *New Left Review* (November–December 1982), is one prominent example of this approach.
6 Albeit that the popularity of *Dracula* grew over time: the novel was a bestseller in Stoker's lifetime, going into paperback in 1901, but its importance was increasingly felt through the twentieth century when the story was embraced in popular myth and film. See Christopher Frayling's 'Preface' to Bram Stoker's *Dracula* (London: Penguin Classics, 2011 [1897]), p. xi.
7 It is questionable whether vampire literature has ever passed into dormancy. However, a 2013 special issue of *Gothic Studies* suggests that while 'vampires have been continually reborn in modern culture' there is a renewed 'recent vogue for vampires and all things undead', which has led projects such as *Open Graves, Open Minds: Vampires and the Undead in Modern Culture* (established in 2010) and to the growth of 'Vampire Studies' as an academic field (Sam George and Bill Hughes, 'Introduction: Undead Reflections', *Gothic Studies* 15(1) (May 2013), 1–7). Much of the literature suggests that the upsurge in vampire offerings in fiction, TV series and films began with the work of Anne Rice in the 1970s and continued to grow in the context of the HIV and AIDS epidemic of the 1980s.
8 Frayling's 'Preface' to *Dracula*, pp. xi–xii.
9 There had been fleeting references in earlier Romantic poetry, for instance, Samuel Taylor Coleridge's *Christabel* (1800) (which was supposedly read by the party at Lake Geneva, and may therefore have been a direct influence on the vampire narrative); Byron's *The Giaour* (1813); and Keat's *Lamia* (1819), which appeared in the same year as 'The Vampyre'.
10 Robert Morrison and Chris Baldick tell us that in anthologies of previous reported sightings, vampires had usually been peasants (Robert Morrison and Chris Baldick, 'Introduction' to John Polidori, *The Vampyre and Other Tales of the Macabre* (Oxford: Oxford World Classics, 2008 [1819]), p. xii). Many of the most famous vampires followed in this aristocratic mould, for instance Rymer's *Varney the Vampire* (1847); Le Fanu's *Carmilla* (1872); and Bram Stoker's *Dracula* (1897).
11 For an exploration of this attribution, see Tom Mole, *Byron's Romantic Celebrity: Industrial Culture and the Hermeneutic of Intimacy* (Basingstoke and New York: Palgrave Macmillan: 2007).
12 John Polidori, *The Vampyre and Other Tales of the Macabre* (Oxford: Oxford World Classics, 2008 [1819]), p. 3. All references in the text are to this edition.
13 Morrison and Baldick, 'Introduction' to John Polidori, *The Vampyre*, p. xii.

14 Frayling is the very 'Baedeker of vampirism', as his book jacket tells us: Voltaire, quoted in Christopher Frayling, *Vampyres: Lord Byron to Count Dracula* (London and Boston: Faber & Faber, 1991), p. 31.
15 Rousseau's position is summarised by Frayling and all quotes are taken from *Vampyres*, pp. 32–34.
16 *Ibid.*, p. 80.
17 All quotations taken from the first English translation of Karl Marx, *Capital: A Critique of Political Economy Capital*, trans. Samuel Moore and Edward Aveling, ed. Frederick Engels (Moscow: Progress Publishers, 1887); pdf version available through www.marxists.org at www.marxists.org/archive/marx/works/download/pdf/Capital-Volume-I.pdf.
18 Keston Sutherland, *Stupefaction: A Radical Anatomy of Phantoms* (London; New York; Calcutta: Seagull Books, 2011), p. 49.
19 *Ibid.*, pp. 44, 45.
20 *Ibid.*, p. 47.
21 Marx, *Capital*, p. 193, quoting Friedrich Engels.
22 Sutherland, *Stupefaction*, p. 48.
23 *Ibid.*, p. 69.
24 *Ibid.*, p. 75.
25 Bram Stoker, *Dracula* (London: Penguin Classics, 2011 [1897]). All references in the text will be to this edition.
26 When Jonathon sees Dracula in London he clings to Mina, who tells us that, 'if he had not had me to lean on and to support him he would have sunk down' (184); similarly, when Arthur sees his fiancée Lucy as an unnaturally beautiful corpse, he 'fell a-trembling' (180); later, her vampiric 'voluptuousness' makes him faint: 'Arthur was next to me, and if I had not seized his arm and held him up, he would have fallen' (225).
27 Van Helsing is described as giving way to 'a regular fit of hysterics ... just as a woman does' (180) under the pressure of dealing with the vampire Lucy.
28 Morton, *Ecology Without Nature*, p. 137.
29 Norman O. Brown, *Life Against Death* (Middletown, CT: Wesleyan University Press, 1985), p. 237.
30 Karl Marx and Friedrich Engels, *Kleine ökonomische Schriften* (Berlin: Dietz, 1955).
31 Morton, *Ecology Without Nature*, p. 126.
32 Anne Rice, *Interview with a Vampire* (London: Sphere, 2001 [1976]). All references in the text will be to this edition.
33 The more recent TV series *True Blood* depicts a similar experience of trance-like suggestibility under the power of a vampire as 'glamouring': Alan Ball's *True Blood* (HBO, 2008–continuing), based on Charlaine Harris's vampire-novel series, *The Southern Vampire Mysteries* (2001–13).

34 Frayling, *Vampyres*, p. 4.
35 Sigmund Freud, *Civilization and Its Discontents*, trans David McLintock (London: Penguin Books, 2002 [1930]), p. 3.
36 *Ibid.*, pp. 5–6.
37 *Ibid.*, pp. 10–11.
38 Freud foregrounds instead the helplessness of the child and a longing for its father as the primary needs that would be met by the illusion of religion (*ibid.*, p. 10).
39 *Ibid.*, p. 3.
40 *Ibid.*, p. 5.
41 Rice, *Interview*, p. 206.
42 This designation is Elaine Showalter's and refers to the period 'between 1870 and World War I': Elaine Showalter, *The Female Malady: Women, Madness and English Culture, 1830–1980* (London: Virago, 1985), p. 129.
43 Nina Auerbach, *Woman and the Demon: The Life of a Victorian Myth* (Cambridge, MA: Harvard University Press, 1982), explicitly draws an analogy between Lucy mesmerised by Dracula and the hysteric woman hypnotised by Freud, suggesting that Stoker could have known the work of the Viennese doctor through reports at the Society for Psychical Research in London in 1893; quoted in Bronfen, *Over Her Dead Body*, p. 323.
44 Charcot visited the Lyceum Theatre where Stoker worked for Henry Irving, and is described in Stoker's *Personal Reminiscences of Henry Irving* (London: Heinemann, 1906), Vol. I, p. 316; for an account of the Tuesday Lessons see Vicky Lebeau, *Psychoanalysis and Cinema: The Play of Shadows* (London: Wallflower Press, 2001), p. 20.
45 Zambreno, *Heroines*, p. 133.
46 Lebeau, *Psychoanalysis and Cinema*, pp. 19–20, 30.
47 'Charcot seems to have been a major source for Stoker's interest in trance-like states, which feature so much in the novel': Frayling, *Vampryes*, fn. 4 to Ch. XIV, p. 448.
48 The theory of mesmerism might be seen as the common predecessor of both the telepathic and the hypnotic trances that so interest Stoker. Charcot's work on hysteria and hypnosis developed at a time when the public was fascinated by the work of the Austrian physician Anton Mesmer (1734–1815), who posited a connective 'universal fluid' animating the world: Franz Anton Mesmer, *Mémoire sur la découverte du magnétisme animal* (Geneva and Paris: Didot le jeune, 1779); in English: 'Dissertation on the Discovery of Animal Magnetism,', in George Bloch (trans. and ed.), *Mesmerism* (Los Altos, CA: William Kaufmann, 1980).

49 Charcot's swooning displays were often suggested by his detractors to be staged, with Charcot depicted as the master choreographer of his hysterics. Showalter describes these contemporary accusations of undue influence, with the 'performances' being attributed to 'suggestion, imitation, or even fraud': *The Female Malady*, p. 150.
50 Carl Gustav Jung, *Collected Papers on Analytical Psychology*, trans. Constance Ellen Long (London: 1916), p. 245.
51 Carl Gustav Jung, *Analytical Psychology: Its Theory and Practice* (London: 1976), pp. 159 and 157.
52 For an investigation of potentially 'unresolved and unresolvable transference' in analysis, which might risk the transmission of the analyst's own images into the analysand's mind, see Ned Lukacher, *Primal Scenes: Literature, Philosophy, Psychoanalysis* (Ithaca, NY: Cornell University Press, 1986), p. 20.
53 For an exploration of this, and of the wider ramifications telepathy, see Nicholas Royle, 'The Remains of Psychoanalysis (I): Telepathy', in Martin McQuillan (ed.), *Deconstruction: A Reader* (Edinburgh: Edinburgh University Press, 2000), pp. 361–369.
54 See Nicholas Royle, *The Uncanny*, p. 310, who cites Max Schur, *Freud: Living and Dying* as a source of discussion on Freud faints (London: Hogarth Press and Institute of Psychoanalysis, 1972).
55 Ernest Jones records one occasion when Jung had to carry Freud to a sofa: Ernest Jones, *Sigmund Freud: Life and Work*, 3 vols (London: Hogarth Press, 1953–57), 1:348.
56 Freud's 'Dostoevsky and Parricide' (1928), quoted by Royle, *The Uncanny*, p. 311.
57 Showalter suggests that hysteria had been the quintessential female malady for centuries, but that during the 'golden age' of hysteria it assumed an especially central role in definitions of femininity and female sexuality, such that by the end of the nineteenth century, 'hysterical' had become almost interchangeable with 'feminine'. Even where doctors, such as Charcot, treated male hysterics, 'hysteria remained symbolically, if not medically, a female malady' (*The Female Malady*, pp. 129, 148).
58 Seward describes Van Helsing falling into 'a regular fit of hysterics [...] just as a woman does': Stoker, *Dracula*, p. 180.
59 Frayling, Introduction' to *Dracula*, p. xx.
60 Maurice Richardson, 'The psychoanalysis of ghost stories' (1959), excerpt reprinted as 'The psychoanalysis of Count Dracula', in Frayling, *Vampyres*, p. 387.
61 Frayling, *Vampyres*, p. 25.
62 *Ibid.*, p. 26: although Frayling tells us that 'it is well to consider the initial reactions of *post-literate* societies to the AIDS epidemic. The

resemblances are startling to say the least' (p. 27), particularly in their emphasis on an accusatory 'who did it' rather than an exploratory attempt to understand the mechanisms of the virus.
63 Ernest Jones, *On the Nightmare* (1931), excerpt reprinted as 'On the Vampire', in Frayling, *Vampyres*, p. 413.
64 'Charlotte Stoker's Account of 'The Cholera Horror', in a Letter to Bram Stoker (*c*.1875)', reproduced as Appendix II in Stoker, *Dracula*, p. 412.
65 OED 'pathology': 'I. Senses to do with feelings. 1.2. The branch of knowledge that deals with emotions'.
66 The *OED* gives as the first meaning of pathology as the (now rare): 'Senses to do with feelings'.
67 Daniel Defoe, *A Journal of the Plague Year* (London: Penguin Classics, 2003 [1722]).
68 Hannah Devlin, 'Happy Hypoxia: Unusual Coronavirus Effect Baffles Doctors', *Guardian* (May 3, 2020).
69 See Chapter 4 for more detail on the Irish Famine in relation to James Joyce's work.
70 Sheridan Le Fanu, 'Carmilla', reproduced in *Three Vampire Tales* (Boston: Houghton Mifflin Co., 2003 [1872]). All references in the text are to this edition.
71 Now part of Austria.
72 Susan Sontag, *Illness as Metaphor and Aids and its Metaphors* (London: Penguin Books, 2002 [1979]), p. 30.
73 Ann Radcliffe's work probably contains the most notable examples of a feminine excess of sensibility carrying over into gothic morbidity: in her first novel, *The Castles of Athlin and Dunbayne* (Stroud: Alan Sutton Publishing Ltd, 1994 [1789]), the queen and princess figures are almost permanently 'overcome' with dreadful sensations, and are frequently to be found succumbing to the sensitivities of their minds, 'lifeless', 'insensible', 'senseless', 'languorous'. Unconsciousness places the young princess several times into the hands of marauders who kidnap her and threaten her virtue. All of this is countered by the 'nerves of resistance' and 'firmness' of the young prince.
74 Jones, *On the Nightmare*, in Frayling, *Vampyres*, p. 405.
75 Morton, *Ecology Without Nature*, p. 21.
76 *Ibid.*, p. 14.
77 *Ibid.*, p. 15.
78 *Ibid.*, p. 51.
79 *Ibid.*, p. 51.
80 Frayling notes that one of the earliest vampire accounts, contained in the Istrian *Ehre des Herzogtum Krains* of 1672, describes a male

vampire who likes to be invited across the threshold, after knocking. This is repeated in many later accounts, where the vampire must be invited into a victim's house (Frayling, *Vampyres*, p. 42).
81 J. Hillis Miller, 'The Limits of Pluralism III: The Critic as Host', *Critical Inquiry* 3(3) (Spring, 1977), 439–447.
82 Hillis Miller, 'The Limits of Pluralism III', 442.
83 *Ibid.*, 442–443.
84 *Ibid.*, 447.
85 Jacques Derrida, 'The Time is Out of Joint', in Anselm Haverkamp (ed.), *Deconstruction is/in America: A New Sense of the Political* (New York and London: New York University Press, 1995), p. 29.
86 Hillis Miller, 'The Limits of Pluralism III', 443.
87 Morton, 'Ecology as Text, Text as Ecology', *Oxford Literary Review* 32(1) (2010), 1–17, at 1.
88 Morton, *Ecology Without Nature*, p. 143.
89 Donna Haraway, 'Companion Species, Misrecognitions, and Queer Worlding', in Noreen Giffney and Myra J. Hird (eds), *Queering the Non/Human* (Farnham: Ashgate, 2008), pp. xxiii–xxvi.
90 *Ibid.*, p. xxiv.
91 This is Alice Kuzniar's term, quoted in Noreen Giffney and Myra J. Hird, 'Queering the Non/Human', in *Queering the Non/Human*, pp. 1–16, at p. 3.
92 Robert Azzarello, 'Unnatural Predators: Queer Theory Meets Environmental Studies in Bram Stoker's *Dracula*', in Giffney and Hird (eds), *Queering the Non/Human*, pp. 137–157, at p. 139.
93 Morton, *Ecology Without Nature*, p. 71.
94 *Ibid.*, p. 185.
95 *Ibid.*, p. 197.
96 See Timothy Morton, *Hyperobjects: Philosophy and Ecology after the End of the World* (Minneapolis and London: University of Minnesota Press, 2013), p. 7.
97 Morton, *Ecology Without Nature*, p. 188.
98 Morton expresses the power of literature as vampiric contagion in his suggestion that the gothic tackiness of Coleridge's *Ancient Mariner* is aesthetics as ecology: its point is to 'infect others', rather than providing a 'moral' ('don't shoot albatrosses!'); it perpetuates violent interrelation through *literature* as contagion (*Ecology Without Nature*, p. 159).

6

Lovesick, lesbian swoons and the romantic art of sinking

In the preceding chapters, we have seen how, since the eighteenth century, swooning clusters in works of literature that examine illness in conjunction with femininity – whether that is under the context of the extra sensitivity lauded and then interrogated under the rubric of sensibility; in the gothic, eroticising and erotophobic swoons of vampire fiction; or in the attempts of writers to channel feminine morbidity in new visions of artistic creation and embodiment. In this final chapter, I focus on a queer romance novel, Patricia Highsmith's *The Price of Salt* (1952) (later known as *Carol*) and the popular romance/erotic fiction series *Fifty Shades of Grey* (2012). I examine the contrasting ways in which feminine swooning has been made to function in relation to romance in these works, arguing that Highsmith uses the figure of fainting to work against heteronormative constructions of health and artistic production, while James deploys swooning as gendered and generic cliché. I suggest that, in twentieth- and early twenty-first-century romance fiction, the swoon might function as a literary strategy of innovation and transformation, but also risks repetition, bathos and cliché. Finally, I consider a transformative faint in Angela Carter's retelling of the necrophilic fairy tale of Bluebeard, 'The Bloody Chamber' (1979) – a faint which pivots the story from recapitulation to reinvention.

Queer, stimulating, romance swoons

In an afterword to her groundbreaking novel, *Carol*,[1] Patricia Highsmith describes her inspiration for writing the text as the experience of a near-faint. '[V]aguely depressed and also short of money'[2] while waiting for *Strangers on a Train* to be published, Highsmith took a job as a clerk in a department store in Manhattan during the 'Christmas rush'. In the midst of this consumerist maelstrom, she experienced something extraordinary:

> One morning, into this chaos of noise and commerce, there walked a blondish woman in a fur coat ... It was a routine transaction, the woman paid and departed. But I felt odd and swimmy in the head, near to fainting, and yet at the same time uplifted, as if I had seen a vision. (309)

That night, Highsmith returned alone to her apartment and wrote out the plot for *The Price of Salt*, the novel that would depict a lesbian relationship with unprecedented intimacy and tenderness. Highsmith describes the early writing of the outline of the work as a spontaneous result of her visionary, swoony experience in the store: 'It flowed from my pen as if from nowhere – beginning, middle and end. It took me about two hours, perhaps less' (309). In Highsmith's account of it, her writing proceeds via a revised version of divine inspiration: the novel flowed from the beatific vision of a woman who 'seemed to give off light' (309) and from Highsmith's resulting physical faintness, which initiated an altered state of consciousness.

The next day, Highsmith felt fainter still. She recalls 'nearly fainting' (309) on the train to work and how she subsequently developed a fever. She realises that she has contracted chickenpox. Queer desire, contagion and writing begin to affect and infect one another in her description of *Carol*'s composition: 'One of the small runny-nosed children [in the department store] must have passed on the germ, but in a way the germ of a book too: fever is stimulating to the imagination' (310).

Highsmith's description of the creative stimulation provided by illness and a pathologically altered state of conscious are especially significant because in *Carol*, the main characters are subjected to repeated attempts to cast female same-sex desire as a kind of sickness. Highsmith's novel anticipates critical work of the twenty-first century that has sought to challenge heteronormativity and constructions of health concurrently – Robert McRuer's work developing 'crip theory',[3] for instance, which shows us that normative versions of sexuality have depended on normative versions of the healthy body. Highsmith valorises her own faintness and fever in order to challenge the construction of 'health'; and these same norms will be tested by Therese Belivet, the main protagonist of *Carol*, specifically in regard to lesbian sexuality and/as pathology.

Therese is a young shop-clerk and aspiring stage-designer in 1940s New York. She falls deeply in love with Carol, an older woman who visits the store in which she's working during the Christmas rush. As Therese attempts to navigate her feelings for Carol, she is subjected to repeated diagnoses of her desire for Carol as a shameful kind of sickness. Richard, Therese's boyfriend at the start of the novel, narrates her own feelings to her in terms of her naivety and regression: 'Don't you think it's pretty silly?' he begins one particularly punishing exchange. 'It's like a crush that school girls get' (161). Richard goes on to describe Therese as being physically affected by Carol in a way that has compromised her ability to think: 'You're in some kind of trance ... it's worse than being lovesick because it's so unreasonable' (162). Richard's aetiology of Therese's desire casts her as infantile, unsteady and unsound of mind. Her feelings for Carol are cast as a kind of debilitation. Richard finally accuses Carol of serious exploitation: 'I think she's committing a crime against you. I've half a mind to report her to somebody, but the trouble is you're not a child. You're just acting like one' (163). It suits Richard now to cast Therese as an exploited minor, though he has clearly construed her, at nineteen, as old enough and competent enough to consent to heterosexual relations with him. Later, in a letter, Richard expresses intense disgust for Therese and her 'pathology':

> the uppermost emotion I feel towards you is one that was present from the first – disgust. It is your hanging on to this woman to the exclusion of everyone else, this relationship which I am sure has become sordid and pathological by now, that disgusts me ... It is rootless and infantile, like living on lotus blossoms and some sickening candy instead of the bread and meat of life. (265)

Therese receives this account of her desire as 'sickening' from an intimate acquaintance, but the censure of her relationship with Carol also operates at the level of legal and political authority within the text. Carol will lose custody of her child as result of her acting on her 'perversity', by sinking to the 'depths of human vice and degeneration' (273), as the legal framework has it. 'In the eyes of the world it's an abomination' (210), Carol tells Therese, warning her that the process of growing up is learning to be careful, learning to hide a desire that the world thinks of as shameful.

Therese has to navigate her feelings for Carol in the context of these pathologising social, moral and legal discourses. Therese's response to these narratives about her feelings is often defiant. When Richard initially accuses her of being in a trance, she asserts her own capacity and perspicacity: 'I'm wide awake. I've never felt more wide awake' (162). In fact, she inverts the patterns of pathology that he attempts to impose on her, beginning to see his attachment to her as itself pathological and potentially violent: 'she had seen him looking at her with that soft, inane smile that in memory now looked cruel, and unhealthy. And its unhealthiness might have escaped her, she thought, if it weren't that Richard was so frankly trying to convince her she was unhealthy' (166). Therese won't accept the terms of health and heterosexuality that are being laid out for her here; in fact, the pathologising of same-sex desire is now interpreted by her as pathological.

Therese constantly interrogates her desire for Carol, trying to make sense of it in the absence of a framework other than pathology:

> Was it love or wasn't it that she felt for Carol? And how absurd that she didn't even know. She had heard about girls falling in love, and she knew what kind of people they were and what they looked like. Neither she nor Carol looked like that. Yet the way she felt about Carol passed all the tests for love and fitted all the descriptions. (100)

Therese's experience of her desire for Carol produces a kind of prismatic effect: life is split apart; her sense of herself refracts away from the different versions of heterosexual and homosexual identity that are visible in the culture around her. This fracturing of identities and experiences is how Eve Kosofsky Sedgwick memorably describes 'queer' in comparison to what she calls 'Christmas effects'. The 'depressing thing about the Christmas season', Sedgwick suggests, 'is that it's the time when all the institutions are speaking with one voice': 'religion, state, capital, ideology, domesticity the discourse of power and legitimacy – line up with each other' to create the 'monolith' in the United States (and elsewhere) that is known as Christmas.[4] Highsmith's Therese is faced with just this monolith: *Carol* begins with the Christmas holiday season, and with Therese's sense of the store where she works, with its regimented systems of consumption and labour, being 'organised so much like a prison' (4) – a state institution controlling and restricting those within it. Sedgwick and Highsmith, in their different ways, propose alternatives to this monolith; Sedgwick gives us 'queer' as a way to break apart the friable components of both Christmas and sexual identity. Queer, she says, can refer to 'the open mesh of possibilities, gaps, overlaps, resonances, lapses and excesses of meaning when the constituent parts of anyone's sexuality aren't made (or *can't be* made) to signify monolithicly'.[5] And in the face of monolithic versions of Christmas and sexual identity, Highsmith introduces Therese. Therese, Carol notes at one point in the novel, is 'free'. She isn't yet inculcated into modes of seeing and behaving and desiring, and of experiencing herself, that are dictated by the heteronormative, consumer-capitalist 'prison' around her.

Therese's attempts to understand her own feelings are charted in the novel as an extraordinary act of resistance to and rejection of the narratives of sickness and shame that might confine her. Therese is in experimental territory in terms of her sense of self and her identity; her feelings for Carol and her concomitant self-identification are not like any of the versions of sickness, love, femininity or lesbianism that are visible to her. Her early experiences of desire for Carol are consequently charged with a sense of wildness and with a near-overwhelming sense of desire as dangerous. This sometimes makes her desire for Carol appear to herself as desiring death. In the early stages of the novel, for instance, she fantasises about being in a car accident with Carol: 'A wild, inexplicable excitement mounted in Therese as she stared through the windshield. She wished the tunnel might cave in and kill them both, that their bodies might be dragged out together' (59). Later, when Carol puts her to bed, she imagines being killed by Carol and 'not caring if she died in that instant, if Carol strangled her, prostrate and vulnerable in her bed' (65). The commingling of intimacy and violence, of desire and danger, continues in the remarkable stream of imagery attributed to Therese as she drinks some warm milk that Carol has prepared for her:

> The milk seemed to taste of bone and blood, of warm flesh, or hair, saltless as chalk yet alive as a growing embryo. It was hot through and through to the bottom of the cup, and Therese drank it down, as people in fairy tales drink the potion that will transform, or the unsuspecting warrior the cup that will kill. (66)

Therese concocts this profoundly ambivalent mixture of taste associations – visceral, magical, pregnant, macabre, mythological, lethal – into a radically creative, 'open mesh' of queer possibility. What happens next could be magical transformation or her destruction.

From this improvised, wild and potentially deadly amalgam of new experiences, emerges a sense of Therese's desire for Carol – once consummated – as a gorgeous, vibrant source of health and happiness. The two women embark on a road trip, and as they grow closer to one another, Therese thinks of them as growing stronger and stronger each day. When they are finally physically intimate with one another, the description of Therese's experience is exquisite:

> Happiness was like a green vine spreading through her, stretching its tendrils, bearing flowers through her flesh. She had a vision of a pale white flower, shimmering as if seen in darkness or through water [...] And she did not have to ask if this was right, no one had to tell her, because this could not have been more right or perfect. (200–201)

Therese no longer needs to question her desire, or fear that it might break her apart or kill her: she now experiences it as lush and organic and an inexorable source of pleasure. Therese and Carol's bodies are overwritten with images of natural and celestial beauty: they are flowers, and then arrows pointing at one another across a wild night sky. There is, finally, in this open, star-shooting imagery, a refusal of all of the narrow narratives of pathology that have attempted to curtail Therese and her desires.

Carol has come to be known as the first lesbian novel with a happy ending. In a recent re-ssue of the novel, Val McDermid describes it as a life-changing work of fiction – not so much filling a 'niche as a gaping void' in terms of literary representations of female same-sex desire that avoided producing characters who were 'miserable inverts or scandalous denizens of titillating pulp fiction'.[6] Highsmith, in her 1991 'Afterword' to the novel, reminds us that it initially had to be published pseudonymously and was rejected by her usual publisher.[7] But the novel sold well, and for months she received large amounts of fan mail. The appeal of the novel, Highsmith suggests, was that it had 'a happy ending for its two main characters, or at least they were going to try to have a future together. Prior to this book, homosexuals male and female in American novels had to pay the price for their deviation by cutting their wrists, drowning themselves in a swimming pool, or by switching to heterosexuality' (311). The 'happy ending' or 'future' offered here is no fairy tale; Carol sacrifices custody of her daughter, Rindy, in order to be able to have relationships with women, and experiences profound grief as a result. But Therese's own experience of her desire for Carol is a triumph over the disciplinary medical, legal and cultural discourses that would have her believe herself to be sick; and the novel is unprecedented in its presentation of a young woman audaciously breaking apart the monolithic version of sexual identity offered to her and creating a vivid, bright new existence from its pieces.

All of this began with a near-faint; with Highsmith experiencing a visionary faintness and with Therese being overwhelmed by her desire for Carol, a desire that plunges her towards desiring death before her feelings are affirmed as gloriously 'perfect'. In her narration of the composition of *Carol*, Highsmith's faint functions in a similar way to Keats's and Joyce's depictions of the swoon: she valorises ill-health contra the norms of 'health' as construed by heteronormative culture. In doing so, she has produced a groundbreaking queer romance, as well as a stimulating version of writing produced through overwhelmed-states and ill-health.

Bathetic swoons: *Fifty Shades of Grey* and other forms of sinking

Highsmith inverts the idea of fainting as feminine weakness, instead presenting her faint as a stimulation. Highsmith's use of swoon-states to depict a lesbian relationship is also a subversion of gendered romance traditions – the popular romance novel has a long and somewhat lurid history of depicting the fainting female form in need of masculine protection and support. In the rest of this chapter, I focus on the most popular romance fiction series of the twenty-first century: the *Fifty Shades of Grey* trilogy.[8] In E. L. James's novels, swooning is eroticised as a specifically feminine art of sinking in front of a rich and powerful man. In the rest of this chapter, I read the swoons in *Fifty Shades* to show that the sinking depicted here might be understood as a form of bathos, or disappointed hope; a falling back into cliché and into received ideas of gender submission.

Bathos: sinking down and falling backwards

Alexander Pope's famous satirical treatise, *Peri Bathous, or the Art of Sinking in Poetry* (1728),[9] lampoons 'low' or '*alamode*' writing by characterising it as a graceful sinking. Bathos, Pope tells us, like the Greek *Altitudo*, 'implies equally *height* and *depth*' (196). Pope uses this altitudinous ambivalence to demonstrate that bathos consists of a contrast between the high and the low, from whence we get the still-current definition of bathos as the 'ludicrous descent from the elevated to the commonplace in writing or speech; anticlimax' (*OED*).[10] Keston Sutherland argues that total destitution is the lowest point in Pope's formulation of the 'downhill way to the *Bathos*; the bottom, the end': bathos is, Sutherland argues, the evacuation of 'truth or beauty' from poetry.[11] To render this effect as merely 'anti-climactic' is itself anti-climactic in Sutherland's account; in Pope's hands, he argues, bathos represents a brutal destitution of poetry's promise to deliver truth.

I want to argue that E. L. James's reincarnation of the swoon can be seen as bathetic, and that the masochism it so famously depicts becomes the bathos of liberation when it functions as an eroticised submission to commodity capitalism. 'Romantic, *liberating* and totally addictive', is how the blurb of the *Fifty Shades of Grey* novels promotes the trilogy.[12] The contradictory coincidence of 'liberation' and 'addiction', the chiasmatic convergence of freedom and compulsion in this seemingly banal copy, intimates some of the problems of the branding of female 'emancipation' in these novels. Improbably virginal 21-year-old literature student Anastasia Steele, meets 'hot, sexy billionaire' (85) Christian Grey, a sexual 'Dominant' in need of a submissive, and discovers sexual pleasure through her orgasmic experiences in his 'Red Room of Pain'. This pleasure, we are encouraged to infer, is the source of her (and the reader's vicarious) 'liberation'.

Criticism of E. L. James's work often reveals a tendency to malign popular female reading habits and tastes; the readers of E. L. James's work have sometimes been castigated as dupes, and the novels stand accused of lulling readers into a dangerous state of masochistic vulnerability (a UK domestic-abuse charity reportedly proposed publicly burning the book).[13] The idea of romance fiction as a 'low', and even a dangerous genre, and of female readers as stupid and/

or vulnerable, is at play in many responses to the novels. I am conscious of this gendered element of *Fifty Shades* criticism as I use the term 'bathos': the tendency to stigmatise female reading tastes in particular as 'low' is apparent in Pope's original work. In initiating the satirical idea of bathos, Pope connects particular types of bathetic lowness to the feminine: a 'principal branch of the *Alamode*', he tell us, is 'the Prurient, a style greatly advanced and honoured of late by the ... encouragement of the ladies not unsuccessfully introduced into the drawing-room'.[14] Sedgwick, among others, has drawn attention to the historical 'devaluation of many aspects of women's characteristic experience and culture' as they are expressed in particular genres.[15] My intention in focusing on *Fifty Shades* as bathetic is not to demean female readers in general or to malign popular contemporary female taste as low. I do not seek, as much criticism seems to, to censoriously produce a generalised, hypothetical female reader as a regressive, masochistic dupe. What I seek to explore is the way in which James's writing allows and contributes to the very construction of femininity as 'lowness': in producing a bathetic depiction of the fainting female body, through travestied moments of past female powerlessness, James's writing is complicit with historical denigrations of female subjectivity and taste.

The different bathetic elements of James's writing (sinking down; sinking backwards; sinking as a specifically feminine habit) are literalised through the figure of the fainting female form. The swoons and faints in James's work metonymically figure a journey to the nadir that is bathos, and give bathos a symbolic gender. In the reading that follows, we will see that to 'fall' in love in these novels is an admission of female physical insufficiency in the face of masculine financial protection and power, a process of feminine disequilibrium that is rebalanced in romance clichés in thrall to the erectness of capital; that to fall in love in James's world is to faint into the bathetic void of the promise of liberation, and into a travestied version of the past.

Pope uses the ironic notion of the 'felicity of falling' to describe a contrast between the high and the low; it is less well-known that he also uses the term to describe a temporal regression, a falling backwards into literary pastiche. Pope describes the manner in which popular work frequently discards the 'rules of the ancients' while also having a magpie eye for the reuse of material. Bathetic literary borrowing distorts and travesties the materials it draws on: the 'Parrots' of the literary world, for instance, 'repeat another's words in ... a hoarse, odd voice, that makes them seem their own', while the ironic figure of the 'true genius', 'when he finds anything lofty or shining ... will have the skill to bring it down, take off the gloss, or quite discharge the colour, by some ingenious circumstance, or periphrase, some addition'.[16] Bathos, then, involves a downwards trajectory that is also a sinking back towards past instances of lofty writing, bringing that writing low in the process of its reuse.

Fifty Shades, through its frequent depictions of feminine faints and its (re)use of swooning as a historical literary trope, has then, I suggest, a bathetic relationship to its literary precedents. *Fifty Shades* began life as *Twilight* (2004) fan fiction, and draws heavily on the conventions of vampire fiction; however, my main focus in the reading that follows will be the relationship between *Fifty Shades* and other historical correspondents, specifically Thomas Hardy's *Tess of the D'Urbervilles* (1891). It is through a blundering re-enactment of Tess's experience of courtship and her swoons that *Fifty Shades* exhibits its most spectacular tendency towards bathetic travesty. Arguing that *Fifty Shades* is bathetic is slightly different from arguing that its gender politics are regressive; these novels involve a simultaneous invocation of and denial of the past, whereby past female abjection is celebrated in a manner that disavows the specificities of that abjection. *Fifty Shades* reuses historical material to produce its own bathetic contemporary; the 'thin' atmosphere of the present moment in these novels is spun out of a repurposed literary past and the texture of history disappears to almost nothing in the process. The bathos of James's writing, then, resides in distorted echoes and amnesiac pastiche.

The felicity of falling

When Anastasia Steele first meets the billionaire CEO Christian Grey, she falls head over heels: tripping at the threshold she finds herself, 'on [her] hands and knees in the doorway to Mr Grey's office'.[17] It is this prone introduction that leads Grey to pursue Ana as a candidate for the role of submissive, and it is her physical fall that begins the domino-clatter of her falling for Grey. This is the first in an array of somatic demonstrations that Ana's control of her body is now ceded to Grey. She admits frequent paralysis in his presence, or in the presence of demonstrations of his wealth, and her first few meetings with him are characterised by repeated expressions of her errant affective and physical reactions to him: she blushes and flushes, she shivers, she quivers, her heart rate accelerates, she flutteringly blinks, her 'eyelids matching [her] heart rate', her legs turn to 'Jell-O'. 'Desperately I scrabble around for my equilibrium', she tells us; but she is rendered profoundly incapable of physically composing herself. And the most extreme example of this disequilibrium is her liability to lose physical balance, and then consciousness.

Her very first experience of desire is articulated in the context of a physical fall: 'It all happens so fast – one minute I'm falling, the next I'm in his arms and he's holding me tightly against his chest … And for the first time in twenty-one years, I want to be kissed.'[18] Grey does not kiss her at this point, and Ana experiences extreme humiliation as a result. She goes to a nightclub with friends and gets drunk to the point of extreme physical disarray. Grey arrives (like the millionaire vigilante Batman, apparently able to track her down whenever and wherever she might be) and she vomits spectacularly in front of him. Her humiliation and abjection in the face of the loss of physical control are crucial factors in her experience of their courtship: she describes herself as 'swamped with shame, disgusted with myself'.[19] This humiliation is the beginning of sexual pleasure for Ana: 'I feel weak, still drunk, embarrassed, exhausted, mortified, and, on some strange level, absolutely off-the-charts thrilled … somewhere deep, deep down my muscles clench deliciously'.[20] Her physical mortification continues and she begins, 'to feel faint. He notices my dizziness and grabs me before I fall and hoists me into his arms, holding me close to his chest like a child … if he wasn't clutching me so tightly, I'm sure I would swoon at his feet'.[21] As soon as he lets go of her, Ana swoons proper: 'My head begins to swim, oh no … and I can feel the floor coming up to meet my face … I pass out in Christian Grey's arms.'[22] Ana's loss of physical control climaxes in this swoon and Grey catches her.

When Ana's relationship to Grey becomes sexual, she describes her newly discovered orgasmic potential in terms of this initiatory disequilibrium: falling in love becomes falling apart. As Grey pins her down, pulling her hair and violently kissing her, he puts all her senses into 'disarray'; when she first comes, she 'fall(s) apart in his hands, [her] body convulsing and shattering into a thousand pieces'; she 'splinter(s) into a million pieces underneath him'; she is 'coming apart at the seams'.[23]

Ana's orgasms are repeatedly described as the experience of shattering and disintegration, terms that recall Leo Bersani's descriptions of sexuality as constitutionally masochistic. As discussed in Chapter 1, Bersani re-reads Freud's key texts on the development of infantile sexuality to suggest that sexuality is the by-product of experiences when they reach a certain level of *intensity*. This intensity, Bersani tells us, is experienced as a shattering for the infant, and any intensity will be experienced as a sexual pleasure when it is strong enough to shatter a certain stability or equilibrium of the self. Sexuality might, therefore, 'be thought of as a tautology for masochism'.[24] And if sexuality is 'constituted as a kind of psychic shattering, as a threat to the stability and integrity of the self', Bersani argues, then: 'sexuality would be that which is intolerable to the structured self'.[25] We are '"shattered" into an ego-shattering sexuality'[26] that is a kind of disintegration of the self rather than its triumph.[27]

For Bersani, in his early work at least, this masochistic shattering of the self, through sex as 'self-abolition', opens the way for radical new modes of selfhood and society. Might we, then, see Ana's introduction to masochism in *Fifty Shades* as an initiation into the radical possibility for transformation that Bersani tracks through self-shattering? The source of Ana's 'delicious' pleasure certainly seems to reside in the intensity of her experience of Grey and of her somatic reactions to him: blushing, vomiting, swooning and ecstatic shattering. And perhaps these descriptions of sexual shattering, or *ébranlement*, are one of the reasons these books have reverberated so spectacularly with female readers.

However, a detailed reading of the *Fifty Shades* novels highlights the failure of a radical or liberatory charge to self-shattering in the *female* subject, when an imputed propensity to shatter becomes the pretext for the patriarchal status quo to protect (control) female bodies. And this reveals to us that it's necessary to inflect Bersani's claims for the radical potential of 'self-abolition' with a bathetic counter-history of the exploitation of woman's imputed 'masochism' and lack of self-possession.[28] Hélène Cixous warns us that: 'One can, of course, as History has always done, exploit feminine reception through alienation. A woman, by her opening up, is open to being "possessed", which is to say, dispossessed of herself.'[29] The kind of radical potential that Bersani glimpses in the 'self-abolition' of the masochistic subject is a potentiality that can also be exploited. And in the disintegrative self-abolition that is Ana's sexual pleasure in *Fifty Shades*, we witness a 'possession'; following the breaking down of her orgasm, Ana will be reconstituted according to Grey's specifications. Her tendency to sink places her at risk of a takeover.

The remaking of Miss Anastasia Steele

Ana, and all other women who encounter Grey, are described as being perpetually on the verge of passing out in his 'swoon-worthy'[30] presence; Ana gets tired of 'watching [the women] all swoon'.[31] When Ana swoons, Grey is always there to catch her, rebalancing her according to his equilibrium – just as when she explodes into orgasm, he pieces her back together into an ever more submissive shape. Ana's pleasure in passing out becomes synonymous with ceding control to Grey: 'I think I'm going to faint', she tells us early in the first novel, as Grey pilots her in a helicopter, 'My fate is in his hands.'[32] This possible faint foreshadows her ceding her 'fate' to him in all directions as the novels progress.

In the first novel, Ana is described at a transformative point in her life: finishing college, giving up her job, her apartment and her car in an attempt to start a working life in a new city (Seattle), she nevertheless describes 'the biggest change of all' as 'Christian Grey'.[33] The change Grey initially proposes is a sado-masochistically codified one: that Ana be the submissive to his Dominant, 'to willingly surrender yourself to me in all things ... To please me.'[34] The first novel revolves around Ana's misgivings about such an arrangement, specifically focusing on a supposedly legal contract of sexual submission (reproduced in detail). As the trilogy progresses, the couple move towards married life, through which Grey is emotionally 'rehabilitated', dispensing with the need for a sado-masochistic contract, which is symbolically superseded by the marriage contract. The dominant/submissive dichotomy remains the blueprint of their relationship, and Ana has realised that what she most wants is to 'please him': '[Y]es, that's exactly what I do want to do. I want him to be damned delighted with me. It's a revelation.'[35]

The later novels, revealing her series of faints and swoons to have been moments of transformative possibility, chart a sort of neo-Pygmalion remaking of Ana according to Grey's turbo-capitalist version of female beauty and civility. This begins with the initiation into a beauty regimen: the submissive contract includes clauses on mandatory exercise (a personal trainer four times a week), clothes (all items to be approved by Grey), and 'Personal Hygiene/Beauty'. By the end of the novels Ana has capitulated to the punishing regime of 'grooming' that she initially felt was 'time consuming, humiliating and painful',[36] and records the results in a way that would make any TV makeover show producer proud:

> My body is so different these days. It's changed subtly since I've known him ... I've become leaner and fitter, and my hair is glossy and well cut. My nails are manicured, my feet pedicured, my eyebrows threaded and beautifully shaped.[37]

Grey's control of Ana's body is yet more invasively exercised in relation to her fertility. He arranges for a gynaecologist to come to his apartment to administer contraception, and despite her initial grumblings ('It's my body'), she relents ('Yes, my body is his ... he knows it better than I do'),[38] agreeing to a contraceptive injection. That both Grey and Ana see her body as his property is emphasised and eroticised everywhere in the novels. He repeatedly touches her intimately, mouthing the claim 'Mine', and by the third novel she joyously claims: 'You own my body and my soul.'[39] 'He is master of my universe', Ana remarks elsewhere, playing on the original title of the online serialisation of the novels, and on the fantasy of masculine omnipotence it perpetuates.[40] This omnipotence is primarily exercised through Grey's power to own everything around him, including Ana. When Grey buys the publishing company that employs Ana, for instance, making him her boss's boss, Ana becomes his employee as well as his 'asset'. He insists that she change her professional name upon their marriage: 'I'm just looking after my assets ... Some of them need rebranding.'[41]

Female jeopardy and the eroticisation of physical vulnerability

In order for Grey's possession and control of Ana's body to seem necessary within the world of the novels, it is incumbent on the reader to see Ana, as female romantic love object, as perpetually at physical risk. This risk increases over the course of the novels, so that they can be read as exercises in escalating female jeopardy. At the beginning of the romance, Ana's inability to stay conscious functions as the early sign of a developing symptomatology of female fragility and insufficiency that will narratively necessitate Grey taking control of Ana's body for her own good. Grey is there to catch Ana when the ground rushes towards her in her swoons; he is there to repeatedly instruct her, 'Breathe, Anastasia', when her body fails, and her 'medulla oblongata has neglected to fire any synapses to make [her breathe]'.[42] The novels suggest that our hapless heroine might actually expire without Grey's timely interventions and instructions regarding basic physical processes, like remaining upright and respiring.

Later in the novels, Ana's pregnancy means that Grey's control of her body is once again figured as necessary. Grey makes the unilateral decision that their second child will be born through elective caesarean because of his perception of the risk involved in natural delivery: 'I am not going through that again,' Grey selflessly decrees, 'You nearly fucking died last time.'[43] He insists upon this, despite Ana's stated desire 'to push him out myself' and her very different assessment of the risk posed during the first birth: 'I did not nearly die.' Grey is implacable in his protectiveness: 'Christian is still treating me like I'm made of glass', Ana tells the reader towards the end of trilogy: 'He still won't let me go to work.'[44]

The risk of swooning, then, is part of the narrative production of rising risk attendant on Ana as her relationship with Grey develops. External risks increasingly threaten our unhappy couple, structuring the plot of the two later novels. Ana is presented as being frequently subject to unwanted male attention, for example, from which Grey always rescues her. These risks necessitate Ana being permanently accompanied by a security team, her confinement to Grey's apartment in his absence, and her obeying Grey's safety instructions. After evading a workplace assault, Ana literally falls into Grey's arms outside her office: 'I haven't eaten all day, and as the very unwelcome surge of adrenaline recedes, my legs give out beneath me and I sink to the ground ... all I can think is *He's here. My love is here* ... He scoops me up into his lap.'[45] Here Ana's faintness, her failure to eat, and her sexual assailability all converge to necessitate Grey's violent intervention on her behalf. Ana's vulnerability – exemplified over and over in these novels in her propensity to swoon and faint, and her implied vulnerability to rape – is the romantic context for Grey's power over her.

The swoon and bathetic rape nostalgia

If Ana's faints spectacularly symptomatise her fragility and insufficiency, they are also a deliberate form of gender anachronism. Ana exhibits a clumsy nostalgia for a romanticised re-imagining of past female powerlessness, largely produced from travestied readings of iconic moments of literary romance. Ana, we should remember, is a student of literature, and her frequent use of the word 'swoon' as a singularly feminine action is one of the ways in which the novels mark themselves as works of nostalgia. Ana's lexicon of female sexual experience (a woman might 'swoon' or 'succumb', be 'comely' or 'compliant') also shows that historical literary precedents are the immediate imaginative context for her experience of romance.

References to Ana's favourite book, Thomas Hardy's *Tess of the d'Urbervilles*, are laced through the novels. At first, Ana seems to straightforwardly lament Tess's circumstances and fate: 'Damn, that woman was in the wrong place at the wrong time in the wrong century.'[46] But perceived similarities between Ana and Tess become increasingly significant to Ana's experience of the erotic. A set of valuable Hardy first editions is one of the first gifts Grey makes to Ana. When she visits his enormous apartment, her awe at his wealth echoes Tess's first sight of the d'Urberville mansion: 'I feel like Tess Durbeyfield looking at the new house that belongs to the notorious Alec d'Urberville.'[47] And the possibilities for her relationship to Grey are apparently the rock and the hard place offered to Tess: 'I could hold you to some impossibly high ideal like Angel Clare or debase you completely like Alec d'Urberville', Grey generously suggests. 'If there are only two choices, I'd take the debasement', Ana replies. Later, following a dream in which Grey feeds Ana strawberries and she is tethered and 'mute', the strawberry scene in *Tess* comes into her mind.[48] And when Grey proposes their dominant/submissive relationship, the range of Ana's possible responses is confined to her (mis)reading of the minds of bygone literary heroines: 'Elizabeth Bennet would be outraged, Jane Eyre too frightened, and Tess would succumb, just as I have.'[49]

After Grey first spanks her, Ana tells him she feels 'demeaned, debased, abused and assaulted'. 'How very Tess Durbeyfield of you,' Grey interposes. 'Do you really feel like this or do you think you ought to feel like this?'[50] Grey's suggestion here is that Ana's response to his physical domination is conditioned by nineteenth-century mores. 'Don't waste your energy on guilt, feelings of wrongdoing, etc.', he counsels. 'You need to free your mind and listen to your body.'[51] But it is not Ana's *reluctance* about Grey's sadistic proposition that is anachronistic; in fact, her willingness to experience this *as erotic* is mediated through the fantasies she produces from romanticised readings of past female sexual powerlessness: her anachronistic travesties are the necessary precondition for their erotic relationship.

Ana's process of aphrodisiacal literary travesty begins with her descriptions of Grey as her 'knight' ('a white knight in shining, dazzling armor – a classic romantic hero – Sir Gawain or Sir Lancelot').[52] That this description rapidly admits the possibility of 'darkness' ('Dark knight and white knight, it's a fitting metaphor'; 'My shining white-and-dark knight'),[53] unwittingly hints at medieval scholar Jill Mann's description of the problem of 'classic romantic' courtship as a problem of mutuality. Mann highlights the ritualisation of female sexual reluctance embedded in some of the earliest Western precedents for our ideas of romantic love: the founding texts of courtly love. Describing Andreas Capellanus's *Treatise on Love* (*c.*1186), widely regarded as expressing 'the thought of a great epoch, which explains the secret of a civilization',[54] Jill Mann describes a cynical guide, containing 'none of the behaviour which is now routinely ascribed to "the medieval code of courtly love"'.[55] This sort of courtship, typified by male sexual aggression and female reluctance, suggests Mann, feeds the male fantasy that 'female acquiescence retrospectively sanctions male coercion, and reveals reluctance to have been a merely ritual female role'. Ritualised male aggression and ritualised female reluctance in certain courtly texts 'preserves the fiction that the woman yields to the man's sexual desire, not her own'.[56] In Mann's reading, the knight is an early motif of coercion rather than gallantry.

In Hardy's *Tess*, written over 700 years later, ritualised female sexual reluctance is depicted as a key problem of heterosexual courtship and a source of potential tragedy. At Tess's first meeting with Alec d'Urberville, the 'strawberry scene' which is the referent of Ana's erotic dream, Alec 'insists' on forcing a strawberry into Tess's mouth. She parts her lips 'in a slight distress' and takes the strawberry, 'half-pleased, half-reluctant'.[57] The possibility for this ambivalence to be interpreted as part of the ritual of courtship forms the background to Alec's rape of Tess. And her indebtedness to him allows her manner to suggest ritualised reluctance to his imagination even when she is most definite in her feelings: she emphatically fails to develop any 'tender feelings' for Alec, we are told, '[b]ut she was more pliable under his hands than a mere companionship would have made her, owing to her unavoidable dependence upon his mother, and ... upon him' (75). The potentially treacherous terrain around perceived female 'coyness' is traversed again when Angel Clare attempts to court Tess:

> His experience of women was great enough for him to be aware that the negative often meant nothing more than the preface to the affirmative; and it was little enough for him not to know that in the manner of the present negative there lay a great exception to the dallying of coyness. (200)

While Hardy's narrator here seems to present the dallying of 'coyness' as an accepted ritual of courtship, at least within the minds of male characters, the obfuscation of female intent or desire that such rituals create is made clear by Clare's failure to understand the situation. The expectation of female coyness is itself part of the brutal violence perpetuated against Tess. 'Her seeming indecision was, in fact, more than indecision: it was misgiving', the narrator tells us elsewhere; but in relation to Alec's ardent pursuit, Tess is forced to develop a 'strategic silence', and is led into a situation in which clearly communicated female consent becomes impossible: '[H]ow can I say yes or no—', Tess exclaims (63, 68, 87). The broken impossibility of Tess's expression of consent is the harbinger of her rape.

In this social and romantic context, the impossibility of effective female expression is figured as a kind of death (Tess is 'Maiden no More') and male desire is haunted by the possibility of its necrophilic urge. The woodland space ('The Chase') in which Alec assails Tess becomes a treacherous place of death and sylvan transformation, from which Tess's sobs have been heard to echo (109). And when Angel Clare discovers Tess's past, the experiences hidden behind his imputation of 'coyness', she is poised to become the dead wife he then fantasises. His altered view is 'deadening' to her, so much that 'she staggered' (260). Angel steps forward, and Tess's swoon and his desire to catch her become a kind of dumb-show of her desired death. A few nights later, Clare sleep-walks into his new wife's bedroom, murmuring, 'Dead, dead, dead!' He wraps her in 'a sheet as in a shroud. Then lifting her from the bed with as much respect as one would show to a dead body, he carried her across the room' (280). Tess suffers herself to be borne out of the house in the manner of a corpse, and 'she lay in his arms in this precarious position with a sense rather of luxury than of terror. If they could only fall together, and both be dashed to pieces' (280–281). Angel holds Tess at the edge of a river bank and she is briefly poised at the point of no return. But he proceeds with her to a ruined church, places her in an empty stone coffin and kisses her.

To fetishise Tess's relation to Alec, as E. L. James's Ana does, is to entirely miss the darkest elements of Hardy's account: that the impossibility of female expression makes corpses of women and symbolic murderers of men. The result of this is Tess's desire for both her and Angel to be smashed to death, to 'fall together'. Tess's masochism is most profound in her continued desire for Angel despite this deathly context. She begs him to kill her ('It is you, my ruined husband, who ought to strike the blow. I think I should love you more if that were possible, if you could bring yourself to do it' (271)) and glories in their somnambulant death procession, hoping for mutual destruction.

Ana's fetishisation of Tess's desire for *Alec* is therefore a spectacular travesty of Hardy's *Tess*, and it eroticises a relation that Hardy describes as abhorrent. E. L. James's Ana is in many ways the antithesis of Hardy's Tess: Tess is frequently described as physically robust, and will not fully swoon or give way in front of men even when she is at the point of physical collapse; she refuses to take any financial support from Alec until she is forced to do so by her poverty, entering into a relationship that is clearly depicted as coercive; she undergoes a self-imposed process of unbeautifying in order to try to repel male attention, attacking her eyebrows and covering her hair so that she resembles a 'mommet' (a scarecrow); she realises that the greatest risks to her come from the men who claim to love her; she murders her 'true' rapist husband and is hanged. This is at total odds with the depiction of Ana, who takes pleasure in her physical fragility and frequent faints, luxuriates in her new-found wealth, finally revels in her makeover, and seeks marriage and protection from the man who violently dominates her. Ana's celebration of Tess's abjection strips Hardy's novel of its most complex and disturbing elements, euphemising a violent and tragic struggle into a swoon of ecstatic submission.

Happy endings: Succumbing to the power of capital

In Grey's version of the world, possession and control of others are his earned right. Grey cites Andrew Carnegie in moral justification of his dominant practices: '"A man who acquires the ability to take full possession of his own mind may take full possession of anything else to which he is justly entitled." I like control of myself and those around me.'[58] In another version of reading as travesty, Grey gives scant consideration to what 'just' might mean here, or to Carnegie's other bon mots, such as: 'A man who dies rich, dies shamed.' There is nothing in Grey's world that is not made available to him through money and he describes himself 'exercising my democratic right as an American citizen, entrepreneur, and consumer to purchase whatever I damn well please'.[59]

The initiation of Ana into Grey's consumerist world-view is the final proof of his exploitation of her swooning receptivity. This initiation begins at the very start of their romance with the proffering of extravagant gifts. Ana is at first troubled by these gifts, the sums of money they represent and the debt to Grey their acceptance might connote. But the novels increasingly glory in describing the gifts and their cost: Ana's shiny new 'iPad',[60] for example; or the whole new wardrobe of luxury clothes Grey buys her, with the price labels helpfully left on, so that we can marvel over a black bustier costing $540 and a pair of Louboutins at $3,295;[61] the diamond earrings from Cartier; the constant popping corks of bottles of 'Cristal' or 'our favorite, Bollinger';[62] the procession of luxury cars (always Audis). Ana's initial consumerist reluctance seems to act as an equivalent to the traditional romance trope of ritualised female sexual reluctance, and the seduction/rape Grey must achieve is partly in terms of Ana's consent to his version of consumer capitalism. Ana must work at accepting the kind of money lavished on her, and her initial 'guilt', 'a familiar unease that's always present when I try to wrap my head around Christian's wealth',[63] is presented as an individualised psychological problem to be resolved rather than an index of structural injustice. Grey's impoverished and abusive early life become the moral justification for his finally 'winning' the game of capitalism, rather than the grounds for any interrogation of its rules. And Ana becomes the perfect consumerist neophyte. She registers her reluctance, but is seduced into enjoyment. In the final epilogue to the novels, Ana describes herself having eradicated all guilt over her lavish lifestyle: 'I relax, my body turning to Jell-O ... I should feel guilty for feeling this joy, this completeness, but I don't. Life right here, right now, life is good, and I've learned to appreciate it and live in the moment like my husband.'[64] The ritualised female sexual reluctance of romance traditions is transposed here onto Ana's reluctance and then seduction by luxury.

What James provides in Ana's final submission to Grey as master and protector, is an eroticised dramatisation of Luce Irigaray's concept of the 'phallic proxy'. Writing critically about the Freudian account of female sexual development that informs much mainstream conjecture about femininity, Irigaray describes the way in which 'the castration complex' casts the young girl as necessarily accepting 'the harsh reality of a sexual "mutilation" or "amputation" ... She must resign herself to the "disadvantage" anatomy has in store for her'.[65] According to this system of development, the only way for the girl to 'redeem her personal value, and value in general', is through the seduction of the father, and consequent father figures, to 'persuade him to express, if not admit, some interest in her'. He might then act as her 'phallic proxy'. Irigaray describes the painful coincidence of guilt and physical illness produced by this perceived (and projected) female insufficiency:

> Mutilated, wounded, humiliated, overwhelmed by a feeling of inferiority that can never be 'cured'. In sum, women are definitively castrated. Their guilt would remain mute: active, of course, but unutterable, ineffable, *to be expressed only by the body*. They would give themselves up to be punished – by the accomplished fact of castration – without knowing what they had done wrong, or even what they were suffering from, what they endured.[66] (My emphasis)

It is an overwhelming sense of inferiority that we can see expressing itself somatically in Ana's swoons, and it is the enforced sense of her insufficiencies that leads her back to becoming the little girl/ little wife who is desirous of a 'Christian Grey Fifty Shades punishment fuck'.[67] Irigaray identifies the 'powerful interests' vested in, and the 'misprision' crucial to, such an account of female sexuality. If this account continues to be adhered to, 'women would remain entangled in a masochistic economy that certain psychoanalysts, male and female, do not hesitate to designate as the condition of women's pleasure. These analysts thus ratify, or enact the status quo into psychic laws, and perpetuate it under the sanction of "normality".'[68] The *Fifty Shades* novels perpetuate this account; they depict Ana's errant somatic expressions (her faints, her stumbles, her nausea) as part of a symbolic economy that designates masochism as the precondition of female pleasure, and the seduction of a powerful man as a form of redemption.

Angela Carter's transformative faint

James's work, I have argued, is preoccupied with the art of a specifically feminine sinking: it repeatedly figures the fainting female form, travestying its literary precedents into bathos. Nostalgia – itself a desire for temporal sinking back – is embedded in these novels as the eroticisation of past female powerlessness, largely produced through (mis)readings of iconic literary moments. And this studied anachronism produces a romanticised re-imagining of past female abjection that denies a material history of suffering.

As a final contrast to this bathetic approach to the past (literary and otherwise), I find myself falling towards the work of Angela Carter, and a story which hinges on a very different depiction of female faintness: 'The Bloody Chamber' (1979).[69] In her non-fiction tract on pornography, *The Sadeian Woman*, Carter sees the Marquis de Sade's Justine as 'the start of a kind of self-regarding female masochism': 'a personification of the pornography' of the self-venerated condition of female *unfreedom* which she sees as an 'aetiology of the female condition in the twentieth century'.[70] The female masochist's obscenity, according to Carter, resides in the 'false expectation' that her submissiveness will do her any good.

As an exploration of female masochism, E. L. James's depiction of Grey's 'Red Room of Pain' was anticipated and already long superseded by Carter's depiction of the Bloody Chamber, the eponymous torture chamber in her reworking of the tale of Bluebeard. Carter's young, poor, virginal narrator marries a marquis, the 'richest man in France', and is given a wedding gift: 'A choker of rubies, two inches wide, like an extraordinary precious slit throat' (11). This choker has been worn by the Marquis's grandmother in a decadent gesture of solidarity with 'the aristos who'd escaped the guillotine' and who developed 'an ironic fad of tying a red ribbon round their necks at just the point where the blade would have sliced it through, a red ribbon like the memory of a wound' (11). The 'cruel necklace', then, is the glittering symbol of the young wife's entry into the grotesque world of obscene and violent wealth. And her admiration of herself wearing the necklace, her self-regard ('the cruel necklace became me'), reveals her potential for corruption within that world: 'I hardly recognised myself' (20). Female desire in the context of this kind of marriage (which makes the marriage bed simultaneously the brothel bed and the butcher's slab, according to Carter)[71] is experienced by the girl with nauseated horror: 'I was aghast to feel myself stirring', she tells us, 'I felt a vague desolation within me … there had awoken a certain queasy craving like the cravings of pregnant women for the taste of coal or chalk or tainted food, for the renewal of his caresses … I longed for him. And he disgusted me' (20–21). There is no pastoralising of masochistic female desire here; the craving for this kind of sexual contract identifies itself as part of a history of female incarceration and nauseated, forced adaptation.

Carter produces a proliferating sense of gothic depth in the layered texture of her writing here; the tale's allusiveness, its baroque surface of imagistic callings back (to fairy tales and to Sade; to mythologised Transylvanian and Italian aristocracies; to the Bible and to colonial conquest narratives; to the occult and to the Symbolists; to The Terror and the Spanish Inquisition; to the Orient and to Paris), mean that we are never just in one place when we read Carter. The queasiness our narrator experiences is reproduced in the reader as a queasy sense of time out of joint, a temporal seasickness. This, of course, is of one of the initiatory features of the gothic as described by Nicholas Royle: 'the making explicit (but therefore also the peculiar enfolding or complication) of a logic of anachrony ... meddling with time, a temporal meddler'.[72] The gothic, Royle has suggested, is always concerned with a temporal unsettling, with a return of the past or the repressed. Carter's writing is composed of resonant repeats, so that the echo of many histories strikes through her prose; 'The Bloody Chamber' reveals James's anachronism to be nothing more than a thin feint of literary allusion. Anastasia Steele presents her literary heroines as minor footnotes to her own situation. She treats her literary precedents as her backdrop; she repapers literary history as though it is the interior of one of her newly acquired recherché residences.

Despite its vampiric roots, then, E. L. James's writing is so bare of effective allusion that it stands as a kind of antithesis to the heavy temporal-tampering texture of the gothic. Carter's work, in contrast, is piled with the affective power of the many different pasts she evokes. And this gives 'The Bloody Chamber' a dreadful sense of building inevitability. The past bricks us into this densely allusive story and the reading experience becomes one of rising claustrophobia, as the castle walls thicken, seemingly inescapably, around our narrator. But at the last moment, Carter surprises us. This is what makes her such a powerful inheritor and transformer of the gothic tradition: she utilises its temporal swoops, but redirects all the power of its taphephobic tendencies towards the possibility of new futures. In 'The Bloody Chamber', the seeming inevitability of masochistic capitulation is transformed at the last moment.

The narrator faces the spectre of past feminine acquiescence to cruelty: when she discovers the Marquis's horde of murdered wives, the greatest horror is their seeming pleasure – the 'worst thing was, the dead lips smiled' (28). 'Were there jewels enough in all his safes to recompense me for this predicament', she lies in 'the lazy, midday bed of the rich' wondering (22). If we do not stir from this imaginative bed, Carter's fairy tale suggests, our prostrate bodies will be glittered over with rubies that will bite into our flesh. The possibility of transformation here stands in stark contrast to masochistic adaptation to the rich husband's murderous exorbitance, and is glimpsed through the figure of an 'indomitable' mother who has 'beggared herself' and will finally save the narrator from her husband. Our narrator, realising she has 'sold [herself] to this fate', directs her imaginative energy towards the possibility of *escape*, rather than accepting the queasy consolation of tainted pleasures. And this gothic détournement is in part achieved through Carter's inventive deployment of a faint. With her 'nerves of steel', our narrator faints only once: she stumbles across a blind boy, her gentle piano-tuner and, 'after the dreadful revelation of that bloody chamber, it was his tender look that made me faint' (32). The narrator swoons at the beautiful possibility of sexual relations transformed from violence into tenderness. She is not fragile; her passing out is not evidence of feminine incapacity, nor of a capitulation to a sado-masochistic economy of desire. Carter gives us a witty reworking of the historically gendered swoon here; the faint becomes a hopeful turning point, occasioned by the surprising gentleness of a boy, an ineffectual piano-tuner, who is loved in all his masculine frailty. There is no bathetic evacuation of, or capitulation to, the past in Carter's writing; the past is powerfully in play here, but is reworked to produce new and surprising endings. Tenderness, this tale suggests, might finally transform gender relations, and render fearful feminine swooning obsolete. But experiences of the past must be felt, in all their strange and painful specificities, in order to make new futures possible.

Notes

1 Patricia Highsmith, *Carol* (London: Bloomsbury, 2010 [1952]), first published pseudonymously as *The Price of Salt*. All references in the text will be to this edition.
2 Highsmith, 'Afterword' to *Carol*, p. 308.
3 Robert McRuer, *Crip Theory: Cultural Signs of Queerness and Disability* (New York: New York University Press, 2006).
4 Eve Kosofsky Sedgwick, 'Queer and Now', in *Tendencies* (London: Routledge, 1994), pp. 1–20 at 5.
5 *Ibid.*, p. 8.
6 Val McDermid, 'Foreword' to *Carol*, p .v.
7 Carol was originally published under the pseudonym Claire Morgan as *The Price of Salt* in 1952.
8 'E. L. James's Fifty Shades Trilogy Sets New Record', *Independent* (July 3, 2012); the trilogy occupied all three top slots of the bestseller lists for a record-breaking length of time in 2012 and made E. L. James the highest-earning author in the world at that time.

9 Alexander Pope, *Peri Bathous, or the Art of Sinking in Poetry* in *The Major Works*, ed. Pat Rogers (Oxford: Oxford University Press, 2008 [1728]), pp. 195–239. All references in the text will be to this edition.
10 For some contemporary, critically astute explorations of bathos, see Sarah Crangle and Peter Nicholls, *On Bathos: Literature, Art, Music* (London: Bloomsbury, Continuum, 2012). See also my previous work on bathos and masochism: Naomi Booth, 'Bathetic Masochism and the Shrinking Woman', *New Formations* 83 (2014), 47–64.
11 Keston Sutherland, 'What is called "Bathos"?', in *Stupefaction: A Radical Anatomy of Phantoms* (London, New York and Calcutta: Seagull Press, 2011). Here Sutherland suggests that the well-known OED definition of bathos as 'ludicrous descent from the elevated to the commonplace in writing or speech; anticlimax', fails to capture the concept's complexity, and is a misreading of Pope's deployment of the term. For Sutherland, both Pope and Marx deploy bathos as an instrument of public attack, to lambast work which has the absolute value nil: bathos is 'put into words by the satirist who attackingly discovers to public view the absolute destitution of truth or beauty' (p. 208).
12 E. L. James, *Fifty Shades of Grey* (London: Arrow Books, 2012) (my italics).
13 '"Fifty Shades of Grey" Copies to be Burned By UK Domestic Abuse Charity, Wearside Women In Need', *Huffington Post* (August 27, 2012).
14 Pope, *Peri Bathous*, p. 228.
15 Her focus being the sentimental in this instance: Sedgwick, *Epistemology of the Closet*, p. 144.
16 Pope, *Peri Bathous*, pp. 206, 212.
17 James, *Fifty Shades*, p. 7.
18 *Ibid.*, p. 48.
19 *Ibid.*, p. 60.
20 *Ibid.*, p. 62.
21 *Ibid.*, pp. 61, 63.
22 *Ibid.*, p. 64.
23 *Ibid.*, pp. 116, 118.
24 Leo Bersani, *The Freudian Body: Psychoanalysis and Art* (New York: Columbia University Press, 1986), pp. 38–39.
25 *Ibid.*, pp. 60 and 38.
26 Bersani, describing in Laplanchian terms his work in the *Freudian Body* in 'Sociality and Sexuality', in *Is the Rectum a Grave?*, pp. 102–119, at p. 108.
27 'The self which the sexual shatters provides the basis in which sexuality is associated with power. It is possible to think of the sexual as, precisely, moving between a hyperbolic sense of self and a loss of all consciousness

of the self. But sex as self-hyperbole is, perhaps, a repression of sex as self-abolition. It inaccurately replicates self-shattering as psychic tumescence' (Bersani, 'Is the Rectum a Grave?', in *Is the Rectum a Grave?*, pp. 3–30, at p. 25).
28 Critics such as Paula J. Caplan, for example, have described the way masochism has been tendentiously applied to women as a social and medical term to serve dominant interests: 'A misogynist society has created a myriad of situations that make women unhappy. And then that same society uses the myth of women's masochism to blame the women themselves for their misery' (*The Myth of Women's Masochism* (Toronto: University of Toronto Press, 1985), p. 9). Feminist objections to the tendentious medical application of the term 'masochism' to women were made when psychiatrists and psychologists in the United States lobbied against the creation of the diagnostic category 'Masochistic Personality Disorder' by the American Psychiatric Association; protestors argued that it would be applied pejoratively, and near-exclusively, to female patients (John Leo, 'Behavior: Battling over Masochism', in *Time* (June 21, 2005), at www.time.com/time/magazine/article/0,9171,1074806-1,00.html (accessed October 17, 2012]).
29 Hélène Cixous, 'Sorties', in Hélène Cixous and Catherine Clément, *The Newly Born Woman* (Manchester: Manchester University Press, 1987), pp. 85–86.
30 E. L. James, *Fifty Shades Freed* (London: Arrow Books, 2012), p. 160.
31 E. L. James, *Fifty Shades Darker* (London: Arrow Books, 2012), p. 347.
32 James, *Fifty Shades*, p. 91.
33 Ibid., p. 302.
34 Ibid., p. 100.
35 Ibid.
36 James, *Fifty Shades*, p. 85.
37 James, *Fifty Shades Freed*, p. 41.
38 James, *Fifty Shades Darker*, p. 168.
39 Ibid., p. 232.
40 Ibid., p. 376. As mentioned earlier, the *Fifty Shades* novels appeared in an earlier serialised version online as *Masters of the Universe*. There are resonances here with the financial power as the delusion of omnipotence as described by Thomas Wolfe in his *Bonfire of the Vanities* (1987), in which a Wall Street financial trader thinks of himself as 'Master of the Universe'.
41 James, *Fifty Shades Freed*, p. 143.
42 James, *Fifty Shades*, p. 68.
43 James, *Fifty Shades Freed*, p. 547.

44 Ibid., p. 547.
45 Ibid., p. 370.
46 James, *Fifty Shades*, p. 21.
47 Ibid., p. 95.
48 Ibid., pp. 442, 444.
49 Ibid., p. 225.
50 Ibid., p. 293.
51 Ibid., p. 294.
52 Ibid., p. 69.
53 Ibid., p. 92; and *Fifty Shades Freed*, p. 89.
54 John Jay Parry, 'Introduction' to Andreas Capellanus, *The Art of Courtly Love* (New York: Columbia University Press, 1990).
55 Jill Mann, *Feminizing Chaucer* (Cambridge: D.S. Brewer, 2002), p. 80.
56 Ibid.
57 Thomas Hardy, *Tess of the d'Urbervilles: A Pure Woman* (Ware, Hertfordshire: Wordsworth Editions, 1992 [1891]), p. 52. All references in the text will be to this edition.
58 James, *Fifity Shades*, p. 12.
59 James, *Fifty Shades Darker*, p. 59.
60 Ibid., p. 39.
61 Ibid., p. 126.
62 James, *Fifty Shades Freed*, p. 88.
63 Ibid., p. 275.
64 James, *Fifty Shades Freed*, p. 533.
65 Luce Irigaray, *Speculum of the Other Woman* (Ithaca, NY: Cornell University Press, 1985), p. 87.
66 Ibid., p. 88.
67 James, *Fifty Shades Freed*, p. 40.
68 Irigaray, *Speculum of the Other Woman*, p. 98.
69 Angela Carter, *The Bloody Chamber and Other Stories* (London: Random House, 1995 [1979]). All references in the text will be to this edition.
70 Angela Carter, *The Sadeian Woman: An Exercise in Cultural History* (London: Virago, 1979), p. 57.
71 The narrator describes the 'formal disrobing of the bride' as 'a ritual from the brothel ... He in his London tailoring; she, bare as a lamb chop. Most pornographic of all confrontations. And so my purchaser unwrapped his bargain' (Carter, *The Bloody Chamber*, p. 15).
72 As described by Nicholas Royle in relation to Horace Walpole's first 'Gothic Story': *In Memory of Jacques Derrida* (Edinburgh: Edinburgh University Press, 2009), pp. 48–49.

Passing out: Contemporary catatonia

You walk into a small, cinema-dark room. The sound of breathing fills the space, though it's not like any breath you've heard before: amplified to fill the room, rasping and athletic, arriving in fast, violent cycles. There is a wall of light; strips of horizontal brightness strobe in sequence, ultra-bright, with each intake of breath. The woman's breathing is too ragged to be safely athletic: she's beginning to hyperventilate. It is so loud and flashing-bright in here that you blink with dizziness; but even then, there is no escape, because the light has strobed your retina and flashes up on the inside of your eyelids. And when you cover your eyes, the sound only gets more intense. You sit down. You sit in the dark against the wall as the ragged breathing becomes more desperate. And then it stops. Silence. Pitch black. An awful dark silence: you're trapped inside a black lung; a closing throat; a collapsing star; a dense, dying interior. Interminable termination. There's a wild flash of light and a low, animal howl. An ugly gargle in the throat. Phlegm and musculature and gummy sounds of the mouth. Broken and horribly intimate. The breath returning. Life coming back from the very brink. And then it starts again: the cycle of quickening breath, hyperventilation, passing out, dense blackness, revival.

Marianna Simnett's *Faint with Light* (2016) is a light and sound installation that records Simnett repeatedly passing out. When I went to see it at FACTLiverpool in May 2019, a gallery attendant came to check on me several times: Most people can only take a few seconds in here, she said.

The exhibition guide describes the installation as follows:

> The gesture of fainting serves as a motif which carries through Simnett's entire practice. *Faint with Light* was provoked by the story of her

Croatian grandfather, who survived a mass execution during the Holocaust when he lost consciousness and collapsed in front of a firing line. On numerous occasions, audience members have fainted in response to her work.[1]

Simnett's work is an intense performance of fainting that animates many of the qualities of swooning that have been of interest to me in proposing a poetics of passing out: aesthetic experience presented as a profound destabiliser of the body; the veneration of fainting as a measure of receptivity to art; experiences at the brink of life and death; excessive feeling, muteness and morbid disturbances of language; gendered and racialised performances of passing out; the power of the past to repeat itself through our bodies and to disturb the present.

Simnett's charged and affecting facsimile of her faints shows us something about the continuing power of the swoon to unnerve, and to function as an index of art and literature's power to affect an audience. But there's another ubiquitous, contemporary current of swooning that might seem to work in an altogether different direction: 'Swoon', *Urban Dictionary* tells us, is now used 'online as an action, to show that someone is attracted [*sic*] or interested in someone or something';[2] as in 'Ryan Gosling ... swoon'.[3] The internet now encourages us 'to swoon' at interior furnishings at swooneditions.com;[4] and at the latest film releases at 'FilmSwoon' blog.[5] Weekend supplements attempt to identify the releases that might cause 'this season's mass hipster swooning'.[6] This new version of swooning constitutes an ironic redefinition of language and 'action', of what verbs might *do*: to swoon can now be to note a consumer or cultural crush; it is an attestation of 'attraction or interest'; it overwrites conventional modes of embodied action with a virtual, ironic signal – it attests to bodily response in the absence of bodily response (typing replaces or displaces the physical swoon).

The swoon, I have argued in this study, has for millennia been deployed by writers who are interested in the extremes of physical and aesthetic experience, and it has often channelled the disruptive energy of the symbolically, morbidly feminine. Online '*swoons*' might at first seem to discharge swooning of this potential power, in (re)producing the swoon as ironic cliché. If, as I suggested in the introduction to this work, swooning can be thought of as paradigmatically literary phenomenon, is this online invocation of *swoon* paradigmatic of something changing – of a new, ironic way to verb in the world of online action?

The irony of the online *swoon*, puts me in mind of David Foster Wallace's critique in 'E Unibus Pluram'[7] of the ironic literary mode he saw in the work of many of his contemporaries. Foster Wallace, in an excoriating description of what he termed 'image-fiction', delineates a mode of writing that has absorbed postmodern literature and TV culture to produce a style of catatonic irony. This irony, Foster Wallace argues, outlasted its usefulness. What was once an effective mode of negation and critique becomes a 'dominant mode of hip expression'.[8] Irony becomes 'tiresome', 'enfeebling' and even oppressive in Foster Wallace's account of it, a sign that crisis has been co-opted into the banal. Foster Wallace objects to writing that institutes 'irony, narcissism, nihilism, stasis',[9] and looks forward a new kind of writing beyond the 'exhaustion' of US fiction, to the next wave of US literary 'rebels' who might treat 'troubles and emotions' with 'reverence and conviction' rather than with sardonic exhaustion.[10]

Foster Wallace's thinking produces an unstable and perhaps unsustainable binary through which irony is now supposed to work in opposition to emotion, reverence, conviction and meaning – a binary that is challenged by the work of the many critics and writers who continue to value irony as a powerful mode of negativity.[11] As my final thought, I want to return to the swoon as a potential crux point for how we might understand some of the effects of the language of social media, language which might seem to share some of the 'narcissism, irony and nihilism' that Foster Wallace diagnoses in image-fiction. Irreverent and self-referring as online swooning may be, I don't think its expressiveness is entirely 'exhausted' in the way that Foster Wallace's thinking about endemic irony wants us to assume. The online *swoon* operates by ghosting the body in the virtual domain; it invokes physical response, even as that mode is complexly constituted and seemingly refuted. Even now, playfully invoked as ironic cliché, the swoon plays around with our systems of meaning. It shares something of the smiley/weeping strangeness of the obligatory emoticons that insert pictorial avatars into our everyday written language. It's a physical glitch in the virtual, a playful palpitation, a parsing problem, a negation of the negation of the body, a shadow-resurrection in a disembodied realm. And it returns us to the beginning of this enquiry, in reminding us that swooning is, and has always been, a literary performance, fictionalising the body in ways that invite further reading.

Passing out.

Notes

1. Ericka Beckman and Marianna Simnett, *Gallery Guide* (FACTLiverpool, March 2019).
2. See www.urbandictionary.com/define.php?term=swoon (accessed August 9, 2013).
3. See http://pinterest.com/edonovan731/ryan-gosling-swoon/ (accessed August 9, 2013).
4. See www.swooneditions.com (accessed July 18, 2019).
5. See 'FilmSwoon', the blog of Buffalo-based movie critic Christopher Schobert: http://filmswoon.com/?tag=frances-ha (accessed August 9, 2013).
6. For the *Guardian*, for instance, in the summer of 2013 this was Greta Gerwig, writer and actor in the newly released *Frances Ha*: see www.theguardian.com/film/2013/jul/13/greta-gerwig-frances-ha (accessed August 9, 2013).
7. David Foster Wallace, '*E Unibus Pluram*: Television and US Fiction', *Review of Contemporary Fiction* (Summer, 1993), 151–194.
8. *Ibid.*, 183.
9. *Ibid.*, 183.
10. *Ibid.*, 193.
11. See, as just one influential instance, Lee Edelman's work on negativity, the death drive and irony in *No Future: Queer Theory and the Death Drive* (Durham, NC and London: Duke University Press, 2004).

Select bibliography

Note: This bibliography comprises only essays and books focused on specifically or extensively in *Swoon*.

Aers, David, *Community, Gender, and Individual Identity: English Writing, 1360–1430* (London: Routledge, 1988)
Ardrey, Caroline, 'A Single Immense Swoon', *The Oxonion Review* 16(4), 201
Austen, Jane, *Love and Freindship* [sic] in Deidre Shauna Lynch and Jack Stillinger (eds), *The Norton Anthology of English Literature* (New York: W.W. Norton & Co., 2006 [c.1790])
——, *Sense and Sensibility* (London: Macmillan & Co., 1926 [1811])
——, *Persuasion* (Ware, Hertfordshire: Wordsworth Editions, 1993 [1818])
Barker-Benfield, George J., *The Culture of Sensibility: Sex and Society in Eighteenth-Century Britain* (Chicago and London: University of Chicago Press, 1992)
Barrett Browning, Elizabeth, *Aurora Leigh* (Oxford: Oxford University Press, 1993 [1856])
Bataille, Georges, *Eroticism*, trans. Mary Dalwood (London: Penguin Books, 2001 [1957])
Behrman, Mary, 'Heroic Criseyde', *The Chaucer Review* 38(4) (2004), 314–336
Berlant, Lauren, *Cruel Optimism* (Durham, NC and London: Duke University Press, 2011)
Bersani, Leo, *The Freudian Body: Psychoanalysis and Art* (New York: Columbia University Press, 1986)
——, *Is the Rectum a Grave? And Other Essays* (Chicago and London: The University of Chicago Press, 2010 [2000])
——, and Phillips, Adam, *Intimacies* (Chicago and London: The University of Chicago Press, 2008)
Bondeson, Jan, *Buried Alive: The Terrifying History of Our Most Primal Fear* (New York, London: W.W. Norton Co., 2001)
Bradbrook, M.C., 'What Shakespeare Did to Chaucer's *Romeo and Juliet*', *Shakespeare Quarterly* 9(3) (1958), 311–319
Bronfen, Elisabeth, *Over Her Dead Body: Death, femininity and the aesthetic* (Manchester: Manchester University Press, 1992)

Select bibliography

Brown, Norman O., *Life Against Death* (Middletown, CT: Wesleyan University Press, 1985)
Burke, Edmund, *On the Sublime and Beautiful* (The Harvard Classics, 1909–14 [1757])
Burnett McInernay, Maud, '"Is this a mannes herte?": Unmanning Troilus through Ovidian Allusion', in Peter Beidler (ed.), *Masculinities in Chaucer* (Boydell & Brewer, 1997), pp. 221–235
Butler, Marilyn, *Romantics, Rebels and Reactionaries: English Literature and its Background 1760–1830* (Oxford: Oxford University Press, 1981)
Callaghan, Dympna, *Woman and Gender in Renaissance Tragedy: A Study of King Lear, Othello, The Duchess of Malfi and The White Devil* (London: Harvester Wheatsheaf, 1989)
Carter, Angela, *The Bloody Chamber and Other Stories* (London: Random House, 1995 [1979]).
——, *The Sadeian Woman: An Exercise in Cultural History* (London: Virago, 1979)
Chaucer, Geoffrey *Troilus and Criseyde* in Larry D. Benson (general ed.), *The Riverside Chaucer*, 3rd edn (Oxford, New York: Oxford University Press, 1988 [*c.*1380])
Cixous, Hélène and Clément, Catherine, *The Newly Born Woman* (Manchester: Manchester University Press, 1987)
Cixous, Hélène, *Insister of Jacques Derrida*, trans. Peggy Kamuf (Edinburgh: Edinburgh University Press, 2007)
Clough, Patricia T., 'The Affective Turn: Political Economy, Biomedia, and Bodies', in Melissa Gregg and Gregory J. Seigworth (eds), *The Affect Theory Reader* (Durham, NC and London: Duke University Press, 2010), pp. 206–225
Coe, Richard N., 'Translator's Foreword' to Stendhal, *Rome, Naples and Florence*, trans. Richard N. Coe (London: John Calder, 1959)
Condren, Edward, 'Transcendent Metaphor or Banal Reality: Three Chaucerian Dilemmas', *PLL* 21(3) (1985), 233–257
Crichlow Goellnicht, Donald, 'Negative Capability and Wise Passiveness' (1976), Open Access Dissertations and Theses. Paper 4675
Davidson, Michael, *Concerto for the Left Hand: Disability and the Defamiliar Body* (Ann Arbor, MI: University of Michigan Press, 2008)
Defoe, Daniel, *A Journal of the Plague Year* (London: Penguin Classics, 2003 [1722])
Dickens, Charles, *Martin Chuzzlewit* (Oxford: Oxford University Press, 1982 [1842–44])
Ellis, Markman, *The Politics of Sensibility* (Cambridge: Cambridge University Press, 1996)
Ely, Steve, *I beheld Satan as lightning fall from heauen* (Leicester: New Walk Editions, 2019)
Fletcher, Alan, 'Lost Hearts: Troilus and Criseyde, Book II, lines 925–31', *Notes and Queries* (June 1990), 163–164

Frayling, Christopher, *Vampyres: Lord Byron to Count Dracula* (London and Boston: Faber & Faber, 1991)
——, 'Preface' to Bram Stoker, *Dracula* (London: Penguin Classics, 2011 [1897])
Freud, Sigmund, 'The Uncanny', trans. James Strachey, in *Pelican Freud Library* (Harmondsworth: Penguin, 1985 [1919])
——, *Civilization and Its Discontents*, trans. David McLintock (London: Penguin Books, 2002 [1930])
Georgianna, Linda, *The Solitary Self: Individuality in the Ancrene Wisse* (London and Cambridge, MA: Harvard University Press, 1981)
George, Sam and Hughes, Bill, 'Introduction: Undead Reflections', *Gothic Studies* 15(1) (May 2013), 1–7
Giffney, Noreen and Hird, Myra J. (eds), *Queering the Non/Human* (Farnham: Ashgate, 2008)
Gillis, Colin, 'James Joyce and the Masturbating Boy', *James Joyce Quarterly*, 50(3) (Spring 2013), 611–634
Görlach, Manfred, *The Textual Tradition of the South English Legendary* (Leeds: University of Leeds, 1974)
Haase, Ullrich and Large, William, *Maurice Blanchot* (London and New York: Routledge, 2001)
Hardy, Thomas, *Tess of the d'Urbervilles; A Pure Woman* (Ware, Hertfordshire: Wordsworth Editions, 1992 [1891])
Harte, Bret, *Gabriel Conroy* (London: Chatto & Windus, 1881)
Hobgood, Allison P., 'Caesar Hath the Falling Sickness: The Legibility of Early Modern Disability in Shakespearean Drama', *Disability Studies Quarterly* 29(4), (2009)
—— and Houston Wood, David (eds), *Recovering Disability in Early Modern England* (Columbus, OH: The Ohio State University Press, 2013)
Hume, David, *A Treatise of Human Nature* (Oxford: Clarendon Press, 1978 [1739–40])
Irigaray, Luce, *Speculum of the Other Woman* (Ithaca, NY: Cornell University Press, 1985)
James, E. L., *Fifty Shades of Grey* (London: Arrow Books, 2012)
——, *Fifty Shades Darker* (London: Arrow Books, 2012)
——, *Fifty Shades Freed* (London: Arrow Books, 2012)
Johnson, Charles, 'Exchange Value', in Joyce Carol Oates (ed.), *American Gothic Tales* (Penguin, 1996 [1981])
Jones, Ernest, *On the Nightmare*, excerpt reprinted as 'On the Vampire', in Christopher Frayling, *Vampyres: Lord Byron to Count Dracula* (London and Boston: Faber & Faber, 1991 [1931])
——, *Sigmund Freud: Life and Work*, 3 vols (London: Hogarth Press, 1953–57)
Joyce, James, *Dubliners* (London: Penguin Books, [1914] 1992)
——, *A Portrait of the Artist as a Young Man* (London: Penguin, 2000 [1914–15])

——, *Letters of James Joyce*, Stuart Gilbert (ed.) (London: Faber & Faber, 1966), Vol. I
——, *Letters of James Joyce*, Richard Ellmann (ed.), (London: Faber & Faber, 1966), Vol. II
Jung, Carl Gustav, *Collected Papers on Analytical Psychology*, trans. Constance Ellen Long (London: 1916)
——, *Analytical Psychology: Its Theory and Practice* (London: 1976)
Keats, John, *The Complete Poems* (London: Penguin Books, 1988 [1838])
——, *The Letters of John Keats, 1814–1821*, ed. Hyder Edward Rollins (Cambridge, MA: Harvard University Press, 1958)
Lawrence, Christopher, 'The Nervous System and Society in the Scottish Enlightenment', in B. Barnes and S. Shapin (eds), *Natural Order: Historical Studies of Scientific Cultures* (London: Sage, 1979)
Le Fanu, Sheridan, '*Carmilla*', reproduced in *Three Vampire Tales* (Boston: Houghton Mifflin Co., 2003 [1872])
Lebeau, Vicky, *Psychoanalysis and Cinema: The Play of Shadows* (London: Wallflower Press, 2001)
Loomba, Ania, *Shakespeare, Race, and Colonialism* (Oxford: Oxford University Press, 2002)
Mackenzie, Henry, *The Man of Feeling* (Oxford: Oxford University Press, 1967 [1771])
Mann, Jill, 'Troilus' Swoon', *The Chaucer Review* 14 (1980), 319–335
——, *Feminizing Chaucer* (Cambridge: D.S. Brewer, 2002)
Marx, Karl, *Capital: A Critique of Political Economy Capital*, trans. Samuel Moore and Edward Aveling, ed. Friedrich Engels (Moscow: Progress Publishers, 1887)
—— and Engels, Friedrich, *Kleine ökonomische Schriften* (Berlin: Dietz, 1955)
McRuer, Robert, *Crip Theory: Cultural Signs of Queerness and Disability* (New York: New York University Press, 2006)
Miller, J. Hillis, 'The Limits of Pluralism III: The Critic as Host', *Critical Inquiry* 3(3) (Spring 1977), 439–447
Mieszkowski, Gretchen, 'Revisiting Troilus's Faint', in Tison Pugh and Marcia Smith Marzec (eds), *Men and Masculinities in Chaucer's* Troilus and Criseyde (Cambridge: D.S. Brewer, 2008), pp. 43–57
Morgan, Oliver, *Turn-Taking in Shakespeare* (Oxford: Oxford University Press, 2019)
Morrison, Robert and Baldick, Chris, "Introduction" to John Polidori, *The Vampyre and Other Tales of the Macabre* (Oxford: Oxford World Classics, 2008 [1819])
Morton, Timothy, *Ecology Without Nature: Rethinking Environmental Aesthetics* (Cambridge, MA and London: Harvard University Press, 2009)
——, 'Ecology as Text, Text as Ecology', *Oxford Literary Review* 32.1 (2010), 1–17
——, *Hyperobjects: Philosophy and Ecology After the End of the World* (Minneapolis and London: University of Minnesota Press, 2013)

——, *Dark Ecology: For a Future of Coexistence* (New York: Columbia University Press, 2016)

Mullan, John, 'Sentimental Novels', in John Richetti (ed.), *The Cambridge Companion to the Eighteenth-Century Novel* (Cambridge: Cambridge University Press, 1996), pp. 236–254

Neff, Amy, 'The Pain of *Compassio*: Mary's Labor at the Foot of the Cross', *Art Bulletin* 80 (1980), 254–273

O'Donnell, Kimberly, 'Feeling Other(s): *Dracula* and the Ethics of Unmanageable Affect', in S. Ahern (ed), *Affect Theory and Literary Critical Practice* (Palgrave Macmillan, 2019), pp. 139–157

O'Farrell, Mary Ann, *Telling Complexions: The Nineteenth-Century Novel and the Blush* (Durham, NC and London: Duke University Press, 1997)

Palmer, Abi, *Sanatorium* (London: Penned in the Margins, 2020)

Pertile, Giulio J., *Feeling Faint: Affect and Consciousness in the Renaissance* (Evanston, IL: Northwestern University Press, 2019)

Poe, Edgar Allan, *The Complete Tales and Poems of Edgar Allan Poe* (London: Penguin Books, 1982)

Polidori, John, *The Vampyre and Other Tales of the Macabre* (Oxford: Oxford World Classics, 2008 [1819])

Pope, Alexander, *The Major Works*, ed. Pat Rogers (Oxford: Oxford University Press, 2008 [1728])

Praz, Mario, *The Romantic Agony*, trans. Angus Davidson (London, New York and Toronto: Oxford University Press, 1954 [1933]), 2nd edn

Pugh, Tison and Marzec, Marcia Smith (eds), *Men and Masculinities in Chaucer's* Troilus and Criseyde (Cambridge: D.S. Brewer, 2008)

Reames, Sherry L. (ed.), 'Early South English Legendary Life of Mary Magdalen', in *Middle English Legends of Women Saints* (Kalamazoo, MI: Medieval Institute Publications, 2003 [*c*.1290])

Rice, Anne, *Interview with a Vampire* (London: Sphere, 2001 [1976])

Richardson, Maurice, 'The Psychoanalysis of Ghost Stories', excerpt reprinted as 'The Psychoanalysis of Count Dracula', in Christopher Frayling, *Vampyres: Lord Byron to Count Dracula* (London and Boston: Faber & Faber, 1991 [1959])

Richardson, Samuel, *Pamela; Or, Virtue Rewarded* (London: Penguin Books, 1980 [1740])

Rickard, John S., 'A Portrait of the Animal as a Young Artist: Animality, Instinct, and Cognition in Joyce's Early Prose', *Humanities* 6(3) (2017), 56

Roe, Nicholas, *John Keats and the Culture of Dissent* (Oxford: Clarendon Press, 1997)

Roos, Bonnie, 'James Joyce's 'The Dead' and Bret Harte's *Gabriel Conroy*: The Nature of the Feast', *The Yale Journal of Literary Criticism* 15(1) (Spring 2002), 99–126

Royle, Nicholas, *The Uncanny* (Manchester: Manchester University Press, 2003)

——, *How to Read Shakespeare* (Granta, 2005)

———, 'The Remains of Psychoanalysis (I): Telepathy', in Martin McQuillan (ed.), *Deconstruction: A Reader* (Edinburgh: Edinburgh University Press, 2000), pp. 361–369
———, *In Memory of Jacques Derrida* (Edinburgh: Edinburgh University Press, 2009),
Sedgwick, Eve Kosofsky, *Epistemology of the Closet* (Berkeley and Los Angeles, California: University of California Press, 2008 [1990])
———, 'Jane Austen and the Masturbating Girl', *Critical Inquiry* (Summer 1991), 818–837
———, *Tendencies* (London: Routledge, 1994)
Siebers, Tobin, *Disability Aesthetics* (Ann Arbor, MI: University of Michigan Press, 2010)
Sinfield, Alan, *Faultlines: Cultural Materialism and the Politics of Dissident Reading* (Oxford: Clarendon Press, 1992)
Siraisi, Nancy G., *Medieval and Early Renaissance Medicine* (Chicago and London: The University of Chicago Press: 1990)
Shakespeare, William, *The Riverside Shakespeare*, 2nd edn (Boston; New York: Houghton Mifflin Co., 1997)
———, *Much Ado About Nothing*, Claire McEachern (ed.), revised edn (London: Bloomsbury, 2015)
Showalter, Elaine, *The Female Malady: Women, Madness and English Culture, 1830–1980* (London: Virago, 1985)
Smith, Adam, *Theory of Moral Sentiments* (Oxford: Clarendon Press, 1976 [1759])
Sontag, Susan, *Illness as Metaphor and Aids and its Metaphors* (London: Penguin Books, 2002 [1979])
Spencer, Jane, 'Women Writers and the Eighteenth-century Novel', in John Richetti (ed.), *The Cambridge Companion to the Eighteenth-Century Novel* (Cambridge: Cambridge University Press, 1996), pp. 212–235
Stendhal, *Rome, Naples and Florence*, trans. Richard N. Coe (London: John Calder, 1959)
Stoker, Bram, *Dracula* (London: Penguin Classics, 2011 [1897])
———, *Personal Reminiscences of Henry Irving* (London: Heinemann, 1906), Vol. I
Sutherland, Keston, *Stupefaction: A Radical Anatomy of Phantoms* (London, New York and Calcutta: Seagull Books, 2011)
Thompson, Ann, '*Troilus and Criseyde* and *Romeo and Juliet*', *The Yearbook of English Studies* 6 (1976), 26–37
Thompson, Harold W., *A Scottish Man of Feeling: Some Account of Henry Mackenzie, Esq. of Edinburgh, and the Golden Age of Burns and Scott* (London and New York: Oxford University Press, 1931)
Tolstoy, Leo, *War and Peace* (London: Penguin, 2007 [1869])
Wallace, David Foster, 'E Unibus Pluram: Television and US Fiction' (1993: Summer) *Review of Contemporary Fiction*, 151–194
Walpole, Horace, *The Letters of Horace Walpole* (Oxford: Clarendon Press, 1903–25)

Weiss, Judith, 'Modern and Medieval Views on Swooning: the Literary Contexts of Fainting in Romance', in Rhiannon Purdie and Michael Cichon (eds), *Medieval Romance, Medieval Contexts* (Cambridge: D.S. Brewer, 2011), pp. 121–134

Williams, Raymond, *Keywords: A Vocabulary of Culture and Society*, revised edn (London: Fontana, 1983)

Wilson, Jeffrey R., 'The Figure of Stigma in Shakespeare's Drama', *Genre* 51(3) (2018), 237–266

Windeatt, Barry, *Oxford Guides to Chaucer:* Troilus and Criseyde (Oxford: Oxford University Press, 1992)

——, 'Introduction' to his translation of *Troilus and Criseyde* (Oxford and New York: Oxford World's Classic, Oxford University Press, 1998)

——, 'The Art of Swooning in Middle English', in Christopher Cannon and Maura Nolan (eds), *Medieval Latin and Middle English Literature: Essays in Honour of Jill Mann* (Cambridge: D.S. Brewer, 2011), pp. 211–230

Wollstonecraft, Mary, *A Vindication of the Rights of Woman* (Oxford: Oxford University Press, 1999 [1792])

Zambreno, Kate, *Heroines* (California: Semiotext(e), 2012)

Žižek, Slavoj, *The Metastases of Enjoyment: Six Essays on Woman and Causality* (London: Verso, 1994)

Index

ableism 72, 74–76, 83–84
Aers, David 41
affect theory 7–8, 14–16, 157
aquatic swoons 2, 30–31, 61, 73, 136, 168, 179–180
Austen, Jane
  Persuasion 93
  Sense and Sensibility 109–117

Barker-Benfield, George J. 108
Barrett Browning, Elizabeth
  Aurora Leigh 123
Barry, Reverend Edward 102
Bataille, Georges
  Eroticism 12, 13, 148–150
Berlant, Lauren
  Cruel Optimism 15–18
Bernini, Gian Lorenzo
  'Ecstasy of Saint Teresa' 1–4
Bersani, Leo 20, 29, 38, 49, 51, 201
birds 43–46, 63, 66, 151
Blanchot, Maurice 12, 13
Bluebeard 190, 212
blushing 12, 21, 67, 69, 94, 114, 121, 200, 201
Boas, Frederick Samuel 71
Boccaccio, Giovanni
  Il Filostrato 36
Bondeson, Jan 131–132
Bright, Timothy
  A Treatise of Melancholie 62
Bronfen, Elisabeth 133, 136, 170

Brookes, Stopford 126
Brouillet, Pierre André 171
Brown, Norman O. 166–167
Burke, Edmund 113
buried alive 131, 132, 135, 175, 176
Butler, Judith 28
Byron, George Gordon (Lord Byron) 159–160

Capellanus, Andreas
  Treatise on Love 206
Carter, Angela 24, 190, 211–214
  'The Bloody Chamber' 190, 213–214
  The Sadeian Woman 211
catalepsy 133, 135
Charcot, Jean-Martin 171, 173
Chaucer, Geoffrey
  Troilus and Criseyde 28–29, 34–52, 128
childbirth 20, 31–34
Cixous, Hélène 13, 14, 201
Clinton, Hillary 75
'Cockney School' Essays 125–126
Coe, Richard N. 6
Condren, Edward 41
consciousness 8, 9, 15, 16, 19, 24, 41, 78, 84, 90, 103, 106, 129, 133, 134, 143, 166, 167, 170, 172, 173, 176, 191, 200, 219

contagion 9, 22, 76–77, 102, 158, 175, 178–181, 191
courtly love 29, 39, 47, 49, 52, 56, 206
COVID-19 158, 176
Crichlow Goellnicht, Donald 127
crip theory 23, 191
Crocker, Holly 37, 49–51

Dalwood, Mary 149
dark ecology 157, 180, 182, 183
Davidson, Michael 124
deconstruction 14, 151, 180–182
definitions of swooning 10, 28, 219
Defoe, Daniel 176
Deleuze, Gilles 14
Derrida, Jacques 13, 14, 182–183
di Bondone, Giotto 33
dialogical scansion 65–66
Dickens, Charles
    Martin Chuzzlewit 11
disability 22, 60, 72–76, 83, 124, 191
Dostoyevsky, Fyodor 172
Dutoit, Ulysse 51

Ellis, Markman 98–100
Ely, Steve 34
epilepsy 2, 14, 25, 72–76, 83, 88, 172
eroticism 1, 2, 4, 10, 12, 13, 20, 22, 24, 29, 35, 40, 45, 46, 47, 48, 50, 51, 95, 100, 101, 108, 116, 124, 146–150, 152, 157–159, 163–168, 174–179, 183, 190, 196, 197, 203–211
eschatology 123, 129

fainting 1, 3–5, 8–19, 23–26, 33–35, 41–43, 53–56, 59, 72, 99, 103, 112, 165, 166, 170, 190, 191, 196, 198, 211, 218, 219
falling sickness 72, 74, 76, 88

Fanu, Sheriden Le
    'Carmilla' 22, 158, 177, 179–183
feminisation of swooning 125–127, 164–165
Fletcher, Alan 45
Florence 6, 7
Frayling, Christopher 159, 161, 168, 174–175
Freud, Sigmund 14, 37, 133–135, 158, 168, 170–172, 201, 210
    '*Das Unheimliche*' 135
    'Oceanic Feeling' 168

Galen 37
gender 10, 19–21, 23, 24, 26, 42, 60, 83–84, 89, 93, 95, 107–109, 116, 125, 159, 190, 196, 198–199, 205, 214, 219
Gogol, Nikolai 161
Gospel of Nicodemus 33, 34
gothic, the 122, 157, 159, 163, 167, 178, 188–190, 212–214
Greenbriar Ghost, the 132
Guattari, Felix 14

Haase, Ullrich 13
haemosexuality 174
Hanway, Joseph
    A Sentimental History of Chimney Sweeps 96
Haraway, Donna 182
Hardy, Thomas
    Tess of the D'Urbervilles 23–24, 199, 205–209
Harte, Bret
    Gabriel Conroy 139–141
hauntology 183
Highsmith, Patricia
    The Price of Salt (later known as *Carol*) 23, 190
Hobgood, Allison P. 60, 72, 74, 75, 76

Index

Houston Wood, David 60
Hume, David 97

intoxication 46, 47, 85, 102
Irigary, Luce 210, 211

James, E.L.
  Fifty Shades of Grey 23, 190, 196–211
Johnson, Alexander 131
Johnson, Charles
  'Exchange Value' 15–18
Jones, Ernest 172, 175, 179
Joyce, James 8, 22, 124, 196
  A Portrait of the Artist as a Young Man 136, 145
  'The Dead' 137–144
Jung, Carl 14, 172–173

Keats, John 22, 124–131, 136, 196
  'Bright Star' 128–129
  Endymion 129–130
  Negative Capability 126–128, 139
  The Fall of Hyperion. A Dream 130–131

Large, William 13
'Life of Mary Magdalen' 28, 29–34
Loomba, Ania 84–85

Mackenzie, Henry
  The Man of Feeling 95–109
Mann, Jill 35–37, 42, 206
Margherini, Graziella 4, 5
Marx, Karl
  Das Kapital 161
masculinity 22, 28, 37, 41–42, 44–52, 61–62, 68, 70, 72, 74, 76, 80, 123–125, 127, 129, 146, 148, 164–165, 178, 196, 198, 203, 214
masochism 29, 38, 49, 51
masturbation 94, 145–146

McDermid, Val 195
McEachern, Claire 62
McRuer, Robert 191
Meyer, Stephanie
  Twilight 199
Michelangelo 7
Mieszkowski, Gretchen
  'Revisiting Troilus's Fate' 28, 34, 41–42, 93
Miller, J. Hillis 181, 182
Morgan, Oliver 65–67
Morton, Timothy 157, 180–83
Moskowitz, Reed 5
Mullan, John 96–98, 105, 115–116

necrophilia 93, 166, 174, 190, 207

O'Brien, Eugene 151
O'Donnell, Kimberley 157
O'Farrell, Mary Ann 12, 114–115

Palahniuk, Chuck
  'Guts' 3, 4, 9
Palmer, Abi
  Sanatorium 1–3
Pecora, Vincent 139
Pertile, Giulio 8, 15
Phillips, Adam 51
Poe, Edgar Allen 22, 124, 131–135
  'Liegeia' 133
  'The Pit and the Pendulum' 133–135
  'The Premature Burial' 132–133, 135
poison 84, 87, 89, 90
Polidori, John
  'The Vampyre' 22, 159–161, 163
Pope, Alexander
  Peri Bathous, or the Art of Sinking in Poetry 23, 197–199
Post-structuralism 13

Praz, Mario
  The Romantic Agony 124–125
Procne and Philomela 43–44, 46
psychoanalysis 23, 158, 169–170, 172
Pugh, Tison 37, 49–51

queer, queerness 9, 23, 158, 163–164, 182–183, 190–196

race 10, 19, 20, 21, 60, 83–84, 89, 90, 104
rape 43, 44, 46–47, 205, 207, 209
Reeve, Clara 102
religion 1–4, 20–21, 29–34, 60, 84, 90, 145, 149–150
Rice, Ann
  Interview with a Vampire 22, 167–169
Richardson, Samuel 101
Rickard, John S. 136, 151
Roe, Nicholas 125–128, 139
Rolland, Romain 168
Roos, Bonnie 139, 141–142, 144
Rousseau, Jean-Jacques 161, 162
Royle, Nicholas 14, 78, 135, 172, 212, 213

Saint Teresa (Teresa of Ávila) 1–4
saintly swoons 1–4, 20, 29–34
Scott, Sir Walter 96
Sedgwick, Eve 94, 95, 115, 116, 193, 198
sensibility 21, 93, 94, 96
sentimental literature 21, 93–117
Shakespeare, William
  Julius Caesar 20, 72–83
  Much Ado About Nothing 10, 20, 60–72
  Othello 20, 83–90
Simnett, Marianna
  Faint with Light 24, 218–221
Sinfield, Alan 60
Smith Marzac, Marcia 39
Smith, Adam 97, 98, 106
Sontag, Susan 177

Spiers, Tobin 124
Spinoza, Baruch 14
Steele, Richard 100
Stendhal Syndrome 4–6, 9
Stendhal, M. de (Henri Beyle)
  Rome, Naples et Florence 6–9
Sterne, Laurence
  A Sentimental Journey Through France and Italy 96, 104
Stoker, Bram
  Dracula 23, 158, 163–167, 169–174
Stuart, Lady Louise 96, 107
Sutherland, Keston 162, 197

Todd, Janet 104
Tolstoy, Alexis 111, 161
Tomalin, Claire 94
Turgenev, Ivan 161

uncanny, the 14, 133–135
unconsciousness 3, 4, 8, 23, 25, 30, 39, 45, 61, 67, 69, 91, 93, 114, 119, 133, 166, 172, 176

vampires 22, 23, 157–183, 190, 199, 213
van der Weyden, Rogier 28
Verlaine, Paul 147
Voltaire 161

Wagner, Richard 179
Wallace, David Foster 24, 220
  E Unibus Pluram 220
Weiss, Judith 31–32
Williams, Raymond 108
Wilson, Jeffrey R. 75
Windeatt, Barry 30, 32, 36, 39, 40, 41
Wineburg, Elliott 5
Wollstonecraft, Mary 113, 114

Zambreno, Kate 19
Žižek, Slavoj 29

EU authorised representative for GPSR:
Easy Access System Europe, Mustamäe tee 50,
10621 Tallinn, Estonia
gpsr.requests@easproject.com

www.ingramcontent.com/pod-product-compliance
Lightning Source LLC
Chambersburg PA
CBHW070816250426
43671CB00037B/2406